ERODING MILITARY INFLUENCE IN BRAZIL

Wendy Hunter

ERODING
MILITARY
INFLUENCE
IN BRAZIL

POLITICIANS
AGAINST
SOLDIERS

The University of North Carolina Press
Chapel Hill and London

The paper in this book meets the guidelines
for permanence and durability of the
Committee on Production Guidelines
for Book Longevity of the
Council on Library Resources.

Library of Congress Cataloging-in-Publication Data
Hunter, Wendy.
Eroding military influence in Brazil:
politicians against soldiers/by Wendy Hunter.
p. cm.
Includes bibliographical references and index.
ISBN 0-8078-2311-2.—ISBN 0-8078-4620-1 (pbk.)
1. Civil-military relations—Brazil
2. Brazil—Politics and government—1985–   I. Title.
JL2420.C58H86   1996
320.981—dc20   96-22285
CIP

01 00 99 98 97   5 4 3 2 1

To my parents

CONTENTS

ACKNOWLEDGMENTS

Many individuals and institutions have contributed to the undertaking and completion of this book. I am deeply grateful to all of them. The Tinker Foundation, the MacArthur Interdisciplinary Group for International Studies at the University of California at Berkeley, and Vanderbilt University provided financial support for the fieldwork on which this study is based. Members of my dissertation committee—David Collier, Philippe Schmitter, Robert Price, and Linda Lewin—gave generously of their time, attention, and criticism. Renato Boschi kindly arranged my affiliation with IUPERJ (Instituto Universitário de Pesquisas do Rio de Janeiro). The Center for Latin American Studies at Stanford University, under the directorship of Terry L. Karl, and the Kellogg Institute of International Studies at the University of Notre Dame provided me with an environment conducive to writing after my return from Brazil.

Numerous Brazilians—military officers, politicians and their aides, academic specialists, and journalists—took my pursuit seriously and shared their experiences, views, and contacts with me. In particular, I thank Geraldo Lesbat Cavagnari Filho, Eliézer Rizzo de Oliveira, and Jorge Zaverucha of the Núcleo de Estudos Estratégicos at UNICAMP; former congressional aides Antonio Carlos Pojo do Rego and Eduardo Jorge Caldos Pereira; and Admiral Mário César Flores and Oliveiros Ferreira.

I have benefited enormously from several scholars in North America who study Latin American militaries. Felipe Agüero, J. Samuel Fitch, Deborah L. Norden, David Pion-Berlin, and Scott Tollefson have offered invaluable encouragement and feedback over the years. At Vanderbilt University, David Bartlett, Paula Covington, and Erwin Hargrove have provided critical encouragement and assistance. For their warm friendship since graduate school I thank James W. McGuire, Yemile Mizrahi, Deborah Norden, Elizabeth Norville, Mina Silberberg, Timothy Power, and Deborah Yashar.

Others I would like to acknowledge include Barry Ames, Gretchen Casper, Lucia and Roberto Brügger da Costa, Emery Lee, Luis Ribeiro, Ruth Ribeiro, Matthew Shugart, and Francisco Weffort.

My husband and colleague, Kurt Weyland, has been a constant source of inspiration and support since we first met in Rio de Janeiro in the early stages of our respective dissertation research. His high energy, positive outlook, and keen insights were decisive in helping me get this project off the ground and bring it to completion. I am fortunate in his personal and professional companionship.

I dedicate this book to my parents, James and Setsuko Hunter, who have encouraged and educated me in so many vital ways.

ACRONYMS AND ABBREVIATIONS

ABIMDE   Associação Brasileira de Materiais de Defesa (Brazilian Association of Defense Materiel Industries)

AMAN   Academia Militar das Agulhas Negras (Military Academy of Agulhas Negras)

ANC   Assembléia Nacional Constituinte (National Constituent Assembly)

APRA   Alianza Popular Revolucionaria Americana (American Revolutionary Popular Alliance [Peru])

ARENA   Aliança de Renovação Nacional (National Renovating Alliance)

ASI   Assessorias de Segurança (Security and Intelligence Assistance Departments)

CCD   Congreso Constituyente Democrático (Democratic Constituent Assembly)

CCPY   Comissão pela Criação do Parque Yanomami (Committee for the Creation of the Yanomami Park)

CEDI   Centro Ecumênico de Documentação e Informações (Ecumenical Center for Documentation and Information)

CENIMAR   Centro de Informações da Marinha (Navy Intelligence Center)

CGT   Central Geral dos Trabalhadores (General Workers' Confederation)

CIE   Centro de Informações do Exército (Army Intelligence Center)

CIMI   Conselho Indigenista Missionário (Missionary Council on Indigenous Peoples)

CISA   Centro de Informações de Segurança da Aeronáutica (Air Force Intelligence Center)

CLT   Consolidação das Leis do Trabalho (Consolidation of Labor Laws)

CNBB   Conferência Nacional dos Bispos do Brasil (National Conference of Brazilian Bishops)

CPD   Concertación de Partidos por la Democracia (Coalition of Parties for Democracy [Chile])

CPHR	Centro de Preparação e Aperfeiçoamento de Recursos Humanos (Center for Training and the Improvement of Human Resources)
CPI	Comissão Parlamentar de Inqúerito (Parliamentary Commission of Inquiry)
CSN	Conselho de Segurança Nacional (National Security Council)
CUT	Central Única dos Trabalhadores (Singular Peak Union Organization)
DIAP	Departamento Intersindical de Assessoria Parlamentar (Interunion Department for Legislative Advising)
DIESSE	Departamento Intersindical de Estatística e Estudos Socio-Econômicos (Interunion Department for Statistical and Socioeconomic Studies)
DINA	Dirección de Inteligencia Nacional (National Directorate of Intelligence [Chile])
DL	decreto lei (decree law)
DSI	Divisão de Informação e Segurança (Divisions of Security and Information)
ECEME	Escola de Comando e Estado Maior do Exército (General Staff and Command School)
EMFA	Estado Maior das Forças Armadas (Armed Forces General Staff)
ESG	Escola Superior de Guerra (National War College)
ESNI	Escola Nacional de Informações (National School of Intelligence)
FUNAI	Fundação Nacional do Indio (National Foundation for Indian Affairs)
IAEA	International Atomic Energy Agency
IBAMA	Instituto Brasileiro do Meio Ambiente e dos Recursos Naturais Renováveis (Brazilian Institute for the Environment and Renewable Natural Resources)
IBGE	Instituto Brasileiro de Geografia e Estatística (Brazilian Institute of Geography and Statistics)
IDB	Inter-American Development Bank
IGPM	Inspetoria das Policías Militares (General Inspectorate of the Militarized Police)
INCRA	Instituto Nacional de Colonização e Reforma Agraria (National Institute for Colonization and Agrarian Reform)
IPEA	Instituto de Planejamento Econômico e Social (Institute of Economic and Social Planning)
IPEN	Instituto de Pesquisas Energétices e Nucleares (Institute for Energy and Nuclear Research)
IUPERJ	Instituto Universitário de Pesquisas do Rio de Janeiro (University Research Institute of Rio de Janeiro)

LSN	Lei de Segurança Nacional (Law of National Security)
MAM	Movimento Anti-Militarista (Anti-Militarist Movement)
MDB	Movimento Democrático Brasileiro (Brazilian Democratic Movement)
MP	medida provisória (provisional measure [with the force of law])
NGO	Nongovernmental organization
OAB	Ordem dos Advogados do Brasil (Brazilian Bar Association)
OCSP	Oficina Coordinadora de Seguridad Pública (Coordinating Agency of Public Security [Chile])
PCB	Partido Comunista Brasileiro (Brazilian Communist Party)
PC do B	Partido Comunista do Brasil (Communist Party of Brazil)
PDS	Partido Democrático Social (Democratic Social Party)
PDT	Partido Democrático Trabalhista (Democratic Labor Party)
PFL	Partido da Frente Liberal (Party of the Liberal Front)
PIN	Programa de Integração Nacional (Program of National Integration)
PM	policia militar
PMDB	Partido do Movimento Democrático Brasileiro (Party of the Brazilian Democratic Movement)
PND II	Plano Nacional de Desenvolvimento II (National Development Plan II)
PPD	Partido por la Democracia (Party for Democracy [Chile])
PRN	Partido de Reconstrução Nacional (National Reconstruction Party)
PSB	Partido Socialista Brasileira (Brazilian Socialist Party)
PSD	Partido Social Democrático (Social Democratic Party)
PSDB	Partido da Social-Democracia Brasileira (Party of Brazilian Social Democracy)
PT	Partido dos Trabalhadores (Workers' Party)
PTB	Partido Trabalhista Brasileiro (Brazilian Labor Party)
RN	Renovación Nacional (National Renovation [Chile])
SADEN	Secretaria de Assessoramento da Defesa Nacional (Advisory Secretariat of National Defense)
SAE	Secretaria de Assuntos Estratégicos (Secretariat of Strategic Affairs)
SEMA	Secretaria Especial do Meio Ambiente (Special Secretariat of the Environment)
SIPAM	Sistema de Proteção da Amazônia (Amazon Protection System)
SISNI	Sistema Nacional de Informações (National Intelligence System)
SIVAM	Sistema de Vigilância da Amazônia (Amazon Surveillance System)

SNI   Serviço Nacional de Informações (National Information Service)
SOF   Secretaria de Orçamento e Finanças (Secretary of Budget and
           Finances)
SUDAM   Superintendência do Desenvolvimento da Amazônia
           (Superintendency of Amazonian Development)
UDI   Unión Democrática Independiente (Independent Democratic
           Union [Chile])
UNCED   United Nations Conference on the Environment and
           Development
UNICAMP   Universidade Estadual de Campinas (State University of
           Campinas)
URC   Unión Cívica Radical (Radical Civic Union [Argentina])

ERODING MILITARY
INFLUENCE IN BRAZIL

INTRODUCTION

The 1980s and 1990s brought a return of civilian rule to many Latin American countries where the military had governed for much of the two previous decades. How the military conduct themselves in the current period critically affects whether democracy can develop and become robust in these countries. Where the armed forces play an active role in politics, they limit popular sovereignty, the guiding principle of democracy. With civilian rule having entered its second decade in Argentina, Uruguay, and Brazil, it becomes imperative to ask and possible to begin answering the question: What impact did the regime changes of the 1980s have on the role of the military in politics? Has democracy motivated and enabled elected officials to diminish significantly the political influence of the armed forces? Or have military elites been able to maintain their political clout in the democratic era and undermine the independence and authority of their civilian successors?[1]

This book probes these questions for the case of Brazil, where the military ruled from 1964 to 1985. The bulk of the literature on civil-military relations in post-authoritarian South America stresses the continuing influence of the military and the limits to democracy's consolidation. Analysts expected that the Brazilian armed forces would be particularly likely to exercise control over a broad range of political and socioeconomic issues after the transfer of power to civilians in 1985.[2] The basis of this expectation lay in the strength of the military government's bargaining position vis-à-vis civilians during the transition to civilian rule, which resulted in the armed forces' retention of numerous political prerogatives, including six cabinet positions and a predominant presence in the National Security Council (Conselho de Segurança Nacional or CSN) and National Information Service (Serviço Nacional de Informações or SNI), agencies synonymous with the dictatorship. These prerogatives were predicted to provide the military with a strong foundation for protecting the privileges of their institution and exercising tutelage over civilians in the new democracy.

My findings, based on evidence that extends to the end of 1994, cast doubt on the expectation that the military would be an extraordinarily powerful force in Brazil's new democracy. Over time, democratically elected politicians have successfully contested the institution over a broad range of issues and narrowed its sphere of political influence. For example, Congress defied the military and vastly expanded the right of workers to strike in 1988 and 1989. It has also steadily reduced military budget shares. President Collor took steps to restructure the military-dominated intelligence service and security council in 1990. Likewise, he confronted the armed forces' previously unchallenged control over nuclear issues, signing an agreement with Argentina allowing for inspections by the International Atomic Energy Agency. Similarly, by endorsing measures to curb ecological devastation and to protect indigenous populations in the Amazon, Collor opposed the military's strong interest in developing and occupying the region. In sum, despite the institutional strongholds the military retained with the regime transition and the influence they enjoyed in the immediate aftermath of the transfer of power to civilians, elected politicians soon came to contest the military and reduce their political clout.

That civilians have successfully begun to erode the influence of a military that was exceptionally well positioned to remain influential is significant. The economic successes associated with Brazil's military governments, the relatively low incidence of human rights violations they committed, and the impressive degree of public support they managed to orchestrate allowed Generals Ernesto Geisel (1974–79) and João Figueiredo (1979–85) to exercise significant control over the terms of the regime transition, preserving important institutional prerogatives for the armed forces. The erosion of military influence in this "most likely case" of continued strength casts serious doubt on the military's capacity to remain a preponderant actor in the everyday politics of Latin America.[3]

The central thesis of this book is that electoral competition creates incentives for politicians to reduce the interference of a politically powerful and active military, and that broad popular support enhances their capacity to do so. The argument rests on the strategic calculations of self-interested politicians, for whom electoral advancement is an overriding goal. The incentives that elected politicians face are both particularistic and programmatic. The former involve the distribution of public resources to gain and keep constituents. The latter concern the endorsement of public policies that are popular among the electorate. In varied ways, both types of incentives generate strong and specific pressures for politicians to contest the entrenchment of the military in the political and economic fabric of the country.

Chapter 1 presents the central argument of the study and the theoretical framework that informs it. It juxtaposes two competing approaches—rational choice and historical institutionalism—to understanding civil-military relations in post-authoritarian contexts. Based on observations about the motivation and capacity of self-interested politicians to shape institutions and modify them once they are created, Chapter 1 advances an understanding of political change couched in rational choice premises.

Chapter 2 documents the political strength of the Brazilian armed forces at the inception of civilian rule in 1985 and analyzes the numerous factors that, in the view of historical institutionalists, positioned the armed forces to remain a decisive political actor under Brazil's new democracy. In this regard, it focuses on the establishment under the bureaucratic-authoritarian regime of additional institutional prerogatives and various rules and regulations designed to safeguard corporate unity. It also illustrates how the role the armed forces played in the transition to civilian rule enhanced their prospects for remaining influential thereafter. In light of the heightened potential for military tutelage created by these factors— high internal unity, extensive institutional prerogatives, and a negotiated transition to civilian rule—the demonstrated ability of civilian politicians to cut back military influence in various areas is especially noteworthy.

Chapters 3–6 analyze the military's diminishing effectiveness in advancing their preferences under the new democracy. The picture that emerges is one of an organization whose interests are subject to strong competing forces. This stands in sharp contrast to the prevailing view of the Brazilian military as an organization well insulated from the broader dynamic of democracy and able to maintain its claims with ease. Indeed, the military's ability to sway civilian decision making is much less than previously imagined and has clearly been pushed back since 1985.

Chapter 3 traces the fate of a broad array of formal military prerogatives from the time of the transfer of power in 1985 until the end of the Franco government in late 1994. It shows that the armed forces' institutional powers have been reduced overall, notwithstanding enduring autonomy in some areas. Politicians have proven especially likely to cut back those provisions that threaten their own political agendas. Military autonomy remains strong mainly over issues judged to interfere less or not at all with the electoral motivations of politicians, such as military recruitment and promotion, education, and training.

Chapters 4–6 investigate military efforts to influence civilian policy making in three substantive areas in which military preferences conflicted with those of key politicians. The cases presented in these chapters demonstrate that the military's retention of certain formal institutional prerogatives does not necessarily give them decisive influence over actual policy outcomes.

Chapter 4 examines civil-military disputes over federal budget allocations. For a politician, gaining shares of the federal budget to distribute to constituents represents a particularistic incentive unleashed by democratization. This chapter underscores the pressure that electoral competition generates for politicians to fund items with a potential for significant electoral return. It shows how the division of the budget has tended to shift in favor of programs that are easily divisible and for which direct credit can be claimed. The logic of political survival employed by most politicians militates in favor of public works projects. Under this political imperative, defense spending has taken a toll.

Chapter 5 analyzes civil-military disputes over the liberalization of labor policy, a central point of contention in Brazil's new democracy. It shows how electoral pressures led the Congress to defeat restrictions on strikes that military lobbyists had sought to impose. For Brazilian legislators, the liberalization of strike law represented a programmatic incentive to gain electoral popularity. In a political era marked by the growing electoral relevance of the labor movement, the pressure felt by legislators to appear sympathetic with workers' demands discouraged them from supporting the relatively stringent labor controls advocated by the military.

Chapter 6 analyzes military efforts to prevent the Brazilian government from responding to international pressures to protect the Amazon rain forest and the indigenous populations that reside there. Concern that foreign governments and lending institutions (who themselves face pressure from environmental groups in their own countries) could jeopardize the economic success of their governments by withdrawing loans or obstructing debt negotiations creates incentives for Brazilian presidents to remain in good standing with these entities. This has entailed resisting military efforts to veto environmental initiatives. Authoritarian leaders would also risk international reproach but would not be as subject to its domestic political consequences. The political battle President Collor fought with the military over the Amazon needs to be understood not only in terms of the incentives that democratic rule unleashed but also the capabilities it conferred on him. Even where no powerful societal interests opposed military interference, a strong and popularly elected president could go a long way in cutting back the military's reach.

The conclusion reexamines the theoretical and empirical basis of the study, discusses remaining enclaves of military autonomy in Brazil, and suggests how the dynamic I have outlined applies to other new democracies of Latin America.

THE REDUCTION OF
MILITARY INFLUENCE IN
POSTAUTHORITARIAN BRAZIL:
ANALYTIC THEMES

What impact does democratic government have on the military's ability to exercise decisive influence over issues of broad social and political significance? Are electoral politicians under democracy likely to preserve or diminish the military's sphere of involvement? What resources can and will the armed forces deploy to defend and advance their claims?

This chapter discusses competing theoretical approaches that claim to provide answers to these questions. The first section presents and probes the central analytic issue of the book: whether and for how long the "pacted" or negotiated nature of the transition to democracy in Brazil inhibited democracy's consolidation. Did the military governments' firm guidance of the transition, which allowed the armed forces to maintain ample institutional powers and play an influential political role in the *initial* phase of the new regime, create a legacy of extensive military influence? Or did the rules and norms of democracy eventually lead elected civilians to rein in the political activities of the military? The framework I present and endorse in this section suggests that the competitive dynamic of democracy unleashes irresistible incentives for civilian politicians to contest a military prone to political interference and endowed with ample institutional prerogatives, and that the popular support certified by electoral victory enhances their capacity to do so.[1]

The second section examines and analyzes the effect of two conditioning factors—civilian political institutions and broader power alignments—in shaping the strategies of democratically elected political actors to extend their power and influence over the military. I argue that the weak institutionalization of Brazil's political system and multiple constraints on the use of military force for domestic political purposes in the current era reinforce the pressures created by democratic competition to reduce military influence.

While recognizing that the definition of democracy is a subject of intense debate,[2] I conceptualize democracy as a system of governance in which an inclusive adult population is free to engage in individual and collective forms of political action and in which rulers are selected through open, competitive, peaceful, and regularly scheduled elections. This is similar to what Robert Dahl calls "polyarchy."[3] Such a minimalist, formal-procedural definition of democracy is necessary because I seek to investigate the impact that democratic procedures have on a substantive issue (the influence of the military in politics). My study would be condemned to uncovering a tautology if it included in the definition of democracy the absence of interference by unelected officials, such as military officers.

CIVIL-MILITARY RELATIONS IN POSTAUTHORITARIAN BRAZIL: CONTINUITY VERSUS CHANGE?

"Confining Conditions" Inhibit Civilian Sovereignty

Many analysts, including Alfred Stepan, Frances Hagopian, Guillermo O'Donnell, and Terry Karl, posited that Brazilian democracy would suffer from a serious "birth defect."[4] They claimed that the negotiated nature of the transition to civilian rule would provide the military, along with other important actors from the authoritarian period, with long-lasting political clout.[5] More specifically, they contended that institutional privileges the armed forces retained in the transition process would give them a strong and indefinite foundation of political leverage. The military would be able to exercise undue influence in nonmilitary spheres as well as resist civilian direction over defense issues. The concern of these authors was not that the armed forces would launch a frontal assault on democracy by waging a coup d'état, but that they would impede democratic consolidation by continual tutelage, causing democracy to die a "slow death."[6] In line with the view that "patterns of politics established in periods of transition have a very real and strong potential to become semipermanent features of the political landscape," Hagopian contends, "[t]he advent of civilian rule in Brazil did not erode military authority, though it may have disguised it."[7] O'Donnell saw Brazil as vulnerable to the development of a *democradura*, a civilian government controlled by military and authoritarian elements.[8] The considerable political interference of the army in the first three years of the civilian regime seemed to provide empirical verification for this theoretical expectation.

Tenets of "historical institutionalism" informed the development of this rather pessimistic view.[9] The influence of branching tree models, such as Krasner's model of "punctuated equilibrium," is particularly observable.[10] These models claim that stable institutional patterns structure political life. By creating vested interests that promote their own persistence, institutions gain considerable autonomy and strength to withstand shifts in the broader political and socioeconomic environment. Even a challenge drastic enough to upset established institutional patterns is conditioned in its impact by the institutional setting in which it occurs. Historical institutionalists therefore view political development as a path-dependent process: following one path channels further development down the same path and precludes other options.

According to this view, significant political change only takes place at "critical junctures" or "turning points," when institutional patterns are challenged by strong socioeconomic or political pressures. Such moments present rare opportunities for political actors to reshape the political landscape by founding new institutions. Periods of regime transition—when the rules of the game are in flux— constitute such moments. If change is to occur, quick action must be taken before the transition period comes to a close and patterns and practices inherited from the previous regime have a chance to congeal. After these windows of opportunity close, stability prevails and profound political change, which would reshape the institutional framework, is unlikely. If left unchallenged during the regime change, previous institutional patterns are believed to be reaffirmed and given a strong foundation to persist. A historical institutionalist perspective would predict that the armed forces would be able to preserve their power and set limits to popular sovereignty in the new democracy if they and other conservative elites managed to retain strong institutional prerogatives throughout a transition from authoritarian rule.

Electoral Competition Leads Civilians to Contest the Military

In contrast to the view described above, my research on postauthoritarian Brazil suggests that countries that return to civilian rule through elite-led negotiations need not be constrained indefinitely by the balance of forces that prevailed in the transition and immediate posttransition period. Civil-military relations in postauthoritarian Brazil have displayed much greater dynamism than a historical-institutionalist framework can account for. The firm hand the armed forces exercised over the transition and the institutional prerogatives they retained did strengthen their political clout in the immediate aftermath of the transition. The army's interference in civilian decision making was considerable and often met with success in this initial period.[11] But as the authoritarian past receded further into the distance, the advantage that military elites could reap from factors stemming from the transition began to erode. Within roughly three years, elected officials began to take gradual yet significant steps to check the military's political inter- ference. Politicians first confronted the military over issues that directly affected their popularity and electoral standing. Later, their actions included efforts to diminish the military's institutional basis for political involvement, for example, by forming civilian-led organs to replace the former National Security Council (Conselho de Segurança Nacional or CSN) and the National Information Ser- vice (Serviço Nacional de Informações or SNI). At the same time, while some of the military's institutional prerogatives remained in existence, leading officers appeared increasingly unable to use them to wield actual political influence.

How do I explain this unanticipated result? I argue that electoral competition creates incentives for politicians to reduce the interference of a politically power- ful and active military, and that electoral victory enhances their capacity to do so. This claim rests on two premises: that politicians are first and foremost interested in their own political survival, and that the broad institutional context in which they operate structures their behavior. These premises suggest that politicians will contest the military when military actions conflict with politicians' opportunity to gain widespread electoral appeal. Thus, in contrast to the view that political arrangements that are founded or reaffirmed during regime transitions will re- main entrenched even as the political landscape around them changes, I contend that broad political and institutional shifts—in this case, the unfolding of the rules and norms of democracy—can disrupt patterns and practices put in place under a different set of circumstances. Rather than creating a static framework, democ- racy unleashes a competitive dynamic conducive to change.

This analysis is inspired by the literature on rational choice, which focuses on actors and their intentions and explains political action with reference to rational interest calculation. Strategic interaction among individuals maximizing their self-interest is seen as the foundation of politics. In the rational choice perspec- tive, institutions result from this kind of interaction among individuals; they are created by actors pursuing their own preferences in instrumental ways. Once established, institutions set parameters for individual actors and their interest calculations, but they are always open to further modification.[12]

These are the explicit premises of arguments that authors such as Barry Ames and Barbara Geddes advance to explain politics and institutional change in Latin America.[13] These ideas are also reflected in Douglas Chalmers's concept of the "politicized state,"[14] which differs fundamentally from Krasner's model of "punc- tuated equilibrium." Whereas Krasner stresses the stickiness of institutions and confines the possibility of change to rare but major moments of reorientation, such as regime transitions, Chalmers emphasizes the ever-present fluidity of Latin American politics, marked by frequent incremental shifts in the balance of power among self-interested actors and the institutional arrangements they establish.

Both historical institutionalism and rational choice focus on the relationship between actors and institutions but differ in their views concerning the malleability of institutions and the direction of the causal relationship between actors and institutions. Historical institutionalism sees institutional arrangements as resistant to change, except during rare crises, and focuses on the constraints that institutions impose on actors. By contrast, rational choice sees institutions as more mutable and underscores the capacity of actors to shape institutions and modify them once they are created. Rational choice theorists recognize that actors are conditioned by their institutional setting, which establishes a strategic context for decision making, but hasten to emphasize that this framework itself is the product of interaction among self-interested individuals.

Insofar as my empirical findings show that self-interested actors began rather quickly to reshape institutional arrangements and to alter the balance of political power in their favor, my study bears out the guiding principles of rational choice and diverges from those of historical institutionalism. The rules of democracy in Brazil have fostered political competition and thus induced and enabled politicians to undermine the terms of the conservative pact made during the transition from authoritarianism. In particular, politicians have begun to remove important constraints on popular sovereignty by contesting the institutional prerogatives of the military and reducing their political influence.

Political Incentives

What, more specifically, are the factors that induce and enable civilian politicians to undermine military tutelage over the new democracy? Why do many efforts by politicians to enhance their electoral chances conflict with positions the armed forces hold? And how do politicians gain the force to advance their preferences even against opposition from the armed forces?

Democratization gives rise to two types of incentives for electoral politicians: particularistic and programmatic. Particularistic incentives concern the use of resources to build and maintain politicians' personal support networks. Programmatic incentives involve the credit given to politicians for advances in public policy (e.g., health, education, welfare, and economic reform). Both types of incentives are operative in Brazil, as in most democracies. And in different ways both generate strong and specific pressures against the persistence of military involvement in politics.

First, democratization in Brazil has reinforced particularistic incentives associated with political clientelism, often at the armed forces' expense. Heightened electoral competition since the early 1980s has motivated politicians to search ever more energetically for economic assets to distribute as political pork barrel, thereby improving their chances of reelection.[15] The dream of clientelist politicians is to build roads, schools, hospitals, sanitation systems, and other public works projects in their electoral districts. These benefits are targeted toward specific, regionally delimited groups of people. The extent to which legislators support local pork barrel projects, and the prevalence of logrolling in congressional voting patterns, strongly suggest that many Brazilians still vote largely with considerations of patronage in mind, or at least that politicians think they do.

Beyond seeking to distribute particularistic patronage, politicians also pursue "categorical patronage." Such benefits are targeted to specific industries and/or categories of people. In principle, benefits are defined in general terms, but the beneficiaries unfailingly "happen" to be concentrated regionally. The rather narrow and regionally concentrated nature of the given categories qualifies these benefits as patronage and not as an integral part of programmatic strategies. The purpose of providing categorical patronage is for politicians to win regionally based electoral support, not to advance universalist goals. Examples of categorical patronage include subsidies for Brazil's sugar alcohol program and coffee sector, and social security provisions for specific types of workers and pensioners, especially those who are concentrated in the country's most developed regions.

The rampant pursuit of patronage resources by politicians not only clashes with the long-standing positivist impulse within the military to "rationalize" the public bureaucracy.[16] It also leads them to enter into direct competition with military elites over state resources. Politicians are tempted to shift budget shares away from the military to civilian ministries better suited for pork barrel. Similarly, where military officers hold key posts in large state enterprises—strategic positions from which to build political allies by distributing jobs and other benefits—patronage-seeking politicians will seek to replace them. The competition for patronage resources unleashed by democratic competition thus generates strong pressures against the continued entrenchment of the military in the political and economic fabric of the country.

Second, in addition to unleashing particularistic incentives associated with political clientelism, democratization reinforces programmatic incentives that frequently work against the armed forces. In Brazil, winning elections often depends on gaining the votes of the country's impoverished yet increasingly mobilized majority. Besides seeking to rise from their own poverty, some of Brazil's poor have visions, albeit often vaguely defined, of a more egalitarian society. Politicians of diverse ideological leanings suggest increasingly in their conduct that they feel pressured to respond to this pool of voters in a symbolic, if not effective, way. This is especially true of politicians who need to appeal to urban electorates; they would quickly be turned out if they merely defended the interests of the privileged. Politicians tend to portray themselves as sympathetic with the plight of the country's poor, despite the deeply conservative tendencies of Brazilian politics. They do so in rhetorical ways; for example, the successor of the government party during military rule, ARENA (the National Renovating Alliance or Aliança de Renovação Nacional), renamed itself the Democratic-Social Party (Partido Democrático Social or PDS). Similarly, Brazilian politicians frequently make reference to *mudança* (change) and to a *novo Brasil* (new Brazil).[17] They also try to gain standing with the mass citizenry by supporting policies that recognize popular desires for change, at least in some highly visible areas, such as labor legislation.[18] Insofar as many of the policies that (even conservative) politicians are tempted to support in order to appear progressive do not ensure universal social rights or effective interest representation for the disadvantaged, they are more "populist" than "programmatic" in nature. Nevertheless, they often run counter to the military's goal of maintaining social order through restrictions on popular mobilization. The military's ultimate fear is that politicians with populist leanings will encourage Brazil's historically quiescent lower classes to become more assertive, thereby jeopardizing political stability and a model of accumulation propitious for Brazil's rapid economic advancement.

In addition to unleashing "populist" tendencies, democracy makes politicians accountable for the success of more strictly programmatic policies. These include social reforms as well as economic measures like privatization, stabilization, and adjustment. Given the importance of performance for public support, politicians seek maximum control over events and processes that occur within their jurisdiction, territorial and functional.[19] Large bureaucratic organizations like the military can compromise this latitude. And unlike alliances with other established groups and institutions, close relations with the armed services rarely enhance a politician's electoral chances. While Brazilian legislators clearly rely less on taking policy stands and more on providing particularistic services, Brazilian presidents depend on enacting public policies that meet the public's approval. They are thus especially concerned with maintaining political autonomy from groups that could interfere with this goal. The constitution bans immediate presidential reelection, but former Brazilian presidents often reenter politics at lower levels. They can also compete for the presidency again after one term has lapsed.

These seeds of conflict that democracy plants between civilian and military interests create strong pressures for elected politicians to reduce the military's sphere of influence. This does not mean that ideology is irrelevant or that all politicians will follow this course of action all of the time. But at the very least the framework presented here suggests that conflict will invariably develop between electoral politicians and soldiers, and that the survival interests of politicians are sufficiently compelling to prompt efforts to contract the military's domain over time.

Political Capacity

If electoral competition unleashes *incentives* for politicians to diminish military influence, the popular support that electoral victory certifies enhances the *capacity* of politicians to do so. A military organization would incur great risk and cost in taking forceful measures against a government with solid popular backing. The greater the mandate a given government enjoys, the less likely military elites will be to aggressively counteract civilian attempts to diminish their political role. All things being equal, a politician's capacity to take measures prejudicial to the armed forces is also enhanced to the extent that the armed forces do not form a united front opposing the measures in question.

In Brazil, capturing 53 percent of the valid vote in the 1989 presidential election (the first direct presidential election in twenty-nine years) helped President Fernando Collor face down the armed forces in the initial stages of his government.[20] Concrete policies to narrow the military's sphere of influence, as well as symbolic gestures such as Collor's frequent references to himself as "commander in chief," met with little resistance. A poll conducted in the spring of 1991, which revealed the three military ministers to be among the least known of anyone in the cabinet, attested to Collor's ability to defuse the military.[21] Rarely did Collor appear at public events alongside his military ministers, a sure sign that the armed forces had lost their place in the inner circle of power.

By contrast, Collor's predecessor, President José Sarney (1985–90), was far more beholden to the armed forces. The military ministers, especially Army Minister Leônidas Pires Gonçalves, were featured regularly in the press commenting on wide-ranging topics and criticizing civilian authorities. Sarney was the rather colorless vice presidential running mate of president-elect Tancredo Neves, who died in 1985 shortly before assuming office. Neves himself was selected by an electoral college rather than by popular vote. The weakness of Sarney's mandate—beginning with the nonelectoral route by which he came to power—deprived him of the necessary authority to stand strong against the military. Notably, however, even President Sarney made some modest efforts to contain the military in the initial stages of his government. These efforts took place at roughly the same time that Sarney pursued a populist line on economic policy. But after his popularity plunged beginning in December 1986 with the failure of the Cruzado Plan, an economic stabilization plan intended to break inertial inflation, President Sarney became captive to the armed forces.

President Itamar Franco suffered from the same basic weakness as President Sarney. Replacing President Collor in the wake of the December 1992 vote of impeachment, former vice president Franco did not come to power with an electoral mandate of his own. Moreover, during his presidency Franco never gained sufficient popularity among the citizenry to defy any established group or organization. President Franco therefore manifested much greater timidity than his predecessor in taking steps to increase civilian dominance.

The dynamic described above suggests that civilian politicians will be motivated to oppose a politically active military as a natural outgrowth of democratization. Even in the absence of a deliberate, principle-driven strategy to remove the military from political roles, the imperatives of electoral competition, together with the legitimation that popular elections confer on winning candidates, set the stage for civil-military conflict and the subsequent adoption of measures to reduce the military's sphere of influence. Some politicians who support the reduction of military prerogatives undoubtedly do embrace the ideal of civilian control over the military. Many, however, appear to be motivated less by principles and more by instrumental considerations of electoral advancement. That former members of ARENA, the government party under authoritarian rule, have been among those who have contested the armed forces attests to the strength of pragmatic calculations. President Collor himself, who launched the most direct attack on the armed forces since 1985, was himself a son of the military regime.[22]

Presidents versus Legislators: Differences in Incentives and Capacities

Both presidents and legislators seek to extend their own power and influence. A military that interferes regularly in politics will invariably constitute an impediment to this goal. The more the armed forces impinge on the electoral interests of executive and legislative politicians, the more they set themselves up to be contested. Beyond the basic interest that presidents and legislators share in their own electoral advancement, a slightly different set of incentives and constraints applies to the two categories of politicians.

Presidents seek to remain in good standing with the electorate even though most Latin American countries bar immediate presidential reelection. In many countries, it is not unusual for former presidents to strive for the presidency anew after sitting out one or more terms. In Brazil, they often seek election to lower political offices. To maximize their long-term influence and chances of reelection, presidents must do three things: govern effectively, build a political organization with strong personal loyalties to them, and survive in power.[23] The presence of a powerful and politically active military can pose a threat to all three of these objectives. A military prone to political meddling is an especially vexing problem for presidents.

The future careers of presidents, more than those of legislators, depend on achieving programmatic goals that resonate well with public opinion. If reelection is at all a goal, presidents must gather cross-regional support. The programmatic incentives facing presidents include a host of public-policy initiatives over which military influence could be problematic and electorally costly. The following constitutes an example of military interference limiting a president's latitude to enact reforms that could boost his government's popularity. The hierarchy's relentless pressure on the Franco government to award higher salaries to the military (which, if granted, would compel the government to provide salary increases for civilian public employees as well) threatened the austerity requirement of the Franco government's economic plan, the Plano Real. President Franco had a vested interest in the plan, an eleventh-hour development that could improve the reputation of his beleaguered government. The success of the plan was also critical to Finance Minister Fernando Henrique Cardoso, who used it to launch his campaign for the presidency.[24]

While more attentive than legislators to broader policy concerns, presidents also need to build and finance personal support networks. They rely on the distribution of large-scale patronage to win support for their programs in the Congress and bureaucracy, and among governors and mayors. Presidents' reliance on patronage is also designed to lay the groundwork for future political candidacies to which they aspire. Thus, presidents too face pressure to direct public funds to where they have the greatest electoral payoff. Having to spend patronage resources on the armed forces in order to ward off the prospect of a coup interferes with this goal. When threatened with imminent military intervention, Latin American presidents have historically redirected vast amounts of patronage resources to the armed forces. But this leaves them with fewer resources to finance social and economic programs essential for maintaining general popularity and legislative support.[25]

In short, through policies as well as electoral patronage, presidents can enhance their long-term influence and subsequent reelection. A politically inclined military is likely to interfere in the dual processes of policy making and patronage distribution. It thus stands to reason that presidents would be motivated to contest the military and push them back from the political sphere. Moreover, by virtue of the impressive administrative powers that Latin American presidents have at their disposal, their ability to enact reforms to contract military influence greatly exceeds that of individual legislators.

But the aspiration of Latin American presidents to contain military influence in order to advance their electoral interests is often counterbalanced by the desire to survive in office. Antagonizing the military remains a widespread concern among Latin American presidents. In the event of a military coup, a prospect that occurs to all Latin American chief executives at one time or another, the president is usually the main target of overthrow. In the decades before the installation of the bureaucratic-authoritarian regime of 1964–85, the military spearheaded several "moderating coups," whose central purpose was to replace one civilian executive by another.

Presidents can be counted on to court the military—even at the cost of political autonomy—when deep economic and political crises put in doubt the survival of their governments. Discretionary funding and other concessions to the armed services are key ways by which debilitated presidents try to secure their governments. Obtaining military support has two objectives: the first is to reduce the likelihood that the armed forces will try to overthrow the government; the second is to enhance governability by fortifying the government. For example, a president who enjoys military backing is better positioned than one who does not to intimidate an uncooperative Congress or an unruly labor movement into becoming more supportive (or at least less defiant) of his administration.

In short, while the desire to extend their own power and influence constitutes a strong motivation for presidents to contest and contain the military, the instinct to protect themselves from overthrow also exists, constituting a countervailing source of pressure. Given the extensive powers of their office, Latin American presidents can affect decisively the civil-military balance depending on which logic and corresponding course of action they follow. As discussed below, in addition to a president's electoral mandate, broader power alignments and the overall political climate can tip the balance in one direction or the other.

Legislators are also constrained by the presence of a powerful and politically active military. In order to improve their chances of reelection, they too want to extend their own control over resources and broaden their latitude over decision making.[26] Compared to executive politicians, however, electoral support for legislators depends less on what programs they support and more on their ability to satisfy constituents through the provision of particularistic services and categorical patronage. As a general rule, the broader policy concerns of legislators will be more important to urban constituencies, who are better informed and more mobilized than their rural counterparts. But even in states with major urban agglomerations, such as São Paulo, Rio de Janeiro, and Minas Gerais, the provision of categorical patronage is important to getting elected. As individuals, legislators can only gain by doling out huge amounts of patronage. Presidents, by contrast, bear a disproportionate burden for relying excessively on patronage for electoral ends. For a president, the costs of pursuing such a policy range from antagonizing the military to ruining the economy.

Legislators also have a strong interest in not antagonizing the military. But a collective action dilemma, which the organizational weakness and fragmentation of Brazil's political party system exacerbates, often prevents them from supporting budgetary and other policies that reflect this interest. For example, legislators cannot be assured that fellow members would contribute to the collective good of safeguarding democracy by satisfying the military's budgetary demands. The moderation of an individual legislator's hunger for patronage resources would barely affect the armed forces' budget share. But by sacrificing patronage, a crucial weapon in electoral competition, the individual politician might risk his or her political future. Thus, the incentive structure militates against an individual legislator's making a contribution to this cause on his or her own.[27] This suggests that the Congress might be the most likely institution to impose political and organizational costs, as well as budgetary restrictions, on the armed forces. The fact that military reprisal is generally directed more clearly at presidents than legislators reinforces this expectation.

The Brazilian Congress has indeed taken bold steps to challenge military power. But Congress's ability to enact reforms aimed at subordinating the military to effective civilian control in the long term hinges on acquiring collective support. Gathering support to promote the common goal of establishing civilian supremacy over the military is difficult where legislators direct their time, energy, and political capital to issues that yield more concrete and immediate political benefit. In short, the problem is that, as individuals, presidents have the greatest capacity to downgrade the military's institutional powers, but they are often inhibited by fear; legislators are less concerned than presidents about antagonizing the military but face greater organizational barriers to bringing about reforms that would advance civilian authority in the long term. Yet despite these constraints, political elites in postauthoritarian Brazil have in fact challenged the military over specific policy decisions as well as certain institutional prerogatives.

While democracy provides universal inducements to pushing back military influence, the strength of the incentives and the capacity of politicians to act on them vary across time and across countries. Institutional differences—for example, electoral rules and internal party procedures that shape politicians' strategies for electoral advancement—explain some of the variation among democratic countries. So do broad domestic and international changes that affect the degree to which politicians view military restiveness as a serious threat. As elaborated below, both factors—institutional differences among polities and broader power alignments in society—condition the process by which civilians contest the military. While the weakly institutionalized nature of Brazilian politics heightens the incentives for political elites to contest the armed forces, the lack of domestic and international support for military intervention in the post–cold war era removes a previous disincentive. Together, they render politicians more likely to push back military influence.

CONDITIONING FACTORS

Institutional Rules

Institutional rules condition politicians' strategies for pursuing reelection, which in turn shape their conduct toward the military. The system of government (presidentialism versus parliamentarism), rules governing elections, the party system, and internal party procedures have an important impact on these strategies. Brazil's political system contains numerous features that impel politicians to act in accordance with electoral exigencies. Under the short time horizons that this system encourages, politicians are especially motivated to adopt policies that impose organizational, political, and budgetary costs on the armed forces.[28]

Comparatively speaking, Brazilian politics is highly personalistic and weakly institutionalized. The party system is extremely fragmented. Parties themselves lack internal cohesion. The 1989 presidential race provided strong testimony to the weakness of party affiliation and the negligible role that parties play in structuring Brazilian politics. Fernando Collor de Mello created a new party, the PRN (Partido de Reconstrução Nacional or National Reconstruction Party), for the sole purpose of running for president. The runner up, Luis Inácio (Lula) da Silva, came from the Workers' Party (Partido dos Trabalhadores or PT), whose representatives comprised a mere 3 percent of the Congress.

Several institutional provisions elevate the importance of personalistic leadership and populist appeals.[29] Presidentialism, coupled with a fractionalized multiparty system, is a foundation for highly candidate-centered politics. The independent basis of power that presidents enjoy allows them (more than prime ministers) to circumvent parties. And because a multiparty system creates special difficulties for the creation of stable majorities, presidents facing this situation are especially likely to try to govern above parties.

The unique combination of proportional representation and open-list candidate selection gives Brazilian parties limited influence over which candidates are elected. Because candidates effectively compete against members of their own party (as well as other parties), open-list proportional representation systems place a high premium on a candidate's personal characteristics (rather than his or her links to a political party) and on a candidate's ability to dole out patronage.[30]

Further weakening the strength of Brazilian parties is the absence of an entry barrier to the formation of a political party (a certain minimum percentage of the national vote that parties must obtain in order to win representation in the legislature). Brazilian politicians thus form new parties when it is opportune to do so, and because no legislation prohibits it, they frequently leave their old parties for other already established parties. Between 1987 and 1990, 40 percent of all federal deputies switched parties, mainly during the Constituent Assembly of 1987–88.[31] Given the electoral importance of patronage, it is not uncommon for legislators to join and abandon given parties based on party connections to clientelist networks, especially those sustained by the government. Many politicians previously of ARENA have switched into centrist or even somewhat progressive parties, mainly to improve their electoral prospects.[32]

It should not be surprising that levels of party identification and loyalty among voters are extremely low in such a system. Because most Brazilian parties have no "reservoir of support" among their followers, politicians are beholden to rank and file demands. The conditional nature of the electorate's support and the high electoral volatility present in weak and fragmented party systems make politicians especially sensitive to immediate electoral considerations.

The ultimate result of Brazil's weak party system is the personalization of politics. Such a system renders the political landscape ripe for the emergence of populist leaders. Prone to demagoguery, they appeal to voters on the basis of diffuse popular images and political patronage. The fluid nature of Brazilian politics and the nonprogrammatic orientation of political parties not only provide politicians with incentives to behave this way, but also offer them great latitude to endorse political platforms in response to shifting public opinion. The weak institutionalization of Brazilian politics selects for those politicians who shun institutional constraints on their rule, whether these constraints assume the form of a stronger party system or a military that is embedded in the state and armed with a broad array of institutional prerogatives.

There is a double edge, however, to the organizational characteristics of the Brazilian political system and their effect on civil-military relations. In weakly institutionalized systems, civilians are more likely to support policies that effectively lead them to challenge the military. When electoral opinion and military preferences come into conflict, politicians are likely to side with the former since few politicians enjoy the reservoir of support that would allow them to act otherwise. But at the same time, politicians in such a system are less likely to build collective support for measures aimed at institutionalizing civilian control over the armed forces. In other words, while the system's fluidity creates special incentives for politicians to contest or challenge the military when their electoral fortunes are at stake, the organizational weakness of political parties militates against efforts to permanently defuse the armed forces as a political actor. The reason for this is twofold.

First, the fragmentation of political parties and the short time horizons of actors in a weakly institutionalized political system create an environment of *imediatismo político* (political immediatism),[33] which makes it difficult to translate the long-term collective *interest* in gaining civilian supremacy into collective *action* of the kind necessary to develop lasting mechanisms of civilian control over the military. Stronger parties, more suitable for overcoming collective-action dilemmas, would help coordinate members around a more deliberate and persistent strategy of gaining civilian control over the military. A less politicized system would enable politicians to look beyond the most immediate crisis and focus their attention on the development of legislation aimed at solving the problem of military interference in a more enduring fashion.

The second general factor limiting a weakly institutionalized political system from going beyond contesting the military to subordinating them permanently concerns the broader impact of such a system on governability. The short-sighted political calculations that drive the actions of clientelist and populist politicians against the military are likely to undermine other goals, such as responsible economic policy. As the economy deteriorates and political turmoil arises, the standing of civilian politicians, most notably the president, is undermined. When these problems erupt into acute crises, presidents, who are held most accountable for the overall condition of the country, risk losing their positions. Under this threat, and because they lack organized bases of civilian support, the capacity of presidents to keep the military out of politics diminishes. They may even turn to and expand the role of the armed forces in order to keep the crisis from spiraling out of control. Thus, the goal to survive in office may eventually induce politicians under threat to restore military power.

Notwithstanding this possibility, military influence has declined overall since 1985 and can be expected to diminish further as Brazilian democracy becomes more consolidated. The dynamic normally unleashed by democratic competition and reinforced by the fluidity of Brazil's political system is for self-interested politicians to contest the military. The countervailing dynamic described above unfolds only under exceptional conditions, stalling or temporarily arresting this process. The dynamic that has transpired in Brazil in the postauthoritarian period suggests that military interference in politics will decline overall with time, notwithstanding certain short-term deviations from this trend. But because the characteristics of a weakly institutionalized system will motivate civilian politicians to continuously challenge the armed forces but not go further and institutionalize control over them, ongoing civil-military tension and conflict can be expected.

The Credibility of Military Force

If characteristics of Brazil's political system strengthen the incentives that lead politicians to contest the military, features particular to the current era and their effect on power relations in the broader society reinforce this tendency. Politicians need to respond to electoral incentives in a democracy, but they must also respond to power relations, which vary across time and national borders. Since basic threats to the socioeconomic and political order are absent in most of post–cold war Latin America, the use of military force for domestic political purposes lacks widespread support and renders civilian politicians less fearful of upsetting the military. The awareness of Brazilian officers that the current political climate is unsympathetic to strong-arm tactics tames their reactions to challenges that they view unfavorably but that do not threaten core corporate interests. Rarely in recent years have the military closed ranks and frontally resisted civilian initiatives to diminish their influence over extramilitary matters. The navy and air force have tended to be more liberal and internationalist, more concerned than the army is to meet narrower professionalist and technological needs and less inclined to combat developments that diminish their overall clout.[34] Even within the army, not all officers have supported a continuation of the institution's influence over broad political, social, and economic questions. Officers' tendency to exercise restraint emboldens politicians to respond more to public opinion than to military opinion. In short, electoral considerations gain in importance and take precedence over considerations of military power when the basic political and economic order is not in question. In the 1990s, winning votes, not military support, is clearly the first principle of political survival.

The basic analytical issue at hand concerns whether and to what extent the armed forces can transform their central power capability—organized coercion—into influence over outcomes. The potential impact of an actor's central power capability (e.g., financial strength, expertise, force, etc.) is a key determinant of how seriously it is regarded by others. It is indeed the case that an actor's potential power is "the price of admission to the political arena,"[35] even though the armed forces' institutional prerogatives may help them articulate and realize their preferences without having to constantly invoke their ultimate weapon, the capacity for physical intimidation.

Organized coercion, the military's central power capability, can be an impressive political weapon. A wide range of military actions—from "shows of force" to *pronunciamentos*, rebellions, and coups d'état—rest on the military's potential to inflict violence. The coup d'état represents perhaps the most outstanding instance of this. Stated starkly by Samuel Huntington, "while other social forces can pressure the government, the military can replace the government."[36]

But the distinction between an actor's potential strength and how likely it is to bring the full force of its power to bear is also critical. Rarely is there a perfect congruence between power as measured by basic capabilities and power as measured by actual effects. Power is not a static attribute, but one that is conditioned by context.[37] Some contexts increase the likelihood and capacity of political actors to transform their potential power into actual influence over outcomes. Others reduce them. When viewed from this perspective, the military's central power capability—organized force—suffers numerous restrictions.

The degree of political influence the armed forces can wield by virtue of their coercive potential depends very much on how willing they are to employ force and, relatedly, on other actors' perceptions of how likely they are to do so. Force can prevail and the military can constitute the ultima ratio if military leaders are willing to assume the costs of unleashing it. Rule by the military as an institution constitutes the clearest expression of the military's willingness to incur the risks of coercive action. Lesser manifestations of military power also carry risks.

The armed forces can indeed overplay their cards by invoking coercion when they lack societal support. Excessive threats and displays of force can erode the reserve of societal good will that the armed forces need to retain long-term credibility. In the words of Guillermo O'Donnell and Philippe Schmitter, "beyond a certain point, kicking or even pounding the table may be counterproductive. It threatens one's allies almost as much as one's opponents, and the committed players may well join forces to eliminate the obstreperous one."[38]

Many South American militaries, including (perhaps especially) the Brazilian, strive to project an image of respect for the public's wishes. Never have the Brazilian armed forces undertaken a major intervention without first seeking civilian support. History has demonstrated the value of civilian allies as a key determinant of the success of military interventions.[39] Even during the height of military rule, the regime went to great lengths to legitimate itself by publicizing its developmental accomplishments and keeping the Congress open (at least in a formal sense).[40] In the postauthoritarian period, the energy the Brazilian army devotes to public relations provides strong testimony to its commitment to projecting an image of responsiveness to public sentiment. If the military's claim to represent "the national interest" or "the will of the people" is to have any credence, intimidation must be used selectively. If the armed forces do not reserve saber rattling for exceptional circumstances, their chances of gaining domestic and international civilian support at critical moments will be reduced.[41] In the absence of substantial societal backing, the use of strong-arm tactics for domestic political purposes can also adversely affect corporate unity, a key military concern. Recent examples of this took place in Venezuela and Thailand, where military commanders ordered soldiers to fire on demonstrators in 1989 and 1992, respectively, provoking internal division.[42]

At various moments, the armed forces in Latin America have chosen to assume the risks of using coercion for domestic political purposes. Over the course of this century, Brazil's military have wielded force in various forms and degrees. Two factors have generally inspired their forceful intervention in politics: strong objections to the extant economic and political order, accompanied by a vision of change; and core corporate concerns, such as unity among the officer corps, obedience to hierarchy (especially between officers and enlisted men), autonomy of the rank and seniority system from political interference, a monopoly of the armed forces over paramilitary organizations, and budgetary resources sufficient to maintain training, education, and equipment.[43]

Developments of the early 1960s constituted a challenge to core corporate principles as well as the military's preferred political and economic order. Labor organizers' efforts to unionize enlisted men and President Goulart's pardon of mutinous sailors put in question the military's corporate preservation.[44] The mobilization of urban and rural popular sectors raised concerns among military officers as well as societal elites about maintaining their privileged socioeconomic positions. The political polarization of the 1960s rendered the domestic use of military force more acceptable and lent credibility to military saber rattling. Conservative and center-right politicians allied with leading officers although it diminished their political independence. Under conditions of high politicization, even populist politicians with ample popular backing could be overthrown by the armed forces.

Does postauthoritarian Brazil present conditions similar to those that led the military to rattle their swords, gain the backing of societal elites, and intimidate civilian politicians in the past? By and large it does not. The demobilization of the anti-system left, the demise of communism worldwide, and the general consensus about democracy and capitalism as preferred political and economic systems have calmed the military and other elites. The armed forces' survival is not currently in question. Since the return to civilian rule, the Brazilian military have experienced no fundamental challenges, such as the existence of a parallel armed institution or the operation of subversive groups seeking to undermine internal discipline.

Certain trends, such as the decrease in defense expenditures and the privatization of military industries, have adversely affected force levels, military training, and re-equipment plans. And certainly the military do resist moves to reduce their influence in some areas more than others. For example, they made no concerted effort to retain control over the SNI, but have challenged civilians over budgetary expenditures and defense projects in the Amazon. The variation of military response rests on how closely the issue impinges on central corporate functions, on the (self-defined) raison d'être of the institution, and on the organization's ability to justify itself to others. With reference to the above examples, spying on citizens of one's own country is not easily justifiable as a corporate military function. Demanding greater resources to defend territorial integrity in the Amazon is. Many recent developments that contract the military's jurisdiction and competence and meet with resistance do not strike at the heart of corporate preservation. Thus, they have not prompted leading officers to go beyond routine complaining and the occasional issuing of rhetorical warnings.

Only with respect to one matter—the legal prosecution of military personnel for human rights violations committed in the authoritarian period—have Southern Cone militaries considered the stakes high enough to warrant forceful action. The issue of corporate autonomy lies at the heart of the armed forces' visceral reaction to efforts by civilians to prosecute them for measures conducted in a context they liken to war. Rebellious factions of the Argentine army reminded civilians that they constituted a power to be reckoned with, effectively putting an end to the trials initiated by President Alfonsín. In Chile, where the military have essentially remained immune from prosecution, efforts to hold officers account-able for past violations met with shows of strength. In Brazil, the self-granted amnesty of 1979 has never come close to being rolled back.

Just as Latin America's new democracies have basically safeguarded corporate military concerns, the broader political, economic, and social climate of the contemporary period does not threaten elite sectors that backed military activism in the past. Research suggests that only a small percentage of Brazilian industrial-ists feels threatened by the left in the new democratic regime,[45] and that the overwhelming majority has adapted to the democratic system. Industrialists do not regard the military as necessary for protecting their interests on a regular basis[46] and have responded to existing dissatisfaction by demanding greater par-ticipation in economic decisions. In fact, their significant economic power and ties to key decision makers have enabled business groups to exert more influence over economic policy making than any other single social group.[47] International condemnation of military solutions in the post–cold war era—manifested, for example, in response to the attempted coup in Guatemala in 1993—doubtless contributes to the use of nonmilitary forms of influence on the part of Brazil's business elites.

In light of the current climate, the armed forces in Brazil and elsewhere in Latin America have exercised notable restraint after retreating from power, save their uncompromising stance to preserve immunity from human rights prosecu-tions. The rigorous distance Brazil's military maintained from the investigations, demonstrations, and other events leading up to President Collor's impeachment was unprecedented in light of their interference in every other major political crisis of the twentieth century.[48] Further testimony of change was the military's nonintervention during the lowest point of the Franco government, when wide-spread corruption, hyperinflation, and low morale among the ranks led many observers to draw parallels with the pre-1964 environment.

To return to the terms of the earlier discussion, despite the military's basic power capability, constraints on the leadership's willingness to use strong-arm tactics limit its influence over actual policy outcomes. Given the array of factors inhibiting the unleashing of force, coupled with the widespread perception that the military are reluctant to call upon their basic power capability, saber rattling has come to lack credibility.[49] Military elites can bluff only so many times before civilians call their bluff. Armed forces that develop a reputation for making threats that are never carried out lose credibility over time. The practice of not taking military claims seriously remains more evident among legislators than presidents. At the risk of exaggeration, conditions of the 1980s and 1990s have rendered the Brazilian military somewhat of a paper tiger.

CONCLUSION

This chapter has sought to address three questions posed at the outset: What is the impact of electoral competition on the political role of the military? How do specific political institutions condition the way in which civilians contest the military? How can the armed forces defend their claims? Contrary to the prevailing view that democracy in Brazil has remained and will remain restricted by virtue of the strong position the military enjoyed at the onset of democracy, my rational choice approach suggests that the installation of democratic competition tends to bring about a gradual expansion of popular sovereignty.

Using the strategic calculations of politicians as a point of departure, this chapter has argued that electoral competition and the incentives it unleashes form a key source of the dynamism that has marked civil-military relations in the postauthoritarian period. The policies that have resulted from these incentives have gradually shifted the balance of civil-military power in favor of civilians. This general trend of eroding military influence is subject to fluctuation depending on the strength of governments and the electoral relevance of issues. Politicians, both executive and congressional, are more likely to challenge the military under governments with widespread support and over issues where military interference threatens their own ability to win elections.

Specific institutional features condition the manner in which civilians contest the armed forces. How democratic competition works to alter the balance of civil-military power depends partly on politicians' strategies of reelection and on the institutional rules that govern these strategies. In a weakly institutionalized political system, as in Brazil, the feebleness of political parties induces politicians to attract voters through the constant provision of patronage and endorsement of popularity-enhancing platforms, practices that are likely to be at odds with military preferences. Such a system also sets the stage for the emergence of politicians who seek to enhance their political autonomy and therefore challenge tutelage by an independent and bureaucratic military.

But while the institutional characteristics of Brazil's political system reinforce the general incentives that electoral competition unleashes and provide special impetus for elected officials to challenge the armed forces, they militate against the development of conditions and measures conducive to ensuring long-term political stability and civilian control. Effective civilian governance, arguably the best antidote to the armed forces' intervention in politics, is more difficult to achieve in a weakly institutionalized party system. Moreover, given the potential of such a party system to produce high levels of politicization, institutionalized mechanisms to break the political role and autonomy of the military are less likely to be enacted and consistently observed by civilians.

The legitimacy and credibility of military force as a domestic political instrument also conditions the willingness of politicians to contest the armed forces. Widespread consensus in favor of democracy and the relative paucity of threats to the military's core political and corporate interests in the post–cold war era inhibit the armed forces as a whole from countering civilian efforts to downgrade their prerogatives by invoking coercion. The cost-benefit calculation made by military elites has generally pointed in favor of accepting their declining political fortunes rather than putting up resistance at the risk of provoking serious civil-military conflict. But simply because the military's actual bargaining power suffers serious limitations in the current period does not mean that the military cannot and do not extract occasional budgetary benefits or other concessions in exchange for supporting the government.

That civilians have contested and managed to reduce military influence in Brazil is especially noteworthy since the military entered the new democracy from a highly auspicious position. Chapter 2 analyzes why the officer corps enjoyed such strong standing in 1985. To explain this strength, the chapter goes back in time and analyzes developments that took place within the institution during the bureaucratic-authoritarian period, and between civilians and the military governments in the transition to democracy. By establishing where Brazil's armed forces stood in 1985, Chapter 2 offers a baseline from which to judge their post-1985 evolution.

MILITARY STRENGTH AT THE INCEPTION OF CIVILIAN RULE

hree factors—corporate unity, institutional prerogatives, and the ability to negotiate with key civilians—gave the Brazilian military a seemingly unassailable position at the time of the transfer of power to civilians. A relatively high level of unity in the army, far-reaching institutional prerogatives over political decision making, and the control by Brazil's military governments over important aspects of the regime transition all paved the way for a departure on terms favorable to the armed forces. An institutionalist analysis would focus on these developments and their role in shaping civil-military relations after the regime transition, emphasizing the resistance of preexisting arrangements to change. The Brazilian case should confirm the accuracy of such an analytical perspective since the advantages the armed forces enjoyed on the eve of the new democracy seemed to confer upon them insurmountable powers.

In this view, organizational unity would allow the military to pursue their corporate and political interests with full force, without being paralyzed by internal divisions. Ample institutional prerogatives would guarantee the armed forces' deep involvement in political decision making, extending far beyond the reach of their corporate interests. Military control over the regime transition would cement these institutional advantages and make it unmistakably clear to civilian politicians that democracy was granted by the armed forces—and that it could eventually be revoked; challenging the military on important issues would therefore be out of the question.

Indeed, the developments described in this chapter did enhance the military's prospects for exercising continued political strength after the transfer of power to civilians. But, as later chapters demonstrate, their ability to sustain military influence over the longer term was limited. The competitive dynamic of democracy soon came to erode the military's institutional prerogatives and, especially, the military's political influence. Driven by the electoral incentives explained in Chapter 1, politicians increasingly contested the armed forces, disregarded some of their important interests and preferences, and pushed back their influence over political decision making. These findings—presented in Chapters 4 to 6—call into question the institutionalist expectation that ample institutional advantages would guarantee the armed forces control over the new civilian regime.

INSTITUTIONAL UNIFICATION

The military regime (1964–85) enacted numerous regulations and norms that transformed the army into a more centralized, hierarchical, and unified organization. As a result of these well-established norms and rigorously applied sanctions, there are no prominent factions—of a personal or ideological nature—to speak of in today's active-duty army.[1] Similarly, virtually all army leaders derive their authority from institutional positions they hold, not from charismatic appeal or personal followings. Organizational changes that took place from 1964 to 1985 deepened the bureaucratic character of the army and helped keep dissidence at bay, contributing decisively to the relatively smooth exit of the military from power.

Military leaders recognized that internal divisions had weakened the corporation from 1945 to 1964. The first military president, General Humberto Castello Branco, used his powers to attenuate internal rivalries that could compromise the military's capacity to govern effectively and to protect the institution from the potentially politicizing effects of authoritarian rule. He began a process of instituting rules and instilling norms designed to discourage caudillos from emerging and wresting control from the bureaucratic leadership of the army.

Compared to its prior condition as well as to many other militaries on the continent, the Brazilian army was indeed able to emerge from authoritarian rule relatively cohesive.[2] The success of the regime helped suppress factionalization. Of course, the inevitable division between "hard-line" and "soft-line" elements and internationalist versus nationalist factions emerged, as did the autonomy of the security community from the central command.[3] Nevertheless, the army managed to maintain an impressive degree of unity. Over the course of twenty years, Brazil saw a succession of five military governments and a return to civilian rule without rupture. In this connection, Thomas Skidmore notes that "with rare exceptions, the losers guarded their silence. This maintenance of unity, at least in public, contrasted sharply with the frequent divisions that had arisen among the officers in the political-military crises between 1945–1964."[4]

In these previous years, army cohesion was undermined by (1) the existence of factions based on ideological differences; (2) the presence of personalistic leaders, who were often at odds with the army's institutional authorities; (3) the highly politicized character of promotions and appointments at the upper levels, especially in times of political crisis; (4) the frequent pursuit by officers of parallel careers in electoral politics; and (5) the persistent defiance of discipline and hierarchy by factions within the organization.[5]

The central political cleavage between 1945 and 1964 revolved around how officers viewed Getúlio Vargas and the reformist, nationalist dimension of the populist platform he developed toward the end of the Estado Novo. The pro-Vargas versus anti-Vargas split surfaced regularly in debates of the highly politicized Clube Militar and at every point of succession between 1945 and 1964.[6] Not confined to backroom discussions, the internal conflicts of the military were widely reported in the Brazilian press. Within the broad division centering around Vargas, personalistic cliques figured prominently.[7] The length of time officers were allowed to hold top-level positions facilitated the emergence of military leaders with personal followings. The army lacked a strict "up-or-out" promotion system and placed no limit on how long generals could remain in active duty. For example, a quintessential military figure of the period, Oswaldo Cordeiro de Farias, was an active-duty general for twenty-five years, more than sufficient time to create an independent base of leadership within the army.[8]

Military personalities jockeyed for power within the organization and also sought to form alliances with like-minded civilian politicians at the national level. Politicians seeking to build a *dispositivo militar* (a group of allies within the military) welcomed their overtures. In addition to forging ties to civilian politicians, several prominent military figures held political office themselves.[9] At the time, the army placed no restrictions on officers conducting political careers while maintaining their military careers. It allowed officers to take long and indefinite leaves from active service. Many of the officers who played a prominent role in the political crises of the period spent much of their time engaged in extramilitary pursuits. Such officers were known as "amphibians" (partly military, partly civilian) among their military colleagues.[10] The military was so deeply involved in partisan politics that the presidential elections of 1945, 1950, 1955, and 1960 all featured military officers as candidates. Members of the officer corps frequently vied for governorships as well, often in states where they had held important command positions.

These factors contributed to fracturing the army's command structure, giving rise to countless crises. In articulating their own agendas, dissident factions often reached out to like-minded civilians and defied the directives of institutional authorities. While the high command officially opposed the existence of independent movements within the organization, it often found itself at a loss to control them. The fear that disciplinary action would provoke a backlash inhibited army authorities in punishing acts of insubordination.[11]

Given the many cleavages and high potential for politicization that existed within the Brazilian military from 1945 to 1964, effective governance during the bureaucratic-authoritarian regime would depend on the emergence of measures designed to create greater organizational cohesion. Some of the policies instituted in response to this imperative applied specifically to the authoritarian period. Others have remained in place to the present.

Presidential Succession

The existence and nature of presidential succession contributed to keeping the military unified and stabilizing the regime, notwithstanding the eruption of short-term crises at certain points of succession. In addition to providing for regular presidential succession, the Brazilian regime was distinguished by the fact that presidents retired from active duty upon assuming office, donned civilian clothes, and never again appeared in uniform.[12] President Castello Branco (1964–67) set the trend to step down when his term expired, sending a strong message that no caudillo would emerge from the Brazilian regime.[13] Thereafter, regular succession occurred through the consensus of officers. Although senior officers made the final selection for president, it was only after regional commanders consulted with officers far down the ranks in order to assure support for their choice.[14] The effort to consult with lower ranks to try to arrive at policy decisions consistent with majority views within the military was a distinctive aspect of the military regime in Brazil.

On two occasions, leaders with political aspirations and personal appeal threatened the staid bureaucratic style of the regime. The first was General Afonso Augusto de Albuquerque Lima, who in 1968 undertook an active bid for the presidency. The second was Sílvio Frota, who as minister of the army under President Ernesto Geisel tried to articulate support for his own candidacy. Neither general succeeded in his quest for the presidency. Army leaders took issue with the overt politicking in which both men engaged and feared their potential to become military strongmen.[15]

New Regulations to Move Officers "Up or Out"

By instituting rules designed to increase turnover at the upper levels of the armed forces, the first military president, Castello Branco, took additional steps to decrease the possibility that personalistic leaders would emerge, vie for internal constituencies, and fragment the organization. In December 1965, he tightened the rules governing promotions and retirements. Thereafter, officers with the rank of general (admiral in the navy and brigadier in the air force) were subject to retirement if passed over for promotion twice. The revision Castello Branco made also prohibited any officer from serving as a general (admiral or brigadier) for more than twelve years and compelled officers at this rank to retire at age sixty-six, even if they had served less than twelve years. In 1980, President João Baptista Figueiredo carried one step further the "up-or-out" system begun by Castello Branco. He reduced from two to one the number of times an officer with the rank of general (admiral or brigadier) could be passed over for promotion, and from three to two the number of times a colonel could be denied ascension to the rank of general. Virtually without exception, all military officers—even key figures in the military regime—were subject to compulsory rules of retirement.[16]

Military presidents took special advantage of these new retirement rules to shape the high command. Both Presidents Geisel and Figueiredo were able to use standard retirement procedures to remove controversial officers, namely those who appeared to pose a threat to the political opening. Rather than keep within the ranks officers closely associated with torture and other repressive aspects of the regime, whose presence could at the very least hurt the military's public image, the high command removed them by quietly passing them over for promotion.[17]

Prohibiting Parallel Careers

Castello Branco was of the opinion that military officers should not hold electoral office or positions in the civilian bureaucracy. Allowing them to do so, in his view, detracted from the professional character of the armed forces and dragged the military into the divisive world of partisan politics. Castello Branco's desire to draw strict boundaries around the "military as institution" and shield it from routine involvement in national politics led to measures of lasting relevance. In July 1964 he instituted a constitutional amendment compelling officers elected to political office to retire from the army. This was followed by a more general ruling in December 1965 that sought to discourage officers from engaging in any kind of extramilitary activity. This new regulation, an important step in the organizational professionalization of the Brazilian military, specified that officers who took time off from the force had to retire permanently or return to active duty after two years.[18] This ruling limited the participation of military officers in the civilian administration during military rule as well as afterwards. After 1983, this rule was even applied to officers serving in the SNI.[19] In short, new rules of promotion and retirement, coupled with the prohibition of parallel careers, were responsible for creating a new generation of army leaders without the political visibility and personal followings of many of their predecessors. In this connection, a veteran observer of Brazilian military affairs proclaimed, "Castello Branco transformed the Brazilian army into a faceless bureaucracy."[20]

Imposing Discipline

The military presidents of 1964–85 ran a tight ship. They imposed strict standards of conduct and were quick to discipline those who spoke out of turn or, worse yet, actively defied the hierarchy. Although sanctions grew less severe with the political opening, the experience of military rule had the general effect of strengthening disciplinary regulations within the armed forces.

With the imposition of Institutional Act 17 in 1968, the president gained the right to transfer to the reserves any officer "who commits or plans to commit a crime against the unity of the armed forces."[21] Officers were thus careful to watch their step as never before, lest they be purged or led to the reserves. President Geisel went a step further in centralizing military authority. Before him, there had existed an unwritten army rule that the commander was sovereign within the limits of his territorial region. In an effort to control the unordered use of torture, Geisel challenged the norm and put regional commanders strictly under his control.[22]

President Figueiredo feared that the final phase of military rule might provoke a last-minute effort by hard-liners to resist the transfer of power to civilians. His concerns extended to the activities of retired officers, who could conceivably influence the views and behavior of active-duty officers. In April 1979 he signed a decree (no. 83.349) that prohibited retired officers from making statements "that could damage the principles of hierarchy and discipline within the military." This meant that even retired officers who criticized the president or his policies would be subject to punishment by the disciplinary code of the armed forces.[23]

Inculcating Common Beliefs

The creation of consensus through the widespread adoption of a single overarching doctrine provides for more enduring cohesion than rules alone. The Doctrine of National Security (Doutrina da Segurança Nacional) guided military rhetoric and decision making over the life of the authoritarian regime.[24] It posited that national security depended on the development of a strong industrial capitalist economy, which could only develop if popular mobilization and "premature" demands were held in check by a strong government. The regime socialized all officers in the doctrine of national security, starting with cadets at the army academy (Academia Militar das Agulhas Negras or AMAN), and extending to higher officers attending the General Staff and Command School (Escola de Comando e Estado Maior do Exército or ECEME) and the National War College (Escola Superior de Guerra or ESG).[25] The inculcation of common beliefs helped submerge personal and factional goals and orient officers toward the collective goals of the military corporation.

The combined effect of these policies was to create and maintain a relatively high degree of unity within the army at a time when deep involvement in politics under authoritarian rule could well have splintered it. Military cohesion contributed to the accomplishments of the regime by enhancing the prospects for consistent policy making and implementation. In turn, the relatively successful performance of the bureaucratic-authoritarian regime in Brazil helped protect the military against internal fragmentation.[26] By allowing the military to wield their substantial power capabilities in a coordinated fashion, this solid institutional unity boded well for the military's pursuit of corporate and political interests in the new civilian regime.

INSTITUTIONAL POSITIONS AND PRIVILEGES

The military entered the new democracy buttressed by a broad network of institutional positions and prerogatives; some had originated prior to the bureaucratic-authoritarian regime and others were added during its course. Here I discuss those of greatest political significance.[27] On the eve of democracy's return, it might have seemed that the institutional bulwark surrounding the military would allow leading officers to advance their goals without having to form close alliances with individual politicians and their parties or to engage in visible forms of saber rattling, as in the previous period of Brazilian democracy. Instead, men in uniform promised to exercise tutelage over civilians in a regular and institutionalized fashion through access they enjoyed to centers of decision making.

The Ministries of the Army, Navy, and Air Force, whose chiefs have served in the cabinet since the 1920s, were maintained throughout the period of military rule. No unified Defense Ministry emerged in their place. Although the presence of a cabinet-level civilian who controls and coordinates the defense sector is an integral part of most modern democracies and most modern military organizations, at the time of the transition to democracy in Brazil there was no question but that the three traditional service ministries would remain intact and headed by officers. All three service chiefs would thus remain members of the cabinet, an important arena of government decision making.

The armed forces managed to carry over into the new democracy two other positions that they held historically: the military household (*casa militar* or *gabinete militar*) and the Armed Forces General Staff (Estado Maior das Forças Armadas or EMFA). During the military regime, these organs gained ministerial status.[28]

The chief of the *casa militar* (always an army general) acts as a liaison between the three service chiefs and the president. He is also responsible for the president's security. EMFA is responsible officially for integrating the doctrine, strategy, and defense operations of the three service branches. Leadership of the ministry rotates among the three branches.

During the period of authoritarian rule, the military's institutional privileges came to include a major personnel and policy presence in two organs closely associated with the national security regime, the National Security Council (CSN) and National Information Service (SNI). Created in 1934, the CSN did not play an important role until after 1964, when it became a key force in policy making vis-à-vis a range of issues broadly conceived under the rubric of national security, including the cancellation of politicians' political rights, industrial wages, land distribution, Amazonian development, and the nuclear program. Its influence was greatest between 1967 and 1979.[29]

The military exercised a preponderant role on the CSN although it formally included all cabinet members.[30] The secretary-general, whose importance on the council was unmatched, formed a crucial link between the civil and military bureaucracy. It was always an army general who held this position. Five divisions of the CSN conducted studies and elaborated policy reports on matters relating to (1) domestic and foreign politics; (2) economic development; (3) social development; (4) external defense; and (5) regionally related problems of significance to national security. Specific subjects studied under the first division included nuclear energy, the environment, space activities, and the law of the sea. Under the second division were scientific and technological development, transportation and communication, agribusiness, the steel industry, and the extraction of minerals. The third division dealt with housing, social security, health, education, employment, and religion. The fourth concerned itself with the development of the arms industry and military technology, and the coordination of the armed services and their mobilization. Subjects studied under the fifth section included land conflicts, internal migrations, the colonization of the Amazon, and indigenous populations. The CSN also had a permanent committee for issues concerning Brazil's borders.

An active-duty officer, normally a colonel, headed each of the above divisions. He reported to the secretary-general, who in turn advised the president. The secretary-general and president consulted with each other on a daily basis. In addition to contracting civilian consultants on specific issues, the CSN received information and analyses from the SNI.

Along with the CSN, the SNI played a leading role in the military's campaign to eliminate the anti-system left and put the country "back on track." Although the agency was not technically a military organization, the army held a predominant position within it.[31] The agency was created in 1964, the first year of the military regime. Before then, intelligence was conducted in a far less systematic or institutionalized fashion.[32] Formally combining domestic and foreign intelligence and counterintelligence functions, the SNI in practice devoted most of its energies to domestic affairs. Leftist political actors and social movements were primary targets of investigation. Beyond merely collecting information, SNI agents played an operational role in repression. The SNI also advised the president on issues relevant to national security, including the activities of ministries, state enterprises, and parastatal organizations. The agency was such a central organ in the bureaucratic-authoritarian regime that two of its former directors, Generals Emílio Garrastazu Médici and João Figueiredo, became presidents. After 1968, the first year of a highly repressive period that lasted roughly four years, the SNI gained increasing autonomy and deployed more and more personnel to carry out operations in the field. There was no routine oversight, legislative or executive, of the SNI's activities.

The SNI, together with other security organs (military and civilian) mobilized to combat the left, comprised the National Intelligence System (Sistema Nacional de Informações or SISNI). Under the SNI were the secret services and intelligence centers of each branch of the military. The Army Intelligence Center (Centro de Informações do Exército or CIE) was created in 1967. The Air Force Intelligence Center (Centro de Informações de Segurança da Aeronáutica or CISA) came into being in 1970. In existence since 1955, the Navy Intelligence Center (Centro de Informações da Marinha or CENIMAR) was notorious for practicing torture. An important extension of the SNI was forged in 1967 through the formation of Divisions of Security and Information (Divisões de Segurança e Informações or DSIs) and Security and Intelligence Assistance departments (Assessorias de Segurança or ASIs) to operate in all the ministries.[33] The DSIs were charged with assessing the impact on national security, broadly defined, of policies produced by the given ministry they were assigned to monitor. They compiled dossiers on the past activities of prospective employees and could exercise veto power over top-level and secondary-level ministerial appointments.[34] The ASIs performed similar functions. They operated in all governmental and parastate agencies, and in all companies under contract with the federal government. With this wide-ranging organizational network, the SNI sought to control Brazil's burgeoning state apparatus. This gave the military rulers inside information on and the capacity to interfere in all areas of public administration, thus allowing them to root out all internal opposition.[35]

The head of the SNI—always an army general—also enjoyed cabinet status. He thus had a direct say in governmental decision making, even outside his specific attributions. The cabinet status of the SNI, EMFA, *gabinete militar* (whose head also led the CSN), together with that of the traditional service branches, brought to six the number of ministerial posts held by the military, a very high number by international standards. Indeed, the armed forces' institutional power in the government was enormous, demonstrating how deeply the military regime tried to infuse the government with its doctrine of national security.

To further consolidate its control over society, the military regime instituted measures to subordinate to the army the militarized police (*polícia militar*), which had been controlled previously by the state governments. In addition to reducing the independence of the states and centralizing power in the federal government, the regime's intention was to eliminate challenges to the military's monopoly on coercion, a historical motivation for the federal army to reduce independent police power in the states. In fact, the authoritarian rulers also sought to harness the operational capacity of a massive police force in the struggle against the left.

The *polícia militar* are completely independent of the civil police in the states. They are also more numerous and heavily armed. In much of their equipment, internal structure, and training, they resemble a military organization more than a police force. Since the beginning of the republic in 1889, tension has existed between Brazil's strong militarized state police forces and the federal army. Until the state-building reforms of the Estado Novo (1930–45), the *polícia militar* in Brazil's larger states, such as São Paulo, Minas Gerais, and Rio Grande do Sul, rivaled the power of the federal army troops in the state. Governors used the militarized state police to resist efforts aimed at political centralization.[36]

After 1964, the *polícia militar* came under army command through the General Inspectorate of the Militarized Police (Inspetoria Geral das Polícias Militares or IGPM), headed by an army general stationed in Brasília.[37] The IGPM became responsible for the instruction of the *polícia militar*, the coordination of their troops, their organization, and armaments. The same decree that created the IGPM dictated that the commander of the *polícia militar* in all of Brazil's states be an active-duty colonel from the federal army, not an officer from the ranks of the *polícia militar* itself. In keeping with the subordination of the *polícia militar* to army command, the constitution of 1969 maintained that they were "ancillary and reserve forces" of the army. The army's policy of employing the *polícia militar* against subversion extended to requiring all of their commanders to take the year-long course on intelligence operations at the SNI's School of Intelligence (Escola Nacional de Informações or ESNI).[38]

Together with the impressive degree of unity the armed forces commanded, these formal prerogatives and institutional structures boded well for continued military influence under Brazil's new democracy. In contrast to the overt engagement in partisan politics during the previous democratic period, the articulation of military interests under the current democracy promised to be more institutionalized. The bureaucratization of the army in organizational terms, coupled with the growth of military-controlled institutions under authoritarian rule, underlay this expectation. But could the military retain these conditions and arrangements in a more competitive context that would expose them to new pressures and influences? The manner in which the regime made the transition out of authoritarianism enhanced the possibility that they could do so.

THE TRANSITION TO CIVILIAN GOVERNMENT

The transition to civilian rule in Brazil was exceptionally prolonged and tightly controlled by the military governments of Presidents Ernesto Geisel (1974–79) and João Figueiredo (1979–85). The authoritarian rulers achieved many of their original goals, successfully contained challenges from civil society, and left power in a position of strength. This command over the process of democratization allowed the armed forces to preserve the institutional advantages analyzed so far and to attain a seemingly unassailable standing at the inception of civilian rule.

President Geisel initiated the difficult and complex process of extricating the military from government power. It was success, by and large, rather than failure that prompted this move. The armed forces had brutally defeated the radical left, quelled any system-threatening mass mobilization, and—as the "economic miracle" of 1968–73 seemed to suggest—propelled Brazil toward rapid industrialization, promoting the military's dream of turning the country into a "great power." Thus, in the view of large sections of the officer corps and wide-ranging civilian sectors that had supported the military coup, the authoritarian regime had achieved the main goals it had set for itself in the mid-1960s.

Paradoxically, this success made the continuation of military rule—by nature of its extraconstitutional initiation, an exceptional regime type—difficult to justify. The authoritarian government could now also consider it unnecessary to keep exposing the armed forces to the strains and dangers of administering the country. Direct responsibility for the government posed the risk of involving the military in political conflicts, thus undermining corporate unity. It also held other temptations, including corruption, that could corrode internal command and discipline. In the eyes of President Geisel and his principal political advisor, General Golbery do Couto e Silva, transferring power to reliable civilians and institutionalizing a "limited democracy," free of leftist radicalism and populist demagoguery, seemed preferable.

While the final outcome of Brazil's regime transition went beyond these restricted goals, Geisel and his successor, João Figueiredo, were largely successful in containing challenges to their main game plan. As a result, the civilian successor regime that they helped construct certainly seemed severely limited by the wide-ranging institutional prerogatives of a powerful military and the strong position of conservative civilian politicians. How did the two military presidents achieve this success?

President Geisel started the liberalization of the authoritarian regime in 1974, accepting the opposition's success in the legislative elections in November of that year,[39] lifting press censorship, and allowing greater freedom of civil association. Cautioned by fresh memories of harsh repression, civil society tested the limits of the regime's tolerance only slowly. In fact, the general-president continued to wield his arbitrary powers, most prominently by closing Congress with the "April package" of 1977. When Geisel rescinded in 1978 the notorious Institutional Act 5 of 1968 (AI-5), which had inaugurated the most dictatorial phase of the authoritarian regime,[40] he made sure that he and his successors would retain wide-ranging institutional instruments for upholding "law and order" as defined in a Law of National Security (Lei de Segurança Nacional or LSN).[41]

Furthermore, Geisel and his successor continued to manipulate electoral rules and the party system in order to slow down the gradual advance of the opposition. Figueiredo, for example, abolished the artificial two-party system that the regime had imposed in 1965. This move was designed to split and weaken the democratic forces by allowing for the emergence of additional parties out of the previous official opposition party, the MDB (Movimento Democrático Brasileiro or Brazilian Democratic Movement). The regime also reacted flexibly to the threat posed by the eruption of major strikes in 1978 and 1979. While it could not prevent the emergence of a "new unionism" that pressed for democracy and profound social reform, it managed to limit the damage to its plans through a skillful mixture of carrots and sticks. As a result, major parts of the state-corporatist system of interest representation, which gave the government considerable control over important societal associations, survived the process of democratization.

Finally, Figueiredo kept a thorny issue from emerging by decreeing in 1979 an amnesty for "political crimes" and "connected crimes" perpetrated since September 2, 1961.[42] This move generated euphoria among many Brazilians, as exiled leaders, such as former firebrand Leonel Brizola, and young militants were allowed to return to the country. Yet the amnesty also covered the human rights violations that the armed forces had committed in their campaign to eradicate the left. Thus it protected the military's corporate interest in heading off any civilian effort to prosecute soldiers for their brutal abuses and deprived the democratic forces of a powerful moral rallying cry. In all these ways, the military presidents were quite successful in controlling the transition to democracy.

The crucial issue at the end of the Figueiredo government concerned how the next president would be chosen. While the armed forces as a whole favored a civilian successor to Figueiredo, they were reluctant to risk the final stage of transition to the uncertainty posed by direct elections and preferred instead that the candidate be chosen by the Congress or electoral college.[43] A pervasive and overwhelming fear was that direct elections would usher in the victory of someone anathema to the military, populist politician and governor of Rio de Janeiro

Leonel Brizola. The opposition mobilized an impressive campaign in 1984 supporting direct elections (*diretas já*), but Congress failed to approve the constitutional amendment proposing the change. Most representatives of the majority party, the PDS (ARENA renamed), viewed the electoral college option as a golden opportunity to place a candidate from their own party in the presidency, though the fact that fifty-four members voted in favor of direct elections suggested that popular pressure was dividing the party.[44]

Yet after this narrow success, the Figueiredo government lost control of the selection of its successor. Its candidate, Paulo Maluf, was tainted by charges of corruption. He was unpalatable even to some factions of his own party, the so-called Democratic Social Party (PDS). Many PDS dissidents broke away, formed their own grouping, later transformed into the Party of the Liberal Front (Partido da Frente Liberal or PFL), and forged an alliance with the major opposition party, PMDB (Partido do Movimento Democrático Brasileiro, the MDB renamed). As a result of this compromise, the PMDB selected a moderate, Tancredo Neves, as its presidential candidate. Neves was an establishment figure who had earned a reputation for honesty and good judgment; he was acceptable to the military, albeit not their ideal candidate. On January 15, 1985, an overwhelming majority of the electoral college chose him to be Brazil's new president.

Neves, however, died in March 1985 without ever taking office. This accident catapulted his running mate and vice president–elect, José Sarney, into the presidency. A member of the breakaway faction of the PDS that had allied with the PMDB in 1984, Sarney had been president of the PDS. He had also been a staunch ally of the military regime. This unexpected succession allowed the military to achieve their last goal: handing over power to a conservative. Thus, after its own machinations involving the electoral college had failed, the outgoing authoritarian regime fortuitously achieved its original aim.

Reinforcing the military's satisfaction with this outcome was a series of limitations that they had managed to impose on the regime transition through a process of negotiation. In secretive talks, Neves, ex-President Geisel, and then President Figueiredo reached a number of agreements. Although the conditions for the transfer of power to civilians assuaged military apprehensions about the future, they were never made formal or public. What took place between the military and key civilian actors at the time of the transition was not an official pact, but a series of understandings or *entendimentos*. Through these understandings, Tancredo Neves won the support of the armed forces for the final stage of the transition: the transfer of power to a civilian executive. But because of its secretive and informal nature, the accord lacked a permanent or institutionalized foundation.

What were the terms agreed to? Although many analysts affirm the existence of some kind of pact, to date no one has written in any detail of its content. Individuals involved in the negotiation process have remained closely guarded on the subject.[45] As far as can be discerned, however, civilians who took part in negotiations with the military committed themselves to (1) upholding the 1979 amnesty protecting the military against prosecution; (2) supporting a constituent assembly comprised of the Congress, rather than independent individuals; (3) preserving some internal security functions for the military; and (4) maintaining the existence of a high degree of military autonomy in the development of sophisticated military technology.

Most crucial to the armed forces was securing a pledge from key civilians to respect the 1979 amnesty shielding them from prosecution for violations of human rights they committed in the authoritarian period. Having recently witnessed the initiation of trials against the military by the Alfonsín government in neighboring Argentina, the high command was determined to prevent the same thing from happening in Brazil. It is a matter of widespread consensus that leading officers promised to lend their support to Tancredo's succession conditional upon the assurance that his government would take no "revenge" against them nor allow others to do so.[46] The trials in Argentina not only threatened to imprison individual officers for lengthy periods; they also had a divisive effect on the corporation as a whole, resulting in the rebellion of junior officers.

A second bargain that was apparently struck stipulated that the Congress, not an independent constituent assembly, be in charge of formulating a new Brazilian constitution.[47] Given the abundance of federal legislators on the political right,[48] the military thought that a document produced by the Congress was likely to be more conservative than one formulated by an assembly comprised of independent political notables. It was also expected that legislators who faced reelection would be more subject to presidential influence than independent members. While the constitution eventually promulgated in 1988 was in fact quite progressive on social issues, in 1984, the composition of Congress led the military to hedge their bets on it. The new constitution would have a significant impact on wide-ranging issues of interest to the military. Within their immediate corporate sphere, it would affect the basis of salaries, budgets, and other material perquisites. Constitutional provisions would also bear on many of the military's institutional prerogatives and the organs embodying them, such as the CSN and SNI.

Evidence suggests that a third concession the army leadership tried to wrest from key figures in the Democratic Alliance involved preserving the military's constitutionally mandated role in maintaining internal security.[49] Since this important provision hung in the balance with the new constitution, along with decisions affecting broader issues that the military associated with national security and development—such as land reform, labor rights, and Amazon issues—it is certainly plausible, if not probable, that the military tried to influence the forum in which the new constitution was decided.

The issue of military autonomy vis-à-vis high-technology industries of relevance to external defense constituted a fourth aspect of negotiations conducted around the transition. Military leaders advocated the maintenance of a strong state presence in informatics and telecommunications, two industries that experienced considerable advancement under the bureaucratic-authoritarian regime. Tancredo Neves made known his commitment to supporting a "market reserve" for Brazil in these areas,[50] although the array of political and economic factors outside presidential control that would impinge on the future course of these sectors undoubtedly precluded any guarantees to this effect. There is also evidence, albeit scant, that Neves pledged to support a continuation of the military's parallel nuclear program, begun in 1979. Given the secrecy surrounding the negotiations, and the fact that many of the terms agreed to undoubtedly died with Tancredo, it is impossible to determine what other deals of this kind were struck.[51] What was clear, however, was the military's resolve to preserve their autonomy in questions of technological development. Well before the final stage of the transition, the military took steps to insulate defense-sector activities from civilian control. For example, a reorganization in 1979 of the informatics sector strengthened the influence of the National Security Council and intelligence community over policies affecting the development of informatics in the country. Likewise, in 1982 the military transferred from state to federal authority the Institute for Energy and Nuclear Research (Instituto de Pesquisas Energéticas e Nucleares or IPEN), a site of extensive nuclear research under military direction. This shift was motivated by the expectation of an opposition victory in the gubernatorial campaign later that year.[52]

The compromises described above greatly alleviated military anxieties about abdicating power. Not only did Tancredo Neves demonstrate a willingness to accommodate the military: the respect he commanded across a broad political spectrum inspired confidence that he might be able to compel the opposition to adhere to these agreements. When José Sarney assumed the presidency after Neves's death, the military felt assured that the former PDS president and long-standing ally of the authoritarian regime would respect the agreements and safeguard the core interests of the armed forces. Brazil's controlled transition thus seemed to further reinforce the iron grip that the military expected to have on the nascent democracy.

CONCLUSION

If the military anywhere had ample reason to feel confident about casting their fate to a new civilian regime, it was in Brazil. From the beginning of the transition in 1974 until the transfer of power to civilians in 1985, the armed forces experienced no fundamental setbacks in their struggle to maintain key prerogatives.

Strong internal cohesion, the retention of various institutional bases from which to advance their preferences, and assurances gained at the time of the transition gave the armed forces reason to believe that they would be able to safeguard their corporate interests and exercise considerable leverage over the conduct of national affairs in the future.

An institutionalist perspective would regard the preexisting arrangements described in this chapter, and the political leverage they conferred on the military, as highly resistant to change. However optimal the conditions under which the Brazilian military left power, would they allow the military to withstand the pressures bound to emerge under a more competitive context? Could the armed forces remain insulated from the changes about to take place in the broader political environment?

First, would the military be able to remain cohesive in the absence of the grave disciplinary risks that officers ran for defying the central command during the period of authoritarian rule, and in an environment that might place less of an imperative on military unity? Would the military remain a united front in the face of new strains created by democracy?

Second, would the military-controlled institutions that held sway during authoritarian rule, such as the CSN and SNI, remain intact as democracy endured and eventually became consolidated? Or would civilian politicians come to regard them as too much of a threat to their own authority and electoral goals? Even if these agencies continued to exist officially, would they be able to exercise the same influence on civilians as they did in a less competitive setting that placed greater restrictions on political rights and civilian liberties?

Third, would the understandings reached in negotiations with key civilian politicians at the time of the transition hold over time? For example, could the armed forces expect to retain autonomous decision-making capacity over the defense sector as a multitude of other interests and considerations gained influence with democracy? Would a secret unofficial accord constrain civilian actors, especially with the passage of time?

As the following chapters illustrate, the answers to these questions are mixed and complex. The Brazilian armed forces have been able to retain some prerogatives that violate the principle of popular sovereignty and that do not exist among militaries where civilian control is well established, as in more advanced democracies. Yet in other areas the dynamic of democracy has created and reinforced new interests with the capacity to reshape old institutions. Notwithstanding remaining enclaves of military autonomy, the armed forces' ability to keep their prerogatives and use them to influence civilian policy making has been less than imagined and has eroded over time.

MILITARY PREROGATIVES
AND INSTITUTIONAL
STRUCTURES UNDER
THE NEW DEMOCRACY

This chapter examines and analyzes how key military prerogatives have fared since 1985. It focuses on debates over the preservation of several institutional structures that increase the latent power of the military in the state, namely, the three traditional service ministries, the National Security Council, the National Information Service, and legal provisions for military involvement in internal security, including military control over the federal police. An examination of the postauthoritarian evolution of these prerogatives suggests that the Brazilian armed forces have had mixed success in preserving formal institutional positions and privileges. Overall, they have experienced a reduction of their prerogatives even though the level they still enjoy vastly exceeds that of their counterparts in advanced Western democracies, the comparative reference point of many scholars. More importantly, as Chapters 4 to 6 show, these institutional prerogatives have not allowed the armed forces to maintain their initially high level of political influence under the new democracy.

This chapter seeks to explain why the military managed to preserve certain prerogatives and institutional structures while experiencing reductions in others. The political-electoral interests of Brazil's postauthoritarian presidents, as well as those of Congress, largely account for this variation. This finding confirms the claim of rational choice approaches that institutional structures reflect and flexibly adapt to changes in actors' incentives and resources; they are not rigid fetters with considerably independent power to persist in the face of change.

THE SARNEY PRESIDENCY

President Sarney did little to challenge military prerogatives and institutional structures. At first, the strong bargaining position of the armed forces—a result of their control over the transition process—and concern about destabilizing the new democracy largely accounted for his caution. The absence of an electoral mandate weakened Sarney's capacity to challenge such a historically powerful institution. As time went on, Sarney's deteriorating political standing contributed to his support for the preservation of military prerogatives. By the inception of serious discussions over the new constitution, a critical forum for defining military attributions, the Cruzado Plan had unraveled and the economic crisis that has plagued Brazil until the present had become more severe. With the failure of the economic plan, Sarney's best hope of winning widespread popular support, he succumbed to the traditional temptation of Brazilian presidents to seek protection in the armed forces, especially the army. Yet with the bureaucratization and organizational unification of the army, no longer was it sufficient to co-opt powerful individual officers by promoting them to plum command posts or state agencies. Sarney needed to fulfill a taller order: to forge an alliance with the institutional leadership of the military. A major aspect of his appeal to its members included support for the institutional prerogatives of the organization. Debates that took place from early in 1987 until October 1988 surrounding the formulation of a new constitution provided a key opportunity for demonstrating this support.

In May 1985, Sarney announced that a constituent assembly would be formed, raising the question of who would comprise it. One option was to choose a body separate from the Congress. Favoring this option were congressional minority groups determined to make a clean break with the authoritarian past: the left wing of the PMDB, the PT, and most members of the Democratic Labor Party (Partido Democrático Trabalhista or PDT). The alternative was to derive the National Constituent Assembly (Assembléia Nacional Constituinte or ANC) from the legislature as it stood after the elections of November 1986. Preferring this arrangement were conservative politicians of the congressional majority: the PDS, the PFL, and the right wing of the PMDB.[1]

Sarney opted to appoint the upcoming Congress as the Constituent Assembly. This reflected the weight of congressional opinion, as well as the president's own interest in influencing the decisions of the assembly. The chances of this were higher with an assembly of legislators looking to get reelected, and who would thus be susceptible to presidential patronage, than with a body of experts or notables. The decision to have the Congress and the ANC be one and the same also corresponded to the preference articulated by the military in negotiations prior to the transfer of power.[2]

The armed forces mobilized to defend their interests. Each service branch organized a lobby consisting of several officers (donning civilian attire) to sway legislators on constitutional issues deemed to affect the armed forces.[3] The hierarchy sought officers who would be discrete yet effective and would help improve the image of the institution after twenty-one years of authoritarian rule.[4] Army lobbyists distributed to all 559 members of the ANC a twenty-nine-page booklet entitled *Temas Constitucionais* (Constitutional themes), which presented the army's perspective on the major constitutional issues affecting the force.[5] This was the first time in the making of any Brazilian constitution since 1891 (other than the authoritarian constitutions of 1967 and 1969) that the military as an institution launched an active and systematic defense of its corporate interests. Undoubtedly contributing to this effort was a concern that popular mobilization around the making of the new constitution might challenge core military prerogatives, undoing the careful steps taken since the inception of *abertura* (political opening) to secure a privileged place for the military in the new democracy.

What did the armed forces seek from the constitution? One issue over which all three forces closed ranks involved preventing the creation of a unified Ministry of Defense to replace the Ministries of the Army, Navy, and Air Force. This core military prerogative enhances the autonomy of the military (as a whole) from civilian decision making and preserves independence among the service branches. A central goal for the army was to preserve a legal basis for intervening in internal security, a bread-and-butter role of the institution historically. By charging the armed forces with the maintenance of law and order, all previous Brazilian constitutions secured this right. A corresponding army demand, which would enhance the institution's capacity to implement this prerogative, was to keep the militarized state police (*polícia militar*) subordinate to army control. Interservice support, though less solid and unified than for the three service ministries, existed to protect the CSN and keep a dominant military personnel and policy presence in this institution.[6] Similarly, some but not all groups within the army sought to protect the SNI from being dismantled. Officers regarded these last two attributions as less central to corporate autonomy and to the core of the military's role definition.

It is worth underscoring the fact that a majority of Congress initially claimed to favor a reduction in the institutionally guaranteed power of the military in the polity.[7] Nevertheless, this same body eventually voted to preserve many of the armed forces' institutional prerogatives. Summarizing briefly before elaborating in greater detail below, the ANC did not eliminate the three separate service ministries and create a unified Ministry of Defense in its place. It upheld the military's mandate to maintain internal order, but made such action conditional upon civilian orders. It also reduced the army's control over the militarized state police. It made provisions for a civilian-dominated organ to replace the CSN, but its creation was impeded by a last-minute subterfuge on the part of President Sarney. The SNI was left virtually intact but the principle of habeas data was approved, thus permitting individual citizens to gain access to personal files in the secret service. What explains these outcomes? After examining the civil-military dynamic that evolved around the five issues in question, I attempt to answer this difficult and complex question.

All constitutional provisions would have to secure the approval of a subcommittee, committee, systematization committee charged with consolidating all committee reports, and the full ANC.[8] The subcommittee and committee constituted critical points of passage. Individuals known to be sympathetic to the armed forces led the subcommittee and committee that treated most military issues. The left, while interested in rolling back military influence, devoted its scarce numbers to heading up subcommittees and committees that dealt with social issues. Deputy Ricardo Fiúza (PFL-Pernambuco), who made his political career as an ARENA politician after 1964, chaired the Subcommittee for the Defense of the State, Society, and Their Security (Subcomissão de Defesa do Estado, da Sociedade e de Sua Segurança). His subcommittee sponsored eight hearings stacked with participants advocating pro-military positions. Many of them were personnel of military institutions, such as the Escola Superior de Guerra and the Conselho de Segurança Nacional.[9] The president of the Committee for the Electoral Organization and Guarantee of Party and Electoral Institutions (Comissão da Organização Eleitoral, Partidária e Garantia das Instituições), Jarbas Passarinho (PDS-Pará), was a retired colonel and ex-ARENA politician who served as minister of labor and social security and minister of education under the military governments of Artur Costa e Silva (1967–69) and Emílio Garrastazu Médici (1969–74), respectively.

Preventing the Creation of a Ministry of Defense

The armed forces achieved a clear victory with the maintenance of the three traditional service ministries in lieu of a unified Ministry of Defense. The armed forces have a collective interest in increasing the political representation of active-duty officers in the cabinet. Furthermore, each branch seeks to maintain its own ministry in order to preserve autonomy from the others. The army fears that a unified civilian-led Ministry of Defense would reduce its political predominance over the navy and air force and favor the other branches in the allocation of budget resources. The navy and air force, long dominated by the army, are concerned that army interests would soon come to dominate a unified Defense Ministry.[10]

The armed forces constructed an elaborate defense against the extinction of the three service ministries. Their first tactic was to play down the necessity of a

Defense Ministry by emphasizing the coordinating function met by EMFA (the Armed Forces General Staff), such as the dissemination of an integrating doctrine and the supervision of joint operations.[11] A second line of argument rested on the remoteness of the prospect of Brazil's fighting an external war. In times of peace, military lobbyists contended, the extensive involvement of the three forces in separate civilian tasks—such as building roads and other civic action functions (army), exploring for oil and other oceanographic pursuits (navy), and controlling air traffic (air force)—renders unnecessary a common organizational umbrella. In fact, allowing each force to preserve its own particular "character" would, in their view, facilitate everyday performance. Military lobbyists also addressed those who argued that abolishing the three military ministries was necessary to diminish the political weight of the armed forces. They maintained that if the service chiefs were deprived of their ministerial status and hence reduced to mere commanders, they would maintain an exclusive sense of loyalty to the armed forces rather than develop solidarity with the government.[12]

Many legislators seemed to favor the creation of a Ministry of Defense. Assembly members advanced a range of arguments for altering the extant arrangement. Limiting military influence, making more efficient use of limited public resources, and increasing external defense capabilities through enhanced integration between the branches constituted the various rationales for creating a single Defense Ministry. A survey conducted two years after the constitutional debates seemed to confirm that a majority of members favored a unified Defense Ministry, at least in principle: 67.1 percent of all legislators polled agreed with the statement "Instead of having various military ministries, Brazil should have a single Ministry of Defense." Approximately the same percentage concurred that if a Ministry of Defense were created, the minister should be a civilian.[13]

Yet, facing unified military opposition, the Subcommittee for the Defense of the State, of Society, and Their Security summarily vetoed the idea of a unified Defense Ministry, effectively ending the discussion for the rest of the constitutional debates. One of the principal concerns that chairman Fiúza raised was that a left-leaning president could come to power and appoint a minister of defense who would generate "subversion" within the armed forces. In this event, the armed forces would either cease to be a reliable defender of "vital national interests," that is, the status quo, or conservative currents within the military might be prompted to spearhead a coup against the government.[14] The deputy played on the anxieties of other civilians to win support for his position. The majority of committee members ultimately opted to accept a lesser degree of civilian control as insurance against these scenarios. No member of the Constituent Assembly pressed the issue thereafter. In addition to reservations that assembly members may have held initially, it had become all too clear in the course of the debates that eliminating the separate service ministries would strike at the heart of the military's influence over executive decision making, a historical and jealously guarded prerogative.[15]

Moreover, civilian politicians saw that confronting the military on this administrative issue would not yield immediate electoral benefits. The overwhelming majority of the Brazilian population was concerned with social and economic issues and could not have cared less about the reorganization of the military ministries. Therefore, even if in principle they favored the creation of a Ministry of Defense, politicians rationally used their energy and "political capital" to press for changes in those areas that could ingratiate them with voters. Meanwhile, they failed to help realize their overarching interest in the subordination of the military to civilian authority. If by chance other politicians backed a civilian-led Ministry of Defense, all politicians would benefit whether or not they as individuals had contributed to this goal. In short, though historical institutionalism would see evidence here of institutions' tendency toward self-perpetuation, what in fact allowed continuity to prevail was the calculation of most politicians that it was not worth disrupting the preexisting arrangement.

Maintaining the Military's Role in Internal Security but Subjecting It to Civilian Command

Whether to maintain the military's right to intervene in matters of internal security proved to be one of the most inflammatory issues of the constitutional debates. All previous Brazilian constitutions had given legal foundation to military interventionism by holding the armed forces responsible for guaranteeing law and order and obeying the president of the republic only insofar as his actions remained "within the limits of the law [dentro dos limites da lei]."[16] These dual attributions were sufficiently ambiguous to sanction conduct ranging from quelling rioters in the streets to overthrowing the president.

A survey of legislative opinion in early 1987, at the beginning of the constitutional debates, suggested that the membership of the large conservative parties (especially the PDS and PFL) strongly favored a continuing role for the armed forces in internal security, whereas virtually the entire membership of the small left-leaning parties—the PT, PC do B (Partido Comunista do Brasil), PCB (Partido Comunista Brasileiro), and PSB (Partido Socialista Brasileiro)—sought to confine military functions to the sphere of external defense. The large centrist PMDB was divided, with 56 percent of the party wanting to restrict the armed forces to external activities, and 42 percent wanting to maintain their internal security attribution. As a whole, a slight majority of constitutional delegates (50.7 percent versus 48.4 percent) claimed to support a constitutional clause sanctioning military participation in the maintenance of internal order and, by extension, intervention in politics.[17] Defenders of such an attribution tended to emphasize the need to guard against the possibility of social convulsion. Opponents stressed the legitimation that such a clause provided for the military to seize power or, more frequently, to intimidate civilians engaged in protest behavior of a kind that should be acceptable in a democracy.

The military lobby, mainly its army representatives, advocated preserving the right to intervene in questions of internal security. After all, such a role constituted the "bread and butter" of the organization, which had historically paid more attention to internal/domestic threats than to external defense.[18] Within the navy and air force, however, some officers intent on enhancing the professionalist profile of the armed forces and moving away from police roles harbored reservations about maintaining the internal security attribution.[19]

The army lobby's defense of an internal mission for the military rested on the grounds that political chaos could erupt and tear apart the social and economic fabric of the country. Army leaders underscored previous challenges to social order that the military was effective in putting down and emphasized the societal backing that existed for previous military interventions. "The military have never been intrusive in the history of Brazil, but rather, have been an instrument of national will," affirmed the army minister.[20] Interestingly, the army also tried to legitimize its position by referring to international examples, namely the United States. Common reference was made to the National Security Act of 1947, which charged the armed forces with "protecting and defending the Constitution of the United States against all enemies, foreign and domestic."[21] Beyond allowing the armed forces to combat concrete threats to internal security, the "law and order" attribution symbolizes a certain acceptance of the military as a watchdog of the government and defender of the nation against domestic "subversion." An internal mission contributes to the organizational purpose of the armed forces, something that is especially important in an era of minimal and declining external security threats.

Under the leadership of the two conservative politicians heading the relevant subcommittee and committee, the armed forces maintained a constitutional mandate to guarantee law and order. Amendments aimed at restricting the military's activities to external defense were soundly defeated.[22] The draft proposal that emerged closely resembled the position advocated by the army leadership and articulated in the booklet distributed to the ANC.[23] It sanctioned an internal role for the armed forces, yet left ambiguous the question of who would determine when they could intervene.

With the committee stage completed, it seemed that the military's position was secure at least until the entire ANC voted on the issue. Yet upcoming events shook this assumption. In the final days of August 1987, the Draft Systematization or Coordinating Committee, headed by Deputy Bernardo Cabral (PMDB-Amazonas) in close consultation with Senator Fernando Henrique Cardoso

(PMDB–São Paulo), produced the first entire draft of the constitution. Unexpectedly, it omitted mention of an internal role for the armed forces and made *any* mobilization on their part conditional on the "express initiative of the constitutional powers."[24] This reflected the personal preferences of the two senators more than any precedent established in the subcommittee and committee. Although Deputy Cabral had not technically overstepped the boundaries of the authority granted to him as head coordinator, the military was outraged that he would defy the decisions reached in the previous stages. Their indignation with Senator Cardoso may have been augmented by the fact that he had participated in negotiations conducted at the time of the transition and thus, in their view, had violated a certain agreement to which he had been party. Army Minister Leônidas Pires Gonçalves called the two men to a private meeting, in which he threatened to shut down the Constituent Assembly unless they reversed the text.[25] Also, in a cabinet meeting devoted to the public deficit, the army minister assumed the floor to declare the constitutional draft "unacceptable" and to issue a warning to the "radical minority" that the armed forces would not tolerate an attack on their historical prerogatives.[26] Although it is not clear what army leaders would have done had Deputy Cabral and Senator Cardoso not eventually accommodated them, the two legislators shied away from testing the limits of their tolerance. In short order, a substitute draft appeared. It gave the military a role in law and order but subjected this role in no uncertain terms to civilian command.[27]

Leading up to the final vote on the issue, President Sarney tried to mobilize support for the substitute draft.[28] PT deputy José Genoino used the last chance available to present an amendment omitting the military's right to intervene in questions of law and order and make any military mobilization conditional upon a *joint* request by all three constitutional powers. Genoino made an impassioned appeal to the assembly, followed by others who strongly supported his views.[29] But the ANC rejected Genoino's amendment by a vote of 267 to 89 with 4 abstentions. Only the leftist parties—the PT, PDT, PC do B, and PCB—solidly backed it. The middle of the road PSDB (Partido da Social-Democracia Brasileira or Party of Brazilian Social Democracy) was divided in its vote. Despite the report of an earlier poll that 56 percent of the PMDB thought the military's role should be confined to external defense, most of the PMDB ended up voting against this position.

Thus the ANC preserved the armed forces' internal security prerogative, but eliminated the previous qualification on their obedience to the president to situations "within the limits of the law." For the first time ever, the constitution makes the exercise of the internal security prerogative conditional upon orders by appropriate civilian authorities, either the executive, legislature, or judiciary. The new constitution thus reads: "Article 142. The Armed Forces, comprised of the Navy, the Army and the Air Force, are permanent and regular national institutions, organized on the basis of hierarchy and discipline, under the supreme authority of the President of the Republic, and are intended for the defense of the Country, for the guarantee of the constitutional powers, and, *on the initiative of any of these*, of the law and order" (emphasis mine).[30] The change noted in italics introduces an important element of civilian control that was absent previously.[31] While this new legal barrier against autonomous military action cannot keep the military from intervening if vital interests are under attack, it does increase the costs of undertaking such action by diminishing the armed forces' claim to legitimacy.

Army Control over the Militarized State Police

The separation of the police from the armed forces is an important feature of all advanced democracies. The control the army came to exercise over the militarized state police (*polícia militar*) during authoritarian rule was an issue that the ANC would inevitably raise. In fact, the question of who would have authority over the militarized state police emerged even before the debates of the ANC began. With the direct election of governors in 1982, army command of the *polícia militar* came under challenge. Governors, especially those from the opposition, resented the control the federal government exercised over public security in the states. The *polícia militar* also disliked their subordination to the army. The federal army, however, wanted its sphere of influence to remain extended to the militarized state police. Direct elections in 1982 strengthened the capacity of governors to challenge army leaders for command of the *polícia militar* by giving them a powerful popular mandate.

For governors, the issue was not merely one of principle but also of vital political self-interest. The army and its allies in the intelligence community had in fact pressured opposition governors from states with large industrial centers, such as Leonel Brizola of Rio de Janeiro and André Franco Montoro of São Paulo, to take a harder line toward social and political unrest. Assuming a more repressive stance would have been inconsistent with the popular profile and appeal of these politicians and would have threatened their electoral chances in the future.[32] When governors in this situation resisted army appeals, the army command and its allies tried to circumvent their obstruction by entering into direct communication with the commander of the *polícia militar*.[33]

Reforming the security apparatus of the authoritarian regime, which included the *polícia militar*, became a campaign pitch for some politicians. Before his election as governor of São Paulo in 1982, Franco Montoro drew explicit attention to his intention to curb the violence committed by the army and police in the course of repressing strikes. Similarly, Waldir Pires, vice presidential running mate of Ulysses Guimarães in the 1989 presidential election, underscored his achievements as governor of Bahia (1987–89) in creating a new kind of *polícia militar*, "purged of officers prone to excessive violence . . . and prepared for the responsibility of ensuring public security in accordance with democracy and individual freedom."[34] Federal interference in the security forces of the states reduced the latitude of governors to reform the institution.

Opposition governor Leonel Brizola of Rio de Janeiro led the campaign against army domination of the *polícia militar*. Under pressure from the governors, the federal government modified the command structure of the *polícia militar* in January 1983. The new ruling eliminated the requirement that state commanders come from the federal army. It gave governors the right to choose the commander of the *polícia militar* from within the ranks of the *polícia militar*. The army retained the right, however, to approve the governor's choice.[35]

This relaxation of federal control did not last long. Determined to keep labor protest in check, the secretary-general of the CSN advised President Figueiredo not to further loosen the regime's grip over the *polícia militar*. Plans for a general strike in 1983 prompted an executive decree allowing the president of the republic to mobilize the *polícia militar* in cases of "grave commotion or the threat of its eruption." When mobilized, the *polícia militar* would become subordinated to the general staff of the army and placed under the direct authority of the army commander of the region in question.[36] Despite criticism by various governors, this policy arrangement remained in place until the constitutional debates began. In practice, between 1983 and the promulgation of the new constitution in 1988, the *polícia militar* responded to both state governors and federal authorities.[37]

What platform did the army adopt vis-à-vis the *polícia militar* in the constitutional debates? Clearly, the army wanted the federal government to retain considerable control over public security in the states and sought to be *the* federal force with special supervisory powers over the police. The specific position stated in the booklet distributed to assembly members and affirmed throughout the constitutional debates was that the *polícia militar* be considered "ancillary and reserve forces of the army" for the maintenance of public order in the states. Furthermore, the army wanted the federal government to control the organization, instruction, armament, and courts of the *polícia militar*. The text the army proposed made no mention of the prerogatives of state governors in relation to the *polícia militar*. The army buttressed its position by arguing that if federal jurisdiction over the *polícia militar* did not prevail, a national guard of 150,000 men would need to be created, costing the federal government a huge sum of money.[38]

The conservative Subcommittee for the Defense of the State, Society, and Their Security advocated maintaining federal control over the *polícia militar* and making them "auxiliary and reserve forces of the army."[39] PT deputies José Genoino and Brandão Monteiro (PDT–Rio de Janeiro) fought against this definition but could not obtain the votes necessary to redefine the relationship between the army and *polícia militar* advocated by their conservative counterparts.[40] Subcommittee chair Fiúza favored a high degree of army authority over the *polícia militar* on the grounds that the federal government would need all the resources it could muster in the event of large-scale social protest. The committee upheld the guidelines set by the subcommittee.

When the Draft Coordinating Committee began to scrutinize the question of the *polícia militar* and their relationship to the army and federal government, committee chair Bernardo Cabral was reportedly still shaken from the reaction of the army minister a few weeks earlier to the (later reversed) elimination of the army's role in guaranteeing internal order. Thus, Cabral was careful to produce a text that would not provoke the army leadership. The first draft of the coordinating committee assigned the organization and maintenance of the *polícia militar* to the federal government. While it referred to them as "ancillary and reserve forces" of the army, it placed them under the command of the state governors, except in times of crisis.[41]

This version of the text sat poorly with several governors as well as the leadership of the *polícia militar*, all of whom preferred greater autonomy from the army. The governors of Rio Grande do Sul, Bahia, São Paulo, and Minas Gerais pressured Cabral to change the text in accordance with their preferences. The next draft was more explicit in subordinating the command of the *polícia militar* to the state governors and dropped their status as an "ancillary and reserve forces of the army."[42]

In the end, after fierce lobbying on the part of governors as well as the army, the Constituent Assembly approved a compromise text. The new constitution defines the *polícia militar* as "ancillary and reserve forces of the army" but places them in normal times under the control of state governors (Article 144, no. 6). At the same time, the constitution charges the Union with the exclusive power to legislate on "*general* rules of organization, troops, materiel, guarantees, drafting and mobilization of the *polícia militar*" (Article 22, XXI; emphasis mine).[43] But the new constitution gives the army leadership no regular means of interfering in the command of the *polícia militar*. Thus, even though the federal government retained certain prerogatives, the army suffered a defeat insofar as it lost the power to directly and regularly coordinate and supervise the operations of the *polícia militar*.

Thus the military lost authority over a powerful coercive force, the force that most naturally was summoned in matters of internal security. From now on, reaction to domestic disturbances would depend on the discretion of the state governors; it would be much harder for the military as such to override their decisions and assume direct responsibility for the maintenance of law and order. On an issue that was of vital interest to powerful electoral politicians—in this case, the state governors—the armed forces suffered a substantial defeat. The significant patronage that state governors command helped them to win over a majority of constitutional delegates and to override the army's pressure tactics.

The army tried to gain more direct authority over the *polícia militar* the following year. On April 28, 1989, a bill that originated in the Army Ministry was sent to Congress via the president. It proposed several amendments in relation to the constitutional text on the *polícia militar*. Among them was the proposal that the "Ministry of the Army exercise control and coordination over the auxiliary forces through the Army General Staff." Furthermore, the bill sought to subject the governors' choice of commander of the *polícia militar* to the prior approval of the army minister, the situation that existed from 1983 until the promulgation of the new constitution in 1988.[44] After vehement protest by the state governments, the Committee for National Defense in the Chamber of Deputies swiftly shelved the bill, declaring it unconstitutional insofar as it represented an "undue affront" to the autonomy of the states.[45] Thus, the provisions stipulated by the original constitutional text remain in effect today.

The CSN: Saved Only by Executive Decree

The military leadership preferred that the new constitution retain the Conselho de Segurança Nacional unmodified. Much more than the SNI, the CSN provided the high command with influence over policies of wide-ranging economic, technological, social, and political significance. The parallel nuclear program, energy issues, the occupation and development of the Amazon, and land conflicts were among the central issues the council attempted to influence in the final military government and initial years of the New Republic. Given the organ's composition and leadership structure, its privileged access to the president, and closed forum of decision making, the CSN had served the interests of all three service branches. Although the military leadership sought to preserve the CSN, it recognized that the organ's close association with the national security state might present an obstacle to this goal. After all, the CSN, in conjunction with various military presidents, had been responsible for cashiering the political rights of a number of parliamentarians who now sat in the National Constituent Assembly.

Many politicians did think that the CSN gave excessive influence to the military. The council decided on issues and possessed powers that would devolve largely to elected public officials in a more democratic system of government, most notably to the parliament. Expanding democracy and extending politicians' latitude and power would require dismantling the CSN and shifting matters formerly within its purview to other government entities. Much more than the SNI, the CSN encroached on the sphere of congressional decision making. In this way, the CSN was like other bureaucracies that centralized power in the executive under military rule, such as the Conselho Monetário Nacional (National Monetary Council),[46] whose functions and resources legislators also wanted to regain control over. The self-interest of politicians to occupy more political space clearly militated in favor of reform.

It fell on two different committees of the ANC to decide the fate of the CSN. The more progressive Committee for the Organization of Powers and the System of Government sought to demilitarize decision making on national security issues. It proposed the extinction of the CSN and its substitution by a consultative body, the Council of the Republic (Conselho da República). Charged with more circumscribed and clearly defined responsibilities than the CSN, this body was to be comprised nearly exclusively of civilians.[47] The more conservative Committee for the Organization and Guarantee of Electoral and Party Institutions, of which Senator Passarinho was president, recognized the public sentiment against the CSN but opted to modify rather than overhaul the organ.[48]

The Draft Systematization Committee endorsed the extinction of the CSN and its replacement by the Council of the Republic, transforming it into an *exclusively* civilian advisory body similar to that proposed by the Committee for the Organization of Powers and the System of Government.[49] Yet counterbalancing the absence of military personnel on this organ, the Draft Systematization Committee created another body, the National Defense Council (Conselho de Defesa Nacional), to serve alongside the Council of the Republic as "an advisory organ to the President on issues related to defending national sovereignty and the democratic state." Together, the two organs were designed to break the extensive power of the CSN and increase the prominence of civilians in vital decisions of national security without unduly antagonizing the military.

On August 28, 1988, the ANC widely approved a restructuring of the national security apparatus by extinguishing the CSN and creating the Council of the Republic and National Defense Council.[50] The Council of the Republic is comprised entirely of civilians.[51] As stated in Articles 89 and 90 of the constitution, this body is charged with advising the president on federal intervention, on states of defense and states of siege, and on matters relevant to the stability of democracy. Article 91 of the constitution charges the National Defense Council, comprised of six high-ranking civilians as well as the ministers of the armed services,[52] with advising the president on the declaration of war and peace; on the decree of states of defense, states of siege, and federal intervention; and on the use of areas indispensable to the security of national territory. It also assigns the National Defense Council responsibility for studying, proposing, and monitoring the development of initiatives required to guarantee national independence and the defense of the democratic state.

A broad current of political opinion celebrated the vote to usher in these changes as an important step in the democratization of Brazil. Yet one month after the crucial vote, a ploy by President Sarney undermined the National Constituent Assembly's decision. On September 28, Sarney took advantage of a legal loophole to sign a decree (no. 96.814) calling for the transformation of the General Secretariat of the former National Security Council into an Advisory Secretariat of National Defense (Secretaria de Assessoramento da Defesa Nacional or SADEN).[53] With attributions nearly identical to those of the CSN, the SADEN would add a top layer to the National Defense Council. The SADEN's administrative structure, staff, and budget were inherited from the old CSN, and its executive secretary was the army general in charge of the military household.[54] It seems that Sarney had become so weak politically that he was willing to risk the antagonism of Congress to curry favor with the top brass.

This underhanded move did indeed provoke outrage on the part of constitutional delegates who fought for the extinction of the CSN and intended the Council of the Republic and National Defense Council to be *the* higher bodies for consultation on national security issues. Senator Fernando Henrique Cardoso denounced the decree as a coup (*golpe branco*) against the ANC and brought the case to the Senate, hoping to find Sarney guilty of overstepping presidential powers. The Senate examined the case but could do little to overturn the decree since Sarney had not technically violated the law.[55] While the new constitution made provision for the Council of the Republic and the National Defense Council, the Sarney government never activated these organs.

Instead, the SADEN, led by executive secretary General Bayma Denys, interfered in a range of political, social, and economic issues during the remainder of the Sarney presidency. Like its predecessor, the SADEN accompanied developments in land reform, nuclear research, and conflicts involving domestic and international actors over environmental devastation in the Amazon. During the presidential campaign of 1989, leading candidates attacked the organ as a bastion of military power, which they, if elected, would make sure to eliminate. As described below, Fernando Collor did act on his promise to abolish the SADEN.

Maintaining the SNI

Even after the return to civilian government in 1985, the SNI kept a close watch on politicians and on civil society. While leftist forces and movements continued to be a primary focus of investigation, SNI agents also kept tabs on the financial activities of individuals and enterprises, public and private. The SNI maintained an office in every ministry, state enterprise, and parastatal. Although the agency was undoubtedly less active and intrusive than in the authoritarian period, it did veto some *técnicos* from assuming positions in the bureaucracy because of their leftist political leanings, and blocked others due to suspected involvement in corruption.[56] In the vacuum of power created by Sarney's weak leadership, the head of the SNI, retired general Ivan de Souza Mendes, became a close advisor to the president on wide-ranging matters judged to affect social and political stability in the country, such as industrial labor strikes and movements for agrarian reform.[57] He spoke daily with the president and appeared frequently at his side in public photographs. Although Mendes had no association with the intelligence community prior to the Sarney government and had a reputation as a political moderate, his influence over President Sarney nevertheless defied the principle of civilian control over the military.

Military opinion toward the SNI was divided. Institutionalist or professionally oriented officers in all forces, even the army, were ambivalent toward the agency. On the one hand, some officers were thankful to have the agency advance a military perspective on extramilitary issues, such as industrial labor strikes, and allow the army itself to keep a lower political profile. On the other hand, they argued that the SNI tarnished the armed forces' image. Moreover, many officers felt threatened by what was essentially a parallel organization that sometimes interfered in what they regarded as within their own domain. At the very least, they wanted to de-link military intelligence (intelligence conducted within the three forces) from the SNI.[58]

The preservation of the SNI in the new regime did not go unremarked by legislators and groups from civil society. In fact, opposition in the legislature about the organization and its activities had been growing since the late 1970s. By 1983, the House alone registered thirty-one denunciations against the SNI. In 1985, two different legislators issued proposals to abolish the agency. Arguments advanced against the continued existence of the agency rested on four somewhat different considerations. The most common criticism of the SNI originated from individuals who themselves had been targets of abuse under the dictatorship. In their view, the agency represented the worst excesses of the authoritarian period and should be abolished once and for all. Their rejection of the agency was nonnegotiable. A second group of opponents emphasized the threat that an unreformed SNI posed to the principle of civil rights and popular sovereignty, but acknowledged a role for state intelligence and was willing to accommodate a reformulated information service. Yet a third type of objection rested on narrow self-interest rather than principle. Across the political spectrum, politicians as well as unelected public officials (such as state ministers and heads of state enterprises) were loath to have intelligence agents watching over their handling of financial matters and investigating corruption. Finally, the SNI came under increasing attack the more the press exposed the material privileges enjoyed by its top ranks. Access to state-funded apartments, cars, swimming pools, and other perquisites created an image of the SNI as the "último reduto dos marajás de oliva-verde [last bastion of the army princes]." Even civilians within the organization quietly protested their status as "second-class citizens" in relation to their military counterparts.[59]

Despite widespread opposition to the SNI and amendments proposing its elimination, the National Constituent Assembly did not abolish the agency: 121 members voted to extinguish it; 197 members voted in favor of its retention, or at least not to assess the SNI as a constitutional issue; and 10 members abstained.[60] As such, the constitution says nothing (one way or the other) about the SNI or any other intelligence service in the country. One important expansion of civil rights that the new constitution did enact, however, was the principle of habeas data, which permits citizens access to their personal files within the secret service.[61] Shortly after the promulgation of the constitution in October 1988, many citizens were able to see their dossiers.

After the constitutional debates ended, an obvious question was whether the SNI would persist as time went on. Did SNI leaders take seriously the opposition in political and civil society to the agency? Would the agency adjust sufficiently in the face of an increasingly assertive Congress? There were indeed signs that SNI leaders recognized the need to gain support among politicians for the agency's policies, and perhaps its very existence. As early as 1987, General Ivan de Souza Mendes initiated some changes to make the intelligence service more acceptable to the public. After meeting with interested members of civil society, Mendes began a process of reorienting the agency toward the investigation of external rather than domestic subjects, and moved increasing numbers of personnel away from operations and into analysis.[62] He also tried to raise the public's consciousness about the vital role that intelligence plays in national security, emphasizing the possible coexistence of effective intelligence with democratic government.[63] But at the same time, there was ample evidence of the SNI's failure to adapt to changing circumstances. For example, only in 1989 did the agency decide to form a lobby, and then it contracted only a single lobbyist at a time when virtually all other major interests were employing hoards of parliamentary agents. Similarly, only at the very end of the Sarney administration—after experiencing intense criticism by both candidates in the final round of the 1989 presidential race—did the SNI invite legislators to visit the central agency and engage in discussion about reconciling the organ with democratic government. General Mendes also went before the Congress to justify the agency's existence and defend some of its activities. Although it was the first time that an SNI minister had done anything of the kind (Mendes's predecessors had not even responded to legislative summons), the fact that the agency did not initiate contacts with the Congress sooner suggested a failure to grasp the importance of legislative approval in determining its future.

Analysis of Military Prerogatives in the Constitutional Debates

On balance, the armed forces had mixed success in Brazil's new constitution. The three military ministers survived. The internal security attribution remained intact, but with the provision that intervention by the military could only proceed on the initiative of civilian authority. As for the military's relationship to the *polícia militar*, notwithstanding emergency powers reserved for the federal government, the constitution gives the army itself no regular and direct authority over the force. The Constituent Assembly abolished the CSN, but President Sarney overrode its efforts and created the SADEN. Nevertheless, by making provision for the Council of the Republic and National Defense Council, the new constitution enhanced the potential for greater civilian participation in matters of security and defense. The SNI survived, but with allowance for habeas data.

What explains this mixed success? Why did the military prevail on some issues while suffering defeats on others? A general characteristic of the ANC contributed to this outcome. Each major political current reigned over issues it considered of highest priority. The left put the lion's share of its energy into social legislation. The priority subcommittees and committees for the small number of delegates representing leftist parties were those that dealt with matters such as workers' rights, social security, and health care. Although most left-leaning parliamentarians opposed and voted against the military prerogatives enshrined in the new constitution, the left as a whole did not devote its scarce numbers and resources to launching an all-out effort to prevent this occurrence. Although centrist and rightist parliamentarians had more pressing concerns than to assure the retention of military prerogatives (the right, for example, channeled its energies into economic issues), by virtue of their greater numbers they figured more prominently in the treatment of military matters. Even constitutional delegates of the center and right who did not particularly endorse military preferences were unwilling to expend much energy to alter preexisting patterns of civil-military relations. This was especially true of those attributions that did not bear directly or immediately on their own political standing.

For these reasons, the armed forces achieved some notable successes. The bargaining power the military enjoyed in the transition, which extended to striking an informal accord with high-ranking party leaders, undoubtedly contributed to this outcome. Several party leaders who also served as influential members of the National Constituent Assembly may well have felt pressured to honor the basic parameters of the understanding reached previously with the top military leadership.

But what explains the variation of outcomes among different prerogatives? What accounts for the fact that the ANC was more willing to challenge the military over the CSN and *polícia militar* than the internal security attribution, three separate ministries, and SNI? In accordance with the rational choice framework, developed in Chapter 1, politicians saw the first two issues as bearing more directly and immediately on their independence and popular standing than the latter three. If democratizing reforms were made, wide-ranging issues within the purview of the CSN—such as land use, the development of industry in urban and rural areas, and social security—would devolve at least partially to the Congress and strengthen the powers of the institution. Legislators in a competitive system would have every reason to want to control decisions that could broaden their area of responsibility, give them access to patronage, and enhance their electoral clout.

Elected governors rejected the prospect of regular army command over the *polícia militar* as an intrusion on their own sphere of decision making. The important role of Brazilian governors in dispensing patronage to legislators from their states, a practice that would gain even greater importance with the decentralization of finances mandated by the new constitution in 1988, also prompted legislators to side with the governors over the question of who would command the *polícia militar*. Results of the struggle over this issue suggest that it was possible even before the formal transition to civilian rule in 1985 for elected politicians to diminish the military's sphere of influence. The fact that civilians were willing to challenge the military and hold their ground over time is no doubt linked to the concrete threat the army's control over the *polícia militar* posed to the autonomy of Brazil's historically powerful state governors, who, in turn, could affect the fate of legislators through the dispensing of patronage.

By contrast, the internal security attribution of the armed forces and the existence of the three military ministries were issues that had little impact on the independence and decision-making authority of specific categories of electoral politicians. At the same time, they constituted high-priority issues for the military. A constitutional clause charging the military with the maintenance of law and order is indeed infused with symbolic meaning and confers some legitimation on military involvement in matters of domestic security. Yet most parliamentarians were not willing to risk antagonizing the army command over a general attribution that was not likely to affect their individual careers in a decisive way.

The persistence of ministerial status for the three service branches can be seen in similar terms. The continued existence of three military ministries has little immediate bearing on the legislature. Thus, it was unlikely that the vast majority of assembly members would have chosen to invest precious "political capital" in creating a unified civilian-led Ministry of Defense, notwithstanding the few parliamentarians committed to advancing civilian control at all cost. The ANC's failure to create a single Defense Ministry has more far-reaching implications for the executive, for whom the presence of several military officers in the cabinet can be highly constraining politically.

What explains why the SNI survived beyond the Constituent Assembly? Given the various objections individual parliamentarians had to the agency, why did the ANC not eliminate it? Although the SNI did pose some threat to the decision-making autonomy of elected politicians, several factors appear to have inhibited legislators from abolishing it. Notwithstanding the SNI's interference in matters of domestic politics in the Sarney government, the agency's role in actual policy making was limited and the range of issues it affected was relatively narrow. Relative to the CSN, which held sway over a broader sphere, the SNI did not encroach upon the powers of parliament in an extensive way. This constitutes a partial but important explanation of why parliamentarians were less determined to eliminate the SNI than the CSN.

Second, there existed considerable fear about how the intelligence agency would react to attempts to dismantle it. The concern was not only that the SNI leadership might, together with the army, imperil the constitutional debates. It was also that the agency would target individual opponents and raise suspicions about their integrity by revealing unfavorable information that had been gathered on them. Certainly, overwhelming support to extinguish the agency would serve to inhibit the SNI from taking recourse of the latter kind. But in the crucial stages of building support before the final vote, the preferences of individual members of the relevant committees would be exposed, making them vulnerable to retribution.

Finally, the fact that the campaign against the SNI was spearheaded by José Genoino, a leading member of the PT and former PC do B militant, undoubtedly diminished the chance that the agency would be extinguished.[64] In the course of debates about the future of intelligence in the country, a polarization of opinion around ideological leanings developed. This may well have prompted conservatives who otherwise opposed the SNI to vote against proposals to abolish it.

Thus only selectively did civilians use the opportunity presented by the formulation of a new constitution to reduce the military's political prerogatives and institutional structures or to establish mechanisms of civilian control over the armed forces. While their success was mixed, the military did suffer some important defeats. The legislature challenged the armed forces over specific policies and decisions several times in the year and a half that remained of the Sarney government. But it did not take active measures to cut down the military's formal prerogatives and structures. The advent of the Collor government, however, promised to change this situation.

THE COLLOR GOVERNMENT

The government of Fernando Collor de Mello represented the most deliberate and large-scale effort made under Brazil's new democracy to reduce the political role of the military. Based on his popular mandate as the first directly elected president of Brazil in twenty-nine years, Collor tried to enhance his autonomy and political standing by putting the armed forces in their place. He skillfully increased his room to maneuver by appointing military ministers identified closely with professionalist goals and interested in diminishing military activism in broader social and political issues.[65] Even though aspects of military autonomy persisted under his presidency, and some prerogatives that were reduced under it later reemerged during the successor government headed by Itamar Franco, the precedent Fernando Collor set in challenging the armed forces was nevertheless significant. That Collor contested the military without provoking much of a backlash was undoubtedly not lost on others interested in the same goal. Collor's successes demonstrate that Brazil's fledgling democracy was able to remove many of the institutional constraints imposed on it during the military-controlled transition process.

The most noteworthy changes that the Collor government instituted were toward the SNI and SADEN. Left unaltered were the internal security attribution, about which little could be done before the constitutional revision scheduled to begin in late 1993, and ministerial status for the three armed services, an arrangement President Collor had promised to change but ultimately did not. In light of the president's motivations for eliminating the SNI and SADEN, elaborated below, it would have been fitting to replace the three traditional military ministries with a unified and civilian-led Ministry of Defense. But Collor may have thought that taking this step, in addition to dismantling the SNI and SADEN, would have tested the limits of the armed forces' tolerance. Insistence on installing a unified Defense Ministry may also have endangered Collor's relationship with the navy and air force, branches whose support was necessary to buffer him against the army, the primary target of reform.

Why was Fernando Collor so adamant about abolishing the SNI and SADEN? Why did the promise to do so form such a central aspect of his political platform during the presidential campaign of 1989? Above all, Collor sought to clear the way of potential impediments to advancing his own political agenda. Dismantling these organs was part of a broader strategy to rid the political landscape of possible obstacles and competitors. Established organizations like the SNI and SADEN posed a particular threat to Collor's authority given the absence of a more permanent support base for his government—institutionalized, for example, in a political party. The extent of Collor's potential vulnerability also prompted the president to surround himself with little-known and relatively inexperienced advisors. Many of the individuals who comprised his first cabinet enjoyed few links to established interests.[66]

Tactics of political marketing—also crucial for Collor's effort to retain and broaden his unorganized support base—further prompted the new president to defy the intelligence and national security community. A central aspect of his popular appeal involved an avowed determination to eliminate remnants of Brazil's elitist and authoritarian past and to usher in a new era in which the ideals of citizenship and popular sovereignty prevailed. Challenging the SNI and SADEN was an integral part of Collor's relentless attack on the political establishment, which included President Sarney, and its tolerance of military interference in politics and the impunity of elites in general. After conducting a campaign in which Collor fueled societal animosity toward the intelligence service and other remaining bastions of military privilege, he proceeded as president to exploit the sentiment he had been instrumental in stirring up. In one move, he extinguished the SNI as well as SADEN. He made this dramatic gesture on March 15, 1990, the first day of his presidency. With little discussion, Congress overwhelmingly ratified the presidential decree (*medida provisória* 150) on April 12, 1990.

President Collor created an organ, the Secretaria de Assuntos Estratégicos (Secretariat of Strategic Affairs or SAE), intended to serve as a substitute for both the SNI and SADEN. He charged the SAE with carrying out intelligence as well as strategic planning and analysis, the core functions formerly performed by these agencies. The government emphasized that a civilian headed the new organ and that many military officers previously employed by either the SNI or SADEN were forced back to their respective service branches. But were the SNI and SADEN fundamentally transformed or merely recast? Much conjecture, though little in-depth analysis, has been devoted to this question. Although the paucity of information available precludes a definitive assessment of the matter, certain conclusions can be drawn.

The abolition of the SNI and the creation of a division of intelligence within the SAE brought several concrete changes. These included, most notably, a reduction of employees overall; a diminution of military personnel in particular; the closing of several regional offices; the elimination of ministerial status for the agency; and the establishment of closer ties with the Congress.

President Collor cut rather significantly the numbers of people employed in intelligence functions. The human and material resources devoted to the former SNI had been immense, a fact that became even clearer in the aftermath of the decree to eliminate the agency. Estimates concerning the shrinking of ranks vary, but available reports suggest that the Collor administration employed within SAE's division of intelligence only between half and three-quarters the number of people that the former SNI did.[67] Special Programs, the division within the SAE that took over many of the responsibilities of the SADEN, employed roughly one-seventh the number of people that the SADEN did.[68]

A related change involved the departure of large numbers of military officers who had worked for the SNI, perhaps as many as eleven hundred.[69] Active-duty officers returned to their respective service branches. Some retired officers lost their positions altogether. Others stayed on within the SAE. Even accounts criticizing the insufficiency of changes within the area of intelligence recognize a reduction of the military's presence within the new agency.[70] Both men to lead the SAE under the Collor presidency, Pedro Paulo Leone Ramos and Eliezer Batista, were civilians. Moreover, the individual appointed to head the intelligence division, Flávio Rodrigues Duarte, was also a civilian. An SNI veteran and specialist in external intelligence rather than domestic espionage, Flávio Duarte had long been critical of military domination within the agency and led a group within it informally known as the MAM (Movimento Anti-Militarista).[71] A civilian was also appointed to head the new division for training intelligence personnel, Centro de Preparação e Aperfeiçoamento de Recursos Humanos (CPHR or Center for Training and the Improvement of Human Resources).

In addition to appointing civilians to direct the SAE, President Collor closed four of twelve regional offices of the former SNI.[72] This represented part of a larger effort to centralize the agency and reduce its role in operations. To decrease SAE's potential to be a springboard of political influence, Collor deprived the organ of ministerial status. This decision, along with the elimination of ministerial status for EMFA and the *gabinete militar*, reduced the number of military positions in the cabinet from six (in existence during the Sarney presidency) to three.[73]

The SAE also behaved in ways different from the SNI and SADEN. Under the Collor government, there were fewer denunciations by Brazilian citizens about intelligence agents meddling in their affairs.[74] Evidently, President Collor was successful in eliminating or drastically reducing the most intrusive forms of investigation conducted previously. In this connection, the SAE under Collor trod more carefully in general than did the SNI under Sarney. Rather than trying to force elected leaders into accepting its policies, as the SNI had done under Sarney, the SAE appeared more interested in building political support for its programs. Evidence of this more flexible and conciliatory stance included the employment of six congressional lobbyists. These changes took place amid a decline of political activism among the remaining military ministries.[75]

One of the most important consequences of Collor's actions was symbolic. His ability to challenge one of the most formidable enclaves of military power and privilege without provoking a serious backlash was an important test of the military's tolerance and a sign of the institution's growing political weakness under the new democracy. Given the restraint the armed forces showed, President Collor helped to create a more favorable climate for contesting remaining domains of military autonomy in the future.

Notwithstanding these shifts, it became evident over time that not everything about the former national security community had changed. Although the SAE was more discreet and projected a less sinister image than the SNI and SADEN, it retained considerable autonomy from elected civilians, and traces of military influence within the organization remained. Legislators did not come to establish institutionalized control over the SAE's budget and activities. No specialized committees in either chamber of Congress were developed for the purpose of routine intelligence oversight. Nor did the extant committees that dealt with military and defense matters (the Committee for National Defense in the House and the Foreign Relations Committee in the Senate) take up the task. The Congress had access to information about the total amount of funding the agency received, but legislators lacked detailed knowledge of how the SAE spent its budget. Although obtainable upon request,[76] this information was not made regularly available even to legislators on pertinent committees. Without controlling the SAE budget, Congress could scarcely begin to restrict the organization's activities. Legislators moved to redress this conspicuous gap in civilian control after August 1991, when the national press revealed the magnitude of funds ($65 million) that the SAE spent on nuclear research, whose exact content remained shrouded in secrecy.[77]

In the aftermath of this public embarrassment, President Collor issued a bill to render the operation of the SAE more compatible with the principles of democratic government. The proposal, *Projeto de Lei 1862/1991*, focused on creating greater legislative control over intelligence and strategic planning; on eliminating an information-gathering function for the military ministries and charging the SAE with the conduct of all intelligence; and on redirecting intelligence activities away from domestic political subjects to issues concerning the protection of Brazil's territorial integrity and its industrial/technological development.[78] But the proposal encountered resistance from numerous groups.

The president's proposal called for reviews on a semester basis by members of a specific committee charged with the oversight of intelligence. Many legislators welcomed the prospect of greater congressional control over the SAE, but raised objections over the stiff penalties specified in the bill for members who violated confidentiality (five to ten years in prison for intentional revelations, and three to five years for accidental disclosures). Some legislators also opposed the lengthy allowances (up to thirty years) for information to remain classified.[79]

Collor's proposal precluded the military ministries from carrying out any kind of intelligence analysis or operations. The military ministries rejected the monopoly over intelligence functions that the bill gave to the SAE. An unintended consequence of demilitarizing the SNI had been to reinforce the information services within the military itself.[80] Many former SNI agents found refuge in the intelligence services of the military ministries. Although there was little evidence that the military ministries were engaged in activities that violated the civil rights of Brazilian citizens during the Collor government, at the same time no civilian monitoring existed over their intelligence-related activities.

Finally, Brazil's Foreign Ministry, the Itamaraty, objected vehemently to the proposal to send intelligence agents abroad for purposes that overlapped with its own sphere of responsibility. Known for their professionalism and esprit de corps, members of the Foreign Ministry shuddered at the thought of having agents from another institution, especially one with a questionable past, intrude in their domain. Other agents would clash and work at cross purposes with the well-trained career diplomats of the Itamaraty. Thus an institution with nonelectoral interests but with a clear sense of identity and mission, like Brazil's Foreign Ministry, regarded the SAE and its agents as a threat to its own autonomy.

In light of the wide-ranging criticism leveled at the executive proposal to regulate the SAE, President Collor ultimately withdrew the bill. In turn, PT legislator José Dirceu put forth in fall 1991 a new bill, *Projeto de Lei 1.887*.[81] Congressman Dirceu's bill underscored the importance of respecting the rights of individual citizens in the course of gathering information, as well as the need to orient the SAE's activities toward the external sphere, but in ways acceptable to the Foreign Ministry. The bill called for two permanent congressional committees (one in the Senate and one in the Chamber of Deputies) to exercise regular oversight of the SAE, and loosened the restrictions on legislators comprising these committees.

Dirceu's bill was carefully conceived and drew praise from legislators across the political spectrum. Key members of the Committee on National Defense within the Chamber of Deputies regarded it favorably. But the proposal never reached the stage of being considered and voted on by the legislature as a whole. Congress had more pressing matters, including maneuvering over federal budget allocations, deciding on numerous executive decrees (*medidas provisórias*), and overseeing various parliamentary inquiry committees (Comissões Parlamentares de Inquérito or CPIs), provisional committees for investigating political scandals. Politicians were unlikely to give priority to a bill aimed at regulating intelligence in a political system that overloaded them with emergency matters and offered them few incentives to pursue long-range programmatic goals (especially if electoral popularity was not at stake).

But beyond this, two immediate developments interfered with the bill's placement on the legislative agenda. The first related to the April 1992 departure of the first SAE head, Pedro Paulo Leone Ramos, under corruption charges and his replacement by Eliezer Batista, who shunned all association with the former intelligence community and sought to transform thoroughly the system of information and strategic planning.[82] His plan to overhaul the SAE diminished the relevance of Congressman Dirceu's bill. A second development further complicated the prospects for congressional examination of the Dirceu proposal. This involved the corruption scandal that led to the most serious crisis Brazil's new democracy has experienced to date and ultimately to Collor's departure from the presidency. From the beginning of June 1992 until the end of the year, legislators were consumed with investigating the accusations leveled against the president and engaging in politics surrounding the scandal. Needless to say, these months were not viewed as a propitious time to raise issues that could antagonize the military, such as regulating intelligence gathering and analysis. Although the armed forces remained uninvolved, their historical tendency to step in and settle major political crises led virtually all political actors to tread more cautiously than usual.

In sum, President Collor's pursuit of political independence from established powers boded well for the reduction of military prerogatives and institutional structures. Not wanting either the SNI or the SAE to constrain his capacity to make policy decisions that would enhance the popular appeal of his government and create an important historical legacy, Collor took the bold step of abolishing these organs and replacing them with a new institution, the SAE.

The SAE did represent a reduction of the armed forces' political prerogatives. Civilian power was advanced despite the persistence of residual enclaves of military autonomy within the agency. Over time, however, President Collor became less able to clear away these traces of military influence. His determination to defy elements of the old regime in general grew weaker when his popularity began to decline after roughly the first year in government. After corruption charges against the president and his inner circle surfaced in May 1992, sending a tremor throughout the country, the only hope for the enactment of greater civilian control rested with the emergence of a new and untainted government. But would the government of Itamar Franco be committed to reducing the military's institutional powers?

THE GOVERNMENT OF ITAMAR FRANCO

In many ways, the government of Itamar Franco was more of a caretaker government than one with far-reaching programmatic goals. Lacking an independent electoral mandate, the former vice president did not have the clout to further diminish military prerogatives. President Franco never made a priority of reforming the SAE or any other military-institutional structure. Preventing a worsening of Brazil's economic and political situation and staying in power until the next regularly scheduled election appeared to be his main concerns. Over time, Franco assumed an ever more cautious stance toward the armed forces. His strategy was one of appeasement.

Creeping military influence in intelligence and strategic planning was evident under the Franco administration. The appointment of a retired naval officer to head the SAE, Admiral Mário César Flores, constituted a visible sign of this trend.[83] Also, rather than confining its attention to matters of national security, strictly defined, the SAE investigated a wide range of domestic as well as international topics.[84] Under Franco, the gathering, analysis, and application of intelligence remained scattered and uncoordinated across various organs: the SAE, the military ministries, the federal police, the *polícia militar,* and the Foreign Ministry. No laws were enacted to mandate a division between the conduct of foreign versus domestic intelligence, nor to regulate the various intelligence-gathering organs' utilizing the information they collected. Under the Franco government, the legislature did not gain institutionalized means of monitoring the conduct of intelligence.

Under Franco, the army also became more deeply involved in one aspect of internal security, suggesting that broader problems of governance can expand the military's jurisdiction. By August 1994, drug trafficking, organized crime, and gang violence in the *favelas* (hillside slums) of Rio de Janeiro had reached alarming proportions. Public authorities looked to the army (viewed as more trustworthy and capable than the police) for a heavy hand. From November 1, 1994, until December 30, 1994, the army commanded Operation Rio, a joint operation of army soldiers, the federal police, and militarized state police. Its purpose was to overwhelm traffickers and gangs and remove the massive amount of contraband arms that had accumulated in the *favelas.* It is crucial to note that Operation Rio was not an independent military initiative,[85] but rather a joint decision by the state governor and president.[86] Doubtless, the operation reinforced common perceptions associating the military with social order.[87]

Despite backsliding in some areas and the failure to enact concrete measures to expand civilian control, the Franco government did not represent a return to the Sarney years, when the military—through the service ministries, the SNI, and the SADEN—took it upon themselves to interfere unabashedly in a wide range of civilian decisions. Even the beleaguered Franco government managed overall to maintain supervision over the military. Evidence that the SAE and the military ministries used the information they gathered in ways deleterious to civil liberties and the democratic process was scant. There was also little indication that high-ranking officers tried to sway the president on many extramilitary matters. To the extent that they assumed a more visible presence under Franco, it was mainly to advance corporate goals, such as higher budgets and salaries.

More positive signs of progress were also evident during the Franco government. The need for greater civilian control over the military, including their role in intelligence, gathered force as a mainstream political notion. On the president's initiative, the constitutionally created National Defense Council met in February 1993 to discuss reforming the extant system of intelligence.[88] In December 1993, PT congressman José Dirceu issued a new bill to expand legislative monitoring over the gathering and application of state intelligence.[89] In May 1994, the Committee on National Defense in the Chamber of Deputies sponsored a four-day seminar, Intelligence Activities in a Democratic State—The Case of Brazil.[90] The first event of its kind in the country, the conference featured Brazilians from numerous civic and political organizations, including several well-known critics of Brazil's military-intelligence complex.[91] Many of the changes they called for overlapped with those proposed in Congressman Dirceu's bill, including a clear separation between organs charged with carrying out civilian versus military intelligence and domestic versus international intelligence; the development of routine legislative monitoring, and the training of parliamentarians in intelligence matters in order to prevent military officers from effectively dominating the issue area. These events suggest a continuing interest among Brazilian politicians in further reducing military autonomy. Whether this interest translates into concrete action, however, is another question. Matters that consumed the attention of Congress during the Franco government—namely, corruption scandals, budgetary politics, and the elections of late 1994 (municipal, legislative, and presidential)—effectively impeded proposals to diminish the military's institutional powers from being placed on the agenda and enacted into legislation.

The constitutional revision scheduled to begin in October 1993, which lowered the vote share required to amend the 1988 charter,[92] promised to provide an opportunity for reform. In preparation for the revision, numerous proposals to contract military prerogatives and influence were formulated. Such proposals included extinguishing the military's right to guarantee law and order;[93] eliminating obligatory military service;[94] narrowing the jurisdiction of military courts;[95] imposing legislative oversight over intelligence activities;[96] and substituting the three service ministries with a civilian-led Ministry of Defense.[97] One congressman even advocated transforming the armed forces into a self-defense force, as in Japan.[98]

The position the military adopted with respect to the constitutional revision was mainly defensive. The armed forces confined their attention to corporate issues, with the exception of trying to reduce the space devoted to indigenous reserves in the Amazon in order to spur the prospects for development and military defense in the region. They sought to keep their internal security attribution, to retain ministerial status for the three services, and to maintain obligatory military service. They also proposed the introduction of a specific clause emphasizing the prohibition of unionization within the armed forces but were otherwise silent on labor issues. The main new item for which the armed forces lobbied involved a legal distinction between military personnel and other categories of public employees, which would make the former eligible for higher salaries and benefits.[99]

Despite the possibilities that the constitutional revision held for advancing civilian control, the revision was thwarted by legislators' inability to coalesce around their common interests. Legislators were so absorbed in other pursuits that the revision did not even take place. The upcoming elections of late 1994 drew parliamentarians across the political spectrum back to their home districts to campaign. Government and party leaders were rarely able to guarantee the quorum required for altering the constitution. In this way, self-interest impeded the collective action necessary to bring about overarching reforms. Also, the left deliberately tried to block the revision from proceeding out of fear that the social achievements of the 1988 charter could be rolled back. In short, these other political considerations effectively prevented legislators from joining together to further diminish military prerogatives and advance other collective goals.[100]

The government of Itamar Franco—while backsliding on some of Collor's policies to reduce military prerogatives—did not bring about a regression to the status quo ante of the Sarney presidency. Even though Franco, like Sarney, lacked the weight to stand firm against the armed forces, a comparison of the two periods suggests that the range of issues in which the military interfere has narrowed over time; that civilians have become more open to reforms to reduce military influence; and that civilians have begun to use some of the formal structures created under the new democracy—such as the Council of the Republic and the Council of National Defense—to decide issues of interest to the armed forces, rather than allowing informal channels of military influence to prevail.

CONCLUSION

The Brazilian armed forces have had mixed success in preserving their initial prerogatives and institutional structures in Brazil's new democracy. A comparison of the institutional powers the armed forces possessed at the beginning of the Sarney government and the end of the Franco administration shows that the armed forces have indeed experienced several significant defeats. Under pressure from state governors, the Constituent Assembly reduced the military's capacity to exercise routine domination over the militarized state police. As a consequence of President Collor's decision to extinguish the SNI and create the SAE, the military's unchallenged control over state intelligence was ended. Similarly, with the elimination of the powerful CSN and SADEN (the CSN's successor, created by President Sarney to reverse the elimination of the CSN by the National Constituent Assembly) and their replacement by the SAE and the Council of the Republic and National Defense Council, the Collor government ended the armed forces' previous monopoly on decisions affecting national security and defense. Where politicians saw a chance to increase their own latitude for decision making, they caused the military to suffer important losses in their institutional powers.

Yet where politicians' electoral prospects were not directly impaired, or where collective action problems undermined efforts to push back the military, the armed forces managed to preserve their institutional prerogatives. These factors explain why a majority of legislators—despite a professed opposition to the military's internal security attribution and to ministerial status for the traditional service branches—did not act to disrupt these arrangements. While legislative interests are not directly hindered by the presence of numerous uniformed officers in the cabinet, the president's latitude certainly is. President Collor clearly wanted to decrease the military's presence in the cabinet, but he backed down on his goal to challenge a key military prerogative by replacing the traditional service ministries with a unified Ministry of Defense.

Like presidents, legislators seek to extend their own power and influence. If the armed forces are judged to interfere with this goal, legislators will want to remove them from relevant institutional spheres and possibly even reduce their reach overall. The more directly the armed forces impinge on the ability of legislators to enhance their electoral interests, the more likely members of Congress will be to enact such reforms to reduce their weight. But congressional initiatives depend on collective action, which is difficult to muster even in the best of circumstances. The absence of solid party organization, a central aspect of Brazil's fluid and weakly institutionalized political system, greatly hinders reform initiatives that compel legislators to think beyond the immediate situation and to organize collectively around long-term interests.

Like legislators, presidents are motivated to remain in good standing with the electorate. Yet the incentives they possess and the constraints they face are somewhat different in degree as well as kind. A president's autonomy is greatly compromised by a powerful and politically intrusive military. This should thus compel presidents, more than legislators, to enact reforms to reduce military prerogatives. Moreover, given the considerable powers of Latin American presidents, their capacity to do so greatly exceeds that of any individual legislator. This motivation is, however, counterbalanced by the persistent fear that executive politicians have of antagonizing the military and jeopardizing the survival of their governments. In the context of poor governance and low public approval, presidents revert to the latter logic and allow military prerogatives and institutional structures to persist unchecked. Thus presidents play a pivotal role. Which logic they employ and course of action they take—either acting on the impulse to push the military back, or "playing it safe" and respecting the status quo—is decisive in determining the extent of institutional privileges the military retain.

To summarize, there are three circumstances conducive to the retention of military prerogatives: (1) where politicians do not perceive military privileges as a threat to their own interests; (2) where collective action is necessary to enact demilitarizing reforms but cannot be realized; and (3) where politicians, mainly presidents, react to problems of governability by backing off from their natural inclination to enhance their own political space by reducing the military's reach. Otherwise, both legislative and executive politicians can be expected to recognize the constraints and inconveniences presented by a politically active and powerful military, and to take measures designed to push them back from the political sphere.

My interpretation of the findings presented in this chapter corresponds to a rational choice perspective. In my view, whether military prerogatives were preserved depended in crucial ways on the interests, incentives, and resources of civilian politicians. Established institutional structures did not automatically prove resilient, as sociological institutionalism would expect. As the regime transition unleashed the competitive dynamic of democracy, some of the military's institutional powers eventually crumbled. Similarly, where military prerogatives were preserved, it was not because of an inherent self-perpetuating tendency on the part of institutions, but instead because politicians were not sufficiently motivated to eliminate or reduce them or because the well-known dilemmas of collective action made it difficult for them to do so.

Despite the continued existence of certain formal institutional prerogatives, the logic of electoral advancement on the part of both legislators and presidents, coupled with the heightened powers of both sets of actors under Brazil's new democracy, has often overridden military attempts to use their remaining prerogatives and institutional structures to sway civilian politicians. As illustrated in the following three chapters, in a dynamic and competitive political context in which politicians must respond to a myriad of factors other than military pressure, military prerogatives do not necessarily translate into effective influence over policy outcomes.

LABOR RIGHTS IN BRAZIL'S NEW DEMOCRACY: POLITICIANS REIN IN THE MILITARY

The value that Brazilian politicians place on satisfying popular opinion on highly visible issues, even over military objections, is well demonstrated in decisions they have made since 1987 to liberalize the corporatist labor legislation installed by Getúlio Vargas in the 1940s and reinforced after 1964 by the military regime. The aspect of this legislation analyzed here concerns strikes, the main economic and political weapon of workers. This chapter demonstrates how military leaders and civilians struggled to advance their own well-defined preferences over strike law under Brazil's new democracy. It argues that the expansion of labor rights in Brazil's new democracy shows the extent to which politicians oppose the military when popular sector support is at stake, and the extent to which popular support enables them to undertake the risks posed by challenging the military.

What is the basis of the armed forces' interest in restricting the right to strike? The goal of a quiescent labor movement has social, political, and economic dimensions in keeping with the positivistic impulses within the Brazilian military. The socially disruptive effects of strikes—the failure to deliver goods and services, protest in the streets—are antithetical to the core military principles of order and discipline. To the extent that union movements are often linked to leftist parties and social movements with a broad political agenda, military leaders regard them as a potential political threat. Brazil's armed forces have also feared that an activist labor movement would demand a "premature" redistribution of the country's wealth and thereby impede its potential to become a major industrial power. In

the National Security Doctrine that guided the military for two decades beginning in the early 1960s, national security and economic development went hand
in hand. The military's perception that the labor mobilization of the early 1960s
constituted a grave social, political, and economic threat led them to reimpose
the strict limits on strikes established in the corporatist legislation of the Estado
Novo and to strengthen these limits in the National Security Law.[1] Business elites
lent their full support to these efforts.

What incentives do elected politicians have to support pro-labor policies, including an expansion of the right to strike? Are the incentives of electoral democracy compatible with controls the military would like to see imposed over the
labor movement? This chapter suggests that they are not. As early as the 1940s,
when Vargas invoked the concept of *trabalhismo*, great numbers of Brazilians
have seen themselves as "working people." They represent a large pool of voters
that politicians in Brazil's fluid party system have proven increasingly interested
in capturing. The ways in which politicians can appeal to this group, through
such measures as loosening strike restrictions, often conflict with the military's
penchant for the rational administration of society.

The opposing preferences of electoral politicians and military elites became
apparent as early as the end of the Estado Novo, when Vargas emphasized *trabalhismo* in anticipation of the post-1945 political opening. The contradictions
between political pluralism and the control aspects of the corporatist system grew
increasingly evident from 1945 to 1964, as labor leaders exploited the vulnerability
of politicians to increase their own leverage within the system. While the military
eventually arrested the growing power of labor with the coup of 1964 and the
authoritarian crackdown that followed, the labor movement experienced a resurgence in the late 1970s. Democratization has led left-leaning as well as mainstream parties to compete more actively for working-class and popular sector
support, bringing them into conflict with conservative military elites, who would
like to keep the labor movement tightly controlled.

The central objective of this chapter is to show how democratic competition
has induced and enabled politicians in Brazil's new democracy to support pro-
labor policies despite the military's persistent efforts to prevent the labor movement from gaining strength. The first section describes Brazil's corporatist tradition of labor organization and analyzes the erosion of corporatist controls over the
course of the previous democratic period. The second examines measures that
the subsequent military governments took to keep a tight lid on the labor movement and explains how they became increasingly unviable in the context of the
political opening after 1974. The final section analyzes the support that Brazilian
politicians have given to pro-labor legislation since 1987 in the face of the military's formidable institutional apparatus and dogged efforts to contain the labor
movement.

THE LABOR MOVEMENT IN BRAZIL'S CORPORATIST TRADITION

The military's vision of labor control in the 1980s stemmed from the corporatist labor code that Vargas imposed during the Estado Novo. The central aim of this legislation, codified in the CLT (Consolidação das Leis do Trabalho or Consolidation of Labor Laws) in 1943, was to co-opt a potentially independent and militant working class into unions that were dependent on and controlled by the state.[2] The CLT covered virtually every aspect of a worker's life, including union organization and operation, mechanisms for wage adjustments, and strike procedures. The state confined workers to one union within a single jurisdiction (*unicidade*) and prohibited direct ties between unions. Unions in the same craft or industry from the same state could form a federation, and state federations could theoretically form a national confederation, but these were usually little more than paper organizations. No single peak confederation existed. The compartmentalization of the labor movement effectively divided and weakened workers.

A further source of state control stemmed from the financial dependence of unions on the state. The state provided strong inducements for workers to join official unions insofar as social welfare benefits were distributed through them and an obligatory tax (*impôsto sindical*) was levied on all workers regardless of whether they were members. This tax comprised an important portion of the Labor Ministry's budget. The Labor Ministry decided what percentage of these funds went back to the union and could even choose to stop funding a union for failing to comply with the CLT.

The state also exercised considerable control over the selection of union leaders. The Labor Ministry appointed the union directorate, which in turn selected union officers, who were subject to approval by the ministry. No provisions were made for shop floor representatives. Within this structure arose a leadership that sought to sustain its position by ingratiating itself with state officials more than by delivering benefits to the base. Leaders who acted in this way were known as *pelegos*.[3]

In keeping with its emphasis on unions as social welfare agencies, the CLT severely limited their role in wage setting and collective bargaining. For all intents and purposes, the CLT withheld from workers the right to strike. It required unions to obtain the endorsement of a regional labor court before embarking on a strike, and gave the Labor Ministry the right to sever the funds and remove the leaders of unions that conducted strikes without this authorization.

The political opening of the mid-1940s provided a new context for working-class politics. Anticipating the end of authoritarian rule and seeking to compete personally under the new democracy, Vargas turned to populism at the end of the Estado Novo. He sought to mobilize labor support by emphasizing the concessions, rather than the controls, of the corporatist framework he had established. He formed the PTB (Partido Trabalhista Brasileiro or Brazilian Labor Party) and invoked *trabalhismo* in speeches. Vargas's appeals to labor fueled concern among conservative military sectors that the one-time dictator might try to establish a "syndicalist republic" along the lines of Juan Perón in neighboring Argentina. This suspicion contributed to the military's increasing antagonism toward Vargas in the period approaching 1945, as well as the distance they kept from him until his death in 1954.

Labor-related conflicts between Vargas and the military at the end of the Estado Novo previewed future tensions between populist politicians and conservative military sectors. Whereas politicians sought to gain electoral support through the extension of benefits to workers, the armed forces wanted to enforce controls over the labor movement. During the period of open electoral competition from 1945 to 1964, labor became a political force of increasing importance. Politicians from mainstream parties, as well as those with a closer association to labor, such as the PTB, became subject to labor demands under the combined pressures of heightened electoral competition, rising labor mobilization, and Brazil's weakly institutionalized system of political parties. Within the country's factionalized and increasingly polarized multiparty system, there was no centrist party that could provide mechanisms of political control over labor. Labor leaders, working from inside as well as outside the official union structure, began to play off different parties (and their factions) against one another.[4] The jockeying for power by labor leaders led to the virtual abandonment of many corporatist controls. Labor protest swelled and labor's demands become more radical.

From 1962 to 1964, the last two years of João Goulart's troubled presidency, labor leaders threatened to withdraw their support for the president and his party (the PTB) if their demands were not met. Recognizing his dependence on these labor leaders, Goulart made concessions to them. Labor support had played a crucial role in his rise to power; it became even more imperative after Goulart became isolated from elite sectors anxious about preserving their privileged status. The armed forces were among these sectors. They turned decisively against Goulart after the labor movement tried to organize soldiers and incite them to rebel against the hierarchy. The prospect of Goulart creating a new political order in which the working class would undermine the military was a key factor motivating the officer corps to mount the coup of 1964.[5] The labor movement's encroachment upon the corporate sphere of the armed forces violated one of the cardinal rules of Latin American politics: that new power contenders coexist with old power contenders rather than attack or try to exclude them.[6]

The conflict between electorally minded populist politicians and control-oriented military officers over labor policy in the previous period of democracy (1945–64) foreshadows recent developments under the current democratic regime (since 1985). The important parallel concerns the contradiction between a military-supported system of control and the incentives of politicians in a competitive and fluid setting to break these restrictions in order to win over an actor of prime electoral importance. The fact that politicians in the previous democratic period were also tempted to court the labor movement over military objections—even though labor mobilization posed more of a threat to political stability than it does in the current (postcommunist) era—suggests that electoral incentives in general, and not a particular aspect of the current period of democracy, stimulate the expansion of labor rights against military preferences.

DEVELOPMENTS IN LABOR RELATIONS UNDER MILITARY RULE

With the imposition of authoritarian rule in 1964, renewed enforcement of the rules and regulations specified within the CLT, coupled with overt repression, served as the basis for demobilizing the labor movement and keeping it firmly in check. The first military government wasted little time in purging dissident union leaders and replacing them with its own choices. It also moved quickly to make several legal changes aimed at decreasing the power of unions.

Among the central changes imposed was a new strike law (Law 4.330 of June 1, 1964), which virtually eliminated the possibility of conducting a legal strike.[7] The antistrike law prohibited all public employees (of the federal, state, and municipal governments) and employees of state-owned enterprises from going on strike. It also banned strikes in "essential" private services and those considered to be of a "political, social, or religious nature," as defined by the government.[8] Outside these areas, the regime theoretically allowed strikes for better working conditions and wages, but the law held them to conditions virtually impossible for unions to meet in practice. For example, for a union to call a legal strike, it had to hold several meetings among the membership, meet extremely high quorums of attendance at these meetings, and secure very high rates of adherence to the proposed action. The law effectively authorized strikes in only two circumstances: to gain back pay and to gain wage levels the labor court sanctioned but employers refused to provide.[9] The punishment for conducting an unauthorized strike was severe. It included suspending or dismissing striking workers without compensation, removing union leaders from their posts, levying hefty fines, and, in extreme cases, canceling the union's legal mandate. Informally, punishment extended to physical repression.

The regime also established a fixed and incontestable wage policy designed to control union wage campaigns. Wages were considered to be a main cause of inflation and a central basis of labor protest. After 1964, the Finance Ministry determined wage increases in the public and private sectors according to a set formula based on government figures. Wages would be readjusted annually, taking into account anticipated inflation and estimated productivity increases. For several years, including the period known as Brazil's "economic miracle" (1968–73), the government underestimated inflation rates as well as rises in productivity, pushing wage levels down in turn.[10]

Another way the military regime reduced the power of unions was to make changes in the administration of social security benefits. Before 1964, social security institutes had become an important part of the political power and patronage base of labor leaders, especially those affiliated with the PTB. By transferring the social security administration back to the hands of state technocrats, the military regime deprived the unions of their main source of patronage and influence. This rationalization of the social security institutes removed a central channel through which the labor movement had penetrated the state bureaucracy.

Together, these measures crippled the power of unions. While workers suffered through adverse conditions, the antistrike law and the full enforcement of the CLT deprived them of their main retaliatory weapon: the strike. The number of strikes fell from 154 in 1962 and 302 in 1963, to 25 in 1965, 15 in 1966, 12 in 1970, to none in 1971.[11] A brief relaxation of controls led to an eruption of militant strikes in 1968 in São Paulo and Minas Gerais, which the military government quickly and forcefully crushed. This set a precedent that deterred further outbursts of activism until the late 1970s.

President Geisel's liberalization of authoritarian rule gave rise to a reawakening of civil society. The "new unionism" or *novo sindicalismo* was born at the crossroads of the political opening. The new unionism sought to abolish the old corporatist framework in favor of an "autonomous" labor movement based on unions led by "authentic" labor leaders (*autênticos*) untrammeled by corporatist shackles. In this vein, the new unionism demanded the right to shop floor organization, direct bargaining between unions and employers, expanded rights to strike, and the elimination of state control over wages. The automobile manufacturing center of São Paulo's industrial suburbs (known as the ABC region) gave rise to this movement in labor. Luis Inácio (Lula) da Silva, president of the Metallurgical Union of São Bernardo dos Campos, was one of the first and most prominent figures to unfurl the banner of the new unionism in the late 1970s.

The new unionism gained widespread attention by spearheading a strike movement that began in 1978. The most immediate concrete motive for these strikes was to protest the government's failure to adjust wage rates in accordance with inflation. Labor protest in 1978 began with a sit-down strike in a truck factory in São Bernardo. It soon spread to ninety firms involving five hundred thousand workers in greater São Paulo.[12] In 1979 a more prolonged strike was held by the metallurgical workers of São Paulo, an event that ignited many more strikes between January and October of that year. Leaders of the new generation of unionism figured visibly in this wave of labor mobilization that affected approximately thirty key economic sectors, including steel production, urban transportation, and trucking.

The new movement in labor became an important and irrevocable part of Brazil's political opening and transition to democracy. The movement's courageous defiance of the regime's highly restrictive labor laws and formidable repressive apparatus earned it sympathetic press coverage. Even moderate newspapers depicted the movement as having legitimate demands. One of the new unionism's major accomplishments during these years was the formation in 1983 of a central union organization, Central Unica dos Trabalhadores or CUT.

With the legalization of new parties in 1979, the new generation of "authentic" union leaders sought to enhance the political power of the labor movement by forming the Workers' Party (PT). They argued that the high degree of state control over Brazil's working class necessitated direct entry into the political system.[13] The PT represents more than the narrow interests of organized workers. It seeks to promote a more democratic and egalitarian political culture in Brazil.

President Geisel's Decree Law against Strikes: 1978

The military regime saw that the political opening would give rise to increased labor mobilization and feared that an unwieldy labor movement, especially one linked to a broader political mobilization, could threaten the military government's control over the political opening. Hence it tried to tame the movement's activities in the transition back to democracy. The dilemma the government faced was between granting too many concessions to labor and thereby possibly inviting labor protest to spiral out of control, and giving too few concessions, posing the risk of an upsurge of demands at a time when the regime's broader goal was to preserve social and political stability. President Geisel formed a group to revise preexisting labor laws. The group included members of the Armed Forces General Staff (EMFA) and General Golbery do Couto e Silva, head of the civilian cabinet and mastermind of the political opening. They assisted in the formulation of a decree law (DL 1632) that President Geisel issued in August 1978. This decree law was designed to relax some of the most draconian aspects of previous legislation, but at the same time make sure that labor protest did not threaten the transition.[14]

Similar to previous legislation, DL 1632 continued to ban strikes in wide-ranging sectors of the economy (those it deemed "essential"), but softened the penalties for those who dared to conduct illegal strikes. It maintained as essential sectors most of the areas listed in the antistrike law of 1964, including water, energy, electricity, gas, sewage, communications, transportation, the loading and unloading of cargo, hospitals, pharmacies, drug stores, and "industries basic to national defense, as specified by law."[15] It added banks (public and private) as well as the provision of petroleum to the list of essential services.[16] The inclusion of an open-ended clause allowing the president to prohibit strikes by decree in additional areas reflected the persistence of an arbitrary element in the regime's style of governing.

With respect to altering the penalties for engaging in illegal strikes, the architects of DL 1632 established a more gradational sequence of punishment, ranging from a simple warning to the suspension of employment for thirty days to dismissal without "just cause" (depriving workers of the right to draw on the government-established fund for job severance pay) to, finally, punishment under the Law of National Security, which could carry up to twenty years in prison.[17] Previously, only two punishments existed: dismissal from employment or prison sentences of four to twenty years for violating the Law of National Security.[18] Since these sentences were too stringent to be widely applied in an era of political liberalization, the regime had mostly ceased to employ them.

Given its status as a decree law, DL 1632 was virtually guaranteed passage. Congress would have sixty days to approve or reject it, with no possibility of amendment. If Congress failed to vote within this period, it would be automatically approved. The constitutions of 1967 and 1969 gave the president of the republic the power to issue decree laws on matters related to national security and public finances. The comprehensive definition the regime gave to "national security" meant that the president could decree almost any legislation.[19]

The issuance of DL 1632 in August 1978 gave rise to a wave of public criticism by union leaders, opposition politicians, and progressive lawyers. Union leaders took issue with the large number of sectors labeled "essential" and attacked the government for perpetuating the notion that strikes were a crime rather than a fundamental right of workers. Echoing their criticisms were mainstream opposition politicians, such as Fernando Henrique Cardoso and André Franco Montoro, who saw the decree law as far too restrictive.[20] One of the platforms of their party, the MDB, included the full restoration of the right to strike. Even some business groups opposed DL 1632 for not allowing more time for direct negotiations between employers and employees before the state intervened.[21]

Legislators of ARENA faced the following dilemma. As members of the government party, they felt obligated to support the legislation; at the same time, however, the criticism targeted at DL 1632 made them fearful that doing so might hurt them in future elections, especially the upcoming legislative contest later that year. On the suggestion of Jarbas Passarinho, an Arenista and staunch ally of the military regime, ARENA legislators chose the easy way out. They would simply not appear at the meetings of the joint committee to examine the bill or for the floor vote.[22] Thus they sought to avoid blame but, given the rules for a decree law, assured approval of the government's bill. DL 1632 passed by default on October 2, 1978.[23] The conduct of ARENA legislators suggests the responsiveness of politicians to electoral incentives even when competition is tightly controlled, as it was under military rule. Heightened electoral competition would only increase their sensitivity to electoral opinion. The terms of DL 1632, however, were enforced only selectively by the last military administration (1979–85), which sought to enhance support for the government party in order to stabilize the transition to democracy.[24]

In the final years of authoritarian rule, politicians were increasingly vocal in their opposition to the restrictive labor legislation of the regime. The grave economic crisis of 1981–83 had dampened labor militancy. Yet by imposing economic losses on workers, the crisis was bound to lead to the articulation of pent-up demands as soon as the economy improved and civilian rule limited the risk of repression. The PMDB gave labor policy a central place in its 1982 manifesto.[25] Targeting labor legislation as the first area for reform, the PMDB proposed an expansion of strike rights. Tancredo Neves echoed his party's view in the presidential campaign of 1984.[26]

THE NEW DEMOCRACY: LABOR GAINS MOMENTUM

Democratization enhanced the political power of labor and set the stage for heightened conflict between army leaders, who would try to keep strike provisions as restrictive as possible,[27] and politicians, who would be encouraged to expand them. Although unionized workers and employees remain the minority in Brazil, in the new democracy labor enjoys a symbolic importance that exceeds its numbers.[28] Since the middle class is quite small in size, a large majority of the population is comprised of "working people," including—besides the organized working class—the vast "informal sector" in the cities as well as rural laborers. Among these "popular sectors," the well-organized categories of labor are relatively better off and therefore provide a model for the millions of poorer people who have a very precarious base of sustenance. Appeals to "workers" and "working people" are therefore attractive to electoral politicians, as the success of Getúlio Vargas's slogan of *trabalhismo* demonstrated in the 1940s and 1950s. The *novo sindicalismo* and the PT helped fuel the growth of expectations and aspirations among workers.[29] Mainstream politicians feel under increasing pressure to play to the themes and slogans these forces have introduced to Brazilian politics, as witnessed by the revival of *trabalhismo*, especially by Leonel Brizola's Partido Democrático Trabalhista (PDT), and appeals made to labor and other popular sectors by such parties as the PMDB. The strength of popular support for labor was revealed in a 1988 opinion poll in which 77 percent of all respondents agreed that strikes should be a legitimate form of political pressure.[30]

As demonstrated in this section, the military and pro-labor political forces clashed in all phases of the redefinition of strike law: during the year in which the minister of labor sought to elaborate a new strike law (mid-1985 to mid-1986); during the constitutional debates of 1987–88; and in a subsequent attempt in the spring of 1989 to roll back the gains that labor had achieved in the constitution of 1988.

Labor Protest in the First Year of the New Democracy

The extensive strike activity of the mid-1980s sharpened the conflict between pro-labor and anti-labor forces. In 1985, the combination of greater political freedom and an improving yet inflation-ridden economy led to rising labor protest. Strikes increased markedly in three dimensions: frequency, duration, and size.[31] At the height of labor protest during the year, union leaders called for the revocation of the decree law imposed by President Geisel.[32] As far as labor leaders and their followers were concerned, workers had legitimate grievances, and legal changes were necessary to ensure their expression.

The military, especially the army, felt otherwise. What Brazil was witnessing, they argued, was "not democracy but disorder," pure and simple.[33] The events of 1985 tested their tolerance for labor activism and their will to influence government policy toward labor. Being out of power did not deter army leaders from following developments in the labor sphere and trying to influence them. Particularly, the labor movement remained one of the central subjects investigated by the SNI.[34] Labor issues also continued to figure prominently in meetings of the army high command. Similarly, the Escola Superior de Guerra continued to include labor issues in courses concerning national security and economic development.[35]

The military pressured the government to crack down on strikes in the initial months of the New Republic. For example, army leaders tried to persuade President Sarney to send in federal troops to curb strikes in various Brazilian states, especially São Paulo. President Sarney and his labor minister, Almir Pazzianotto, however, kept them at arm's length. The presidency was not yet beholden to the military for support. Sarney's popularity in the first year of the new democracy allowed him to withstand the pressure tactics of the army minister.[36] He did not apply the strike legislation of the military regime to the strikers. Nor did he insist on challenging the authority of state governors by calling in federal authorities to repress labor protest.

While President Sarney refrained from employing the tactics of the authoritarian regime to keep labor protest from spiraling out of control, he concluded that it was necessary to start limiting strike activity. The president, much more than individual legislators, needed to be concerned about the daily disruption and economic damage caused by strikes. Elites such as business and the military, as well as nonelite actors affected by the consequences of widespread strike activity, would hold him accountable. Thus the Sarney government sought to replace the strict strike law of the previous period, which it hesitated to apply, with restrictions that were more compatible with the rules and norms of a democratic regime.

A New Strike Law on the Agenda

The first minister of labor in the new civilian regime, Almir Pazzianotto, was charged with drafting a new strike law that would ease Brazil into a more open, less state-controlled form of labor relations until the new constitution made definitive decisions on labor-related issues. The bill Pazzianotto produced became a serious point of contention even though it was intended only as a temporary measure.

Efforts to shape the bill before it reached the Congress are worth examining for what they reveal about the importance of the forum in which interest articulation takes place. The conservative nature of the bill that Pazzianotto produced—contrary to what many expected from the progressive labor lawyer who once defended a leading union in the movement for greater union autonomy—suggests that the influence of nonelectoral elite actors, such as the military, is greatest in closed political settings. The military's ability to sway decision making undoubtedly weakens when and if the stage of open public debate is reached, as occurred in the last two phases of the redefinition of strike law.

Pazzianotto wrote and revised the strike bill from mid-1985 to mid-1986. The military leadership, business elites, and unions sought in a central way to influence the terms of his proposal. Leading generals—the army minister, the director of the SNI, and the head of the military cabinet—insisted that the bill prohibit strikes in the public sector and in a long list of "essential" services. They succeeded in pressuring Pazzianotto to make the draft bill more restrictive.[37] Leaders of the business community also opposed early drafts of the bill for being too sympathetic to workers. They were less concerned than the military with prohibiting strikes and more concerned with finding efficient solutions to labor disputes and instituting measures to protect employers' rights (for example, through employer "lockouts"). Unions and numerous politicians reviled Pazzianotto for heeding the demands of military and business leaders. Union leaders of all stripes—of the new "authentic" as well as the old corporatist variety—argued that the first draft of the bill represented little improvement over existing legislation. They protested the continued ban on strikes among all public workers and insisted on a narrower definition of "essential" services.[38]

The final version of the bill remained restrictive. To the military's relief, it prohibited strikes among a broad range of groups: all public employees and those in most of the sectors deemed "essential" as specified in Decree Law 1632. In sectors deemed "nonessential," it authorized strikes only under the condition that at least 50 percent of union members vote by secret ballot in favor of a walkout. The bill did, however, reduce the punishment for participating in an illegal strike mainly to warnings and dismissals, assigning prison sentences only for the most flagrant violations. It also shortened the time legally required for a union to advise employers of a strike. On a number of other details, the government proposal trimmed the bureaucratic obstacles necessary for calling and resolving walkouts.[39] Yet since constitutional deliberations were already underway before Congress could consider the Pazzianotto bill, the energy expended to produce the strike law proposal was all for naught. The constitution of 1988 would yield a more binding decision on strike law.

Labor Rights in the Constituent Assembly

The next step in the evolution of labor policy was the constitution of 1988. Notwithstanding the disappointments of 1985–86, workers won tremendous gains under the new constitution. The open political forum of the Constituent Assembly (operative from early 1987 to late 1988) redounded to their advantage. Among labor's greatest victories was the unrestricted right to strike. Even public servants and employees in sectors previously considered essential were not excluded from this right, at least until a complementary law was instituted to regulate it.[40]

Labor victories in the new constitution could not have been anticipated by the composition of assembly members. Approximately 52 percent of the Constituent Assembly belonged to the conservative block, the Centrão, which formed in late 1987. Early calculations suggested that organized labor could count on only about 22 percent of all assembly members to represent working-class interests. One-time workers themselves comprised no more than 3 percent of the assembly, versus the approximately 32 percent that represented members of business.[41]

Against these odds, however, organized labor was able to convince politicians across the political spectrum to side with many of its demands. Three factors explain labor's success in swinging a sufficient number of assembly members— including politicians whose conservative affiliations did not predispose them toward pro-labor policies—to vote in favor of an expansion of workers' rights: (1) the concentration of energy and resources by the electoral left and center-left on labor issues; (2) the adept lobby that defended workers' interests; and most importantly (3) the electoral motivations of politicians to support a pro-labor stance.

The important role that Brazilian constitutions traditionally played in establishing the legal framework for labor relations led organized labor to seize the opportunity to defend its future. The left and center-left devoted its energies to committees dealing with social issues, including the Subcommittee for the Rights of Workers and Public Servants (Subcomissão dos Direitos dos Trabalhadores e Servidores Públicos), and the Committee of Social Order (Comissão da Ordem Social), while conservative forces concentrated their efforts on committees to examine questions concerning the economic order and political institutions that would guide Brazil's future.[42]

The labor lobby, coordinated by the Interunion Department for Legislative Advising (Departamento Intersindical de Assessoria Parlamentar or DIAP), defended the rights of organized labor. By the time of the constitutional debates, DIAP represented over 350 unions throughout Brazil. At the outset of these debates, it proposed an expanded definition of the right to strike, greater job security provisions, a reduction in the work week, an increase in the minimum wage, and other benefits to labor.[43]

Military leaders rejected virtually all of DIAP's proposals except minimum wage increases. They expressed vocal opposition to the prospect of a liberal strike law and attacked the notion of job security as a "disservice to the country." The army minister predicted that industries would simply dismiss workers shortly before the point at which job tenure would set in and that capital would be diverted from productive activities to economic speculation.

Business groups were prepared to compromise on most measures. This flexibility is not surprising in light of recent survey research, which suggests that most industrialists regard labor as pragmatic rather than radical and threatening.[44] Nevertheless, business groups objected fiercely and unanimously to the constraints that job security measures in the private sector would impose on firms, and entered into an alliance with the military to combat proposals for employment guarantees.[45] Yet while business groups and the military have entered into occasional alliances over labor issues in Brazil's new democracy, these alliances have been forged over specific issues of shared interest. Even though the military have tended to support the interests of business, industrialists do not on the whole support the military's claims to tutelary powers.

Pro-labor interests predominated in the relevant committees of the National Constituent Assembly. The Subcommittee for the Rights of Workers and Public Servants and the Committee on Social Order drew up proposals that extended the right to strike to all employees (conditional upon adequate warning and provision for the continued functioning of services) and recognized the need for greater job stability (leaving the details to be decided at a later date), shorter working hours, better working conditions, and higher material benefits.[46]

Many observers thought that labor's successes in the early stages of the constitutional debates, when pro-labor elements were preponderant in the above-mentioned committees, would not be maintained in the plenary session of the Constituent Assembly, when conservative elements would be represented. Yet the labor lobby managed to defy the expectation that conservative forces would emerge victorious in the final stages of the constitutional debates and overturn the decisions reached by progressive forces in earlier stages. Following a strategic plan of action, the labor lobby preserved the right to strike in the final two stages of decision making: the draft coordinating committee and the plenary session. The labor lobby played on electoral interests. It also played on the concerns of business groups and their political allies about the job security provision. Supporters of the labor lobby, which included politicians from the PT and PMDB, threatened to hold out for farther-reaching proposals, such as guarantees of job security, if conservatives did not support the (more moderate) proposal that had been approved hitherto.[47] In this way, they succeeded in marshaling conservative support for other pro-labor policies, including the unrestricted right of workers to strike.[48]

By contrast, the army lobby found itself at a loss. As negotiations unfolded, it became evident that it did not have the resources necessary to gain adequate leverage over congressional votes.[49] Lacking positive sanctions, unwilling to use intimidation, and without the full support of the more narrowly professionalist navy and air force, the army was indeed constrained in what it could do to combat the pro-labor current. At one point, when the army minister announced that the country would be better off without so many demagogic legislators making laws on the basis of their electoral interests, several constitutional delegates protested the military's interference in issues that lay outside of their own narrow corporate sphere.[50] Notably, only where business elites forged an explicit alliance with the military—over the issue of expanding job security—was the labor lobby thoroughly defeated. Business groups, which had contributed funds to the electoral campaigns of many assembly members, appeared to have more sway than the military.[51]

Thus, the constitution of 1988 met most of labor's basic demands, as articulated in DIAP's original proposal. Brazilian workers—even public servants and employees in sectors previously considered essential—won the unrestricted right to strike, pending later regulation through a complementary law. The only employees categorically excluded from this right were military personnel, an unnegotiable point for the armed forces. Workers also gained a reduction in the work week from 48 to 44 hours (the original demand was 40 hours), with a maximum of six-hour shifts in the event of no work breaks; an increase in overtime pay; maternity leave of 120 days; advance notice of dismissal; and many other improvements on preexisting legislation.[52] Support for the reform package was solid: 436 in favor versus 38 objections and 19 abstentions.[53] The only major pro-labor policies that the constitution failed to endorse concerned guarantees of job security and the abolition of the corporatist organizational structure of unions. To the extent that aspects of the corporatist structure remained—such as the requirement that all workers pay a union tax, now called *contribuição sindical*, and the prohibition of more than one union representing a category of workers per territorial unit (*unicidade*)—military pressure was not responsible. Rather, many established union leaders advocated these corporatist features. Guaranteed finance and the prohibition of competition strengthened established unions after the government lost its power of interference.

Few of the legislators who voted against the majority on labor reforms publicly denounced the decision of the Constituent Assembly. Among the few dissenting voices was Deputy Luís Roberto Ponte (PMDB–Rio Grande do Sul), who accused his fellow assembly members of being too oriented to the "vote of November 15," that is, the day of the upcoming municipal elections.[54] The military hierarchy echoed these sentiments, objecting vehemently to the decision reached by the National Constituent Assembly.[55] Even the navy, which tended to be more concerned with protecting its organizational and professional interests than shaping broader political developments, manifested anxiety about the consequences of an unrestricted right to strike.[56] Army general Bayma Denys, head of the *gabinete militar*, publicly announced that the military would not tolerate the chaos that an unrestricted right to strike would unleash. While the high command was determined to set in motion a complementary law regulating the right to strike as provided in the constitution, even within the armed forces doubt existed about the capacity to significantly alter the trend toward expanded labor rights.[57] These doubts proved to be well-founded. It was not simply the celebration of social rights and DIAP's lobbying power in the context of the Constituent Assembly. The underlying strength of electoral motivations continued to work in favor of the labor movement.

Regulating Strike Law

Labor victories in the constitution of 1988 did not deter military leaders from persisting in their efforts to dampen labor protest. They had not yet resigned themselves to increased worker mobilization in Brazil's new democracy. The next attempt the military made to control the labor movement involved regulating the right to strike as provided by the constitution.

Strike activity surged in the initial months of 1989. In January and February alone, 387 strikes occurred, 30 percent more than registered in the same period the year before. While the military ministers were preoccupied with questions of social instability, the attention of ministers concerned with the economy focused on the effect of wage increases on inflation and the public budget. Under pressure from both military and civilian members of his cabinet, President Sarney initiated measures in April of 1989 to curb strike activity. Taking the nation by surprise, he appeared on national radio and television to make a special announcement: the gravity of the strike wave, combined with the failure of Congress to treat it accordingly, gave him little choice but to issue an emergency measure to restrict strikes. If Congress failed to endorse it into law, he threatened, the government would reissue the measure time and time again. Sarney appointed the counsel general to draft a "provisional measure with the force of law" or *medida provisória com força de lei* to begin the process of restricting strikes. At his side was the army general who headed the SNI.[58]

Under Brazil's new democracy, the president can issue a *medida provisória* under "exceptional circumstances." Congress has thirty days to approve or reject such a measure. In the event of congressional approval, the measure becomes law. In the event of congressional rejection or inaction, it becomes invalid. During the thirty days, the terms of the measure are binding. While leaving the president considerable power, this legal innovation of Brazil's new democracy represents a large decrease in executive power relative to the decree law under military rule. Whereas Congress previously needed to actively reject a decree law for it to be disqualified, it now needs to actively approve a *medida provisória* for it to remain in effect.

The executive issued a *medida provisória* (MP 50) in late April 1989 that made it difficult to carry out a legal strike. First, it established a high quorum (the presence of at least one-third of all union members) for deciding whether to embark on a strike. Of this percentage, it demanded that half vote in favor of a walkout. Second, the MP enumerated a long list of essential services (thirteen in all) in which unions leaders were required to communicate the intention of a strike at least forty-eight hours in advance. Third, it obligated unions in sectors defined as essential to assure the continued functioning of basic services for the duration of the strike. In the event that they failed to do so, it gave the president the right to summon members of the population to keep services in operation. Fourth, MP 50 specified a number of penalties—warning, dismissal, and arrest— that would be applied to those who violated the legal criteria for a strike.[59] Military leaders applauded the MP. They would go to great lengths to try to persuade Congress of its merit.

How did Congress react to the MP? While the parties appealing to labor attacked it as downright draconian, moderate politicians likened it to the restrictive legislation of the military regime. Conservative legislators remained silent, suggesting their reluctance to take a stand. They recognized, on the one hand, the existence of constituencies who were increasingly frustrated with the paralysis resulting from strikes and who felt that labor should be "kept in its place." On the other hand, they were aware of the possible risks of antagonizing pro-labor groups.[60] The army had deployed its lobbyists with full force, yet few legislators were receptive to those who knocked on their doors. After the rules of the game became more open and competitive, any loyalty that former ARENA politicians may have had to the military for once fostering and protecting their political careers seemed to evaporate.[61]

Congress rejected MP 50 by failing to vote on it within thirty days. But given the provisions of a *medida provisória*, conservative legislators could no longer assure the passage of unpopular legislation by simply avoiding the issue, as they had done with Decree Law 1632 in 1978. The president immediately reissued the MP.[62] Congress needed to place some restrictions on strikes in order to prevent an endless repetition of issuance and defeat of the MP, and because the constitution would need to be regulated at some point anyway. The chair of the joint congressional committee that would produce the replacement or *substitutivo* was Senator Ronan Tito, leader of the PMDB in the Senate. Tito walked a tightrope. He needed to make the new law restrictive enough to prevent the government from trying to limit strikes through the use of *medidas provisórias*, yet liberal enough to not jeopardize his own standing with voters and his party's candidate for the upcoming presidential elections later that year, Ulysses Guimarães.[63]

In his draft, Tito omitted those aspects of the MP that provoked the most widespread opposition, namely, the high quorum required to decree a legal strike, the presidential prerogative of requisitioning civilians to guarantee the functioning of essential services, and the stiff penalties for workers who participated in illegal strikes. The version that Congress passed in June 1989 respected these omissions. It gave individual unions the right to determine their own quorums for decreeing a strike. It excluded some areas from the list of essential services specified by the government's original proposal, including postal and telegraphic services, the loading and unloading of port cargo, and functions connected with the central bank. It allowed strikes to occur among the remaining essential services, but required unions in these sectors to communicate their intentions seventy-two hours in advance. The congressional substitute also permitted the summoning of employees, but not members of the general population, to keep essential services in operation. Last, it drastically softened the penalties for abuses of the right to strike. In short, while the new law that Congress passed does place limits on the right of workers to strike, its terms are far less restrictive than the government's original proposal.[64]

The vote in the Chamber of Deputies was solidly in favor of the new law (244 for, 82 against, and 4 abstentions). In the Senate, only two senators cast negative votes.[65] Legislators from labor-oriented parties acknowledged the new law as a vast improvement over the government's previous proposal to regulate the right to strike, but still had reservations about the extent of its restrictions.[66] Conservative politicians by and large supported the new law. But the military regarded it as excessively permissive. The new legislation was a serious blow to their efforts to keep strike law restrictive. Notably, however, President Sarney did not attempt to veto the new strike law. He was realistic about the goals and powers of Congress, which militate against army tutelage and control over the labor movement.

Military Force as a Measure of Last Resort

In addition to influencing congressional deliberations in their effort to contain the labor movement, the army advocated that strikes be repressed on a number of occasions during the Sarney government. But use of the military's essential power capability—organized coercion—for this purpose carried risks. In fact, it aroused opposition in society, damaged the reputation of the military, and raised questions about the politicians close to them.

The most noteworthy examples of military force being used to quell strikes in Brazil's new democracy occurred in March 1987 and November 1988. In March 1987, 40,000 dock workers went on strike, paralyzing 177 ships. The navy deployed 1,400 marines to occupy the country's principal ports after the superior labor court declared the strike illegal. In the same month, 55,000 workers threatened to cut off oil production and processing if the government did not meet their demands for a wage increase. Army troops moved in and occupied major oil refineries in the country. The formidable show of force they presented, complete with tanks and armored personnel carriers, was intended not only to protect these installations but also to deliver the unequivocal message that neither the government nor the military would tolerate strikes in strategic sectors of the economy.

Whose decision was it to deploy military troops in March of 1987? The director of the SNI, the chief of the military cabinet, and the army minister appear to have been critical in pressuring Sarney to respond to labor unrest in such a way.[67] From their perspective, Brazil's ailing economy did not need the added aggravation of a defiant labor movement. These military leaders accused elements of civil and political society of selfish motives and praised the armed forces as being singularly committed to the national interest.[68] Markedly less popular since the failure of his economic stabilization plan, the Plano Cruzado, Sarney lacked the resolve to stand firm against the top brass. In return for their backing, he allowed the generals' preferences to weigh heavily in the government's handling of labor disputes. As events unfolded in the early months of 1987, Sarney maintained close contact with the director of the SNI and the ministers of the military and civilian cabinets. Notably, the labor minister was not consulted on the government's decision to roll out the tanks. Only after the occupation became a fact did Sarney invite the minister of labor to take part in negotiations.[69]

Union leaders and politicians alike reacted vigorously to the military's intervention. CUT and the leadership of the parties most closely linked to labor, the PT and the PDT, denounced the military's assumption that labor issues lay within their legitimate sphere of action. Leader of the PT Luis Inácio (Lula) da

Silva gave a fiery address before Congress charging the government with gross overreaction. Various more moderate members denounced the interference of the military in the political life of Brazil. Notably, conservative members of Congress refused to publicly support the government's actions. When asked to comment on the military's occupation of the ports and refineries, conservative deputies and senators preferred to remain silent.[70] These reactions show that politicians of all persuasions considered it costly in electoral terms to antagonize Brazil's vast number of working people and support unpopular military actions.

The other major instance of military force being used against labor unrest in Brazil's new democracy was even more damaging to the military's reputation. In November 1988, army troops moved against striking workers at Brazil's National Steel Company in Volta Redonda, Rio de Janeiro. Their actions resulted in three dead and twenty-three wounded. Captured on film, the repression of the strike was aired by all of Brazil's major television networks. Although the Brazilian public had been growing weary of the strike wave engulfing Brazil at the time, many citizens disapproved of the handling of events at Volta Redonda. They objected to the pressure the army minister had been putting on the government to take more aggressive action to control workers (despite the formal protections offered to them in the new constitution), to the use of army troops in such a situation, and later, to the fact that no one would be held accountable for the deaths. A surge of editorials appeared in Brazil's major newspapers denouncing the army and the Sarney government. Lawyers of Brazil's progressive bar association, the Ordem dos Advogados do Brasil (OAB), and politicians from a broad ideological range joined in the disapproval expressed by ordinary citizens. The PT and PDT scored unexpected victories in the municipal elections of November 15, held in the aftermath of the Volta Redonda invasion. Some observers interpret their surprising electoral gains as a show of symbolic support for the values the labor movement represents and the goals for which it strives, which include an end to elite impunity.[71]

The minister of justice ordered a trial of the soldiers implicated in the casualties at Volta Redonda. The army minister, General Leônidas Pires Gonçalves, refused to have them stand trial, claiming that the army had simply carried out its constitutionally sanctioned duty of maintaining "law and order."[72] Insofar as the general's refusal stood, civilian supremacy did not prevail. At the same time, however, the reaction of the Brazilian public suggested that the army may have won the battle but lost the war. In a meeting of the army high command shortly after the incident, some generals spoke out against the army's conduct, suggesting the existence of divided opinions about military involvement in labor issues even within the most politically active branch of the armed forces. They argued that the army needed to adapt to the new democratic order and that repression like that wielded at Volta Redonda would only turn society against it.[73]

Thus the labor movement scored impressive victories in the first postauthoritarian government, and the military suffered a series of blows in keeping strike activity restricted. Would the movement be able to preserve its achievements as time went on? Would army leaders adjust to new realities and come to accept the expanded rights of workers as part and parcel of Brazil's new democracy? The governments of Fernando Collor and Itamar Franco provided evidence for an affirmative response to both questions.

The Collor Government

Military interference in labor issues during the two and a half years of the Collor government was conspicuously absent. General Carlos Tinoco, army minister under Collor, announced at his inauguration that the right to strike was recognized in the constitution and that the army would no longer play a role in quelling labor protest.[74] This noninterventionist stance was couched in terms of the army's resolve to focus on more "professional" pursuits and let civilians deal with such matters henceforth. Under the Collor presidency, army leaders did not try to roll back the legal gains the labor movement had achieved. Nor did they ever deploy troops for the purpose of breaking up a strike.

In September 1990, the government contemplated submitting a bill to Congress that would tighten restrictions on strikes in essential economic sectors. Walkouts scheduled to take place among bank employees and oil workers prompted the government to consider this course of action in the absence of military pressure. Extant legislation did not impede unions in essential sectors from going on strike. The executive, not the legislature, bore the political brunt of the disruption caused by strikes in these sectors. Yet in the end, President Collor did not try to alter the strike law approved at the end of the Sarney government.[75] Imposing stringent legal restrictions on organized workers would conflict with his general policy goal of loosening state control over business and labor[76] and would make it difficult to secure the backing of this important group, which would be required for future governmental programs. Moreover, such action might compromise the public image of empathy for the common Brazilian that Collor had tried so hard to cultivate.

The Franco Government

The armed forces continued to keep a low profile vis-à-vis labor issues in the Franco government. From the beginning of 1993 until the end of 1994, there were no independent military initiatives, either legally oriented or coercive, toward the labor movement. Although military troops were deployed on two occasions to break up labor protest—in October 1993 and in May 1994—both times civilian authorities ordered the military to act and remained in charge of the operation.

The first incident of this kind was aimed at disbanding protesting taxi drivers who had set up a blockade of the main exit roads out of Rio de Janeiro. City residents, angered by the inconvenience the blockade caused, overwhelmingly applauded the military action. The second incident took place in response to a wave of strikes instigated by the stabilization package of then finance minister and presidential aspirant Fernando Henrique Cardoso. In order to have the economic plan bear successful results in time for the November 1994 election, measures had to be taken that would provoke immediate wage losses for salaried workers. The determination of Fernando Henrique Cardoso (virtual head of the government by that time) to prevent labor protest from undermining his economic program, the failure of essential services to keep operating, and a strike by the federal police that had lasted over fifty-two days all contributed to the decision to order military shows of force in several of Brazil's major cities.[77]

The treatment of labor issues in preparation for the constitutional revision of 1993 reflected an important change in military conduct since the constitutional debates of 1987 and 1988. To the extent that the military lobby even raised the labor issue, it was only to try to prevent unionization and strikes from occurring within the military corporation itself. A poll that tapped legislative opinion in October 1993 indicated that the majority of deputies and senators felt that little or nothing should be altered with respect to labor policy. Only 11 percent of members thought that workers' rights should undergo serious alteration. Within this group, opinion was divided as to whether they should be contracted or expanded. Asked explicitly about the right to strike, 74 percent of members felt that tight restrictions against strikes should pertain only to essential sectors. In short, the survey found ample legislative support for preserving labor conquests in the constitution of 1988. While legislators on the left felt that economic considerations rendered imprudent further efforts to expand workers' rights, the fear of alienating voters inhibited legislators on the right from advocating a reduction of labor privileges.[78]

In short, the scant participation of the military in labor affairs under the Collor and Franco governments and the apparent consensus among Brazilian legislators to adhere to the labor policies enshrined in the 1988 charter suggest that workers' rights will remain secure in the country's new democracy. Neither the military nor conservative politicians are likely to roll back the labor movement's recent progress any time soon.

CONCLUSION

In the face of tremendous military opposition, the labor movement made significant legal gains even in the first postauthoritarian government. These gains have remained intact until the present despite the military's enduring concern about labor protest. Politicians seeking to "represent" the great numbers of Brazilians who see themselves as working people were evidently motivated to oppose military efforts to keep the rights of labor tightly restricted. The incentives unleashed by democracy were sufficiently powerful to persuade even many members of Brazil's conservative political class to vote in favor of liberalizing strike legislation. While electoral motivations did not persuade all politicians, they affected a sufficient number to yield an outcome that would not be expected on the basis of ideological leanings and political affiliations. The growing electoral strength of the labor movement and the prominent role that Luis Inácio (Lula) da Silva played in the 1989 and 1994 presidential races suggest that many Brazilian politicians will continue taking into account the concerns of labor and other popular sectors.

Even as early as 1978, when ARENA's electoral standing was still relatively secure, Arenista legislators manifested reluctance to endorse the government's attempt to crack down on strikes. Torn between the recognition that support for anti-labor policies could hurt them at the polls and the compromised relationship they had to the military government, ARENA politicians hid behind the provisions of the decree law. The coming of the New Republic, however, would remove this cover and force legislators to take a more visible stand on labor issues.

Heightened electoral competition, coupled with a stronger labor movement, intensified the pressure that politicians felt to embrace a group at the center of the struggle for a more democratic Brazil. Minister of Labor Almir Pazzianotto took timid steps in the beginning of the New Republic to elaborate a law relaxing previous restrictions on strikes. By the time the constitutional debates were in full swing, however, politicians in the Constituent Assembly were prepared to defend the rights of labor in a more assertive way, even if it meant confronting military opposition. The electoral incentives they faced contributed decisively to the expansion of labor rights in the constitution of 1988. The competitive dynamic of democracy also had an impact on keeping labor controls moderate when a proposal to regulate strike law emerged in the spring of 1989.

Efforts the military made to stem the advancement of labor rights did not bear fruit. Since the military ultimately needed to persuade Congress, the branch of government whose powers increased the most with democratization, even the weakness of President Sarney did not sufficiently aid their cause. While lobbying did not work to stem labor rights, neither did coercion, as exemplified in the aftermath of the Volta Redonda incident. It only worsened the military's image. After Congress defeated several of the central terms of MP 50, military leaders appear to have recognized and accepted the empowerment of labor and its political allies in Brazil's new democracy.

It is in the military's interest not to intervene in strikes in the current period. In fact, the likelihood that some leading officers would not support such intervention would weaken such efforts anyway. If the social order remains relatively peaceful, refraining from attempts to quell labor protest will help promote the army's self-styled image as an institution that respects democracy. However, if labor protest and social activism eventually spiral out of hand, civilians will be apt to call on soldiers to save the day. In this event, the high command will undoubtedly justify the military's intervention as a response to the nation's desires.

BUDGETARY POLITICS: SOLDIERS AND POLITICIANS COMPETE

Many observers anticipated that the military would be a strong contender for state funds under the democratic regime.[1] In fact, however, the armed forces, strongly united on this core corporate issue, have encountered considerable difficulty in convincing the country's politicians to meet their budgetary demands. The share of military expenditures in total public spending has actually diminished considerably under civilian rule, especially after the promulgation of the new constitution in late 1988. The dynamic of negotiations over the budget also bears out the military's weakness in this area. Defense spending has been among the most sensitive and contentious issues between the military and civilians in Brazil's new democracy.

Civil-military conflicts over defense appropriations are common in countries that have recently undergone a transition from authoritarian to democratic rule. In such contexts, the armed forces are intent on protecting their core organizational interests, which include defense expenditures. After holding political power for a lengthy period, many officers look forward to returning to explicitly military activities and expanding their capabilities in external defense. Yet military modernization depends on budgetary resources sufficient to obtain and/or uphold reasonable levels of equipment, training, personnel, and salaries.[2] Acquiring these resources often leads the armed forces into direct contention with civilians.

Why is this so? Some politicians want to punish the military (or at least not appear to reward them in any way) for the exercise of arbitrary power and abuses they committed during the period of authoritarian rule. They are therefore tempted to withhold funds from them. This source of civil-military conflict over defense spending indeed exists in countries where the armed forces devastated the economy and committed extensive human rights violations, as in Argentina.[3]

Much more enduring and widespread are the competing demands for state funds that democracy creates, and the inducements democracy provides for politicians to expand social and economic spending at the expense of military funding. Electoral competition gives politicians virtually irresistible incentives to attract voters through patronage. In order to finance these "goodies," they need to claim resources, even at the expense of the military. This effort to guarantee electoral success compels politicians who do not have any particular aversion to the armed forces to reduce their share of the budget. This political incentive, a direct result of democratization, has been crucial in fueling civil-military tension over defense spending in Brazil, where public animosity toward the military regime was relatively low and where competition for government finances is fierce. If the expansion of labor rights in Brazil's new democracy shows the extent to which politicians will oppose the military over programmatic proposals that command electoral support, cuts in defense expenditures suggest how far politicians will go to gain electoral support by distributing political patronage.

This chapter analyzes the weakness of the military's budgetary claims in Brazil's new democracy. It emphasizes the political calculations behind the funding priorities of legislative and executive politicians, and how they militate against awarding high budget shares to the armed forces. The focus on budget shares rather than absolute expenditures has a theoretical as well as practical foundation. The core analytical issue—the *relative* priority politicians accord to the armed forces versus other groups—is best captured by budget shares. On a practical level, data on absolute expenditures are highly conflicting and distorted by differences stemming from rampant inflation and exchange rate fluctuations. It is nevertheless important to note that declining budgetary shares that translate into smaller real expenditures are more likely to meet with military resistance, and hence provide a stronger measure of civilian steadfastness. For this reason, although data on absolute expenditures are highly conflicting and distorted by economic fluctuations, I consider them along with budgetary shares.

The first section explains in general terms that allocating smaller percentages to the military frees up funding for purposes that carry a greater electoral return. The second section demonstrates how this logic produced a trend toward declining shares of military expenditures over the course of the last democratic period in Brazil (1945–64). After briefly discussing the dynamics of the budget under authoritarian rule, the chapter analyzes in depth the reduction of military budget shares under the new democracy. Finally, it assesses the impact of these restrictions on the prospects for stable civil-military relations in Brazil.

THE LOGIC OF LEGISLATORS AND PRESIDENTS

Budget allocations constitute a critical indicator of the priorities of politicians and their strategies for political survival.[4] For politicians, two types of patronage incentives exist with respect to federal budget allocations: particularistic and categorical. Particularistic patronage concerns the use of resources to finance politicians' personal support networks. Categorical patronage involves politicians' efforts to provide additional benefits to generally defined categories of people (such as certain societal groups or economic sectors) and thus attract their voting support. While politicians rationally channel these favors to categories that are strongly represented among potential voters, they usually do not have personal links to the targets of this strategy. In contrast, particularistic patronage is reserved for personal followers, whom the politician—as patron—tries to integrate in a stable clientelist network. While this type of clientelism is still fairly entrenched in many rural areas, it is weaker, though by no means absent, in the cities. In contrast, the identification of people as members of general categories is stronger in urban centers, as evidenced by the formation of many interest associations. Therefore, the considerations and strategies of legislators and presidents vary somewhat based on the different constituencies they represent as well as the responsibilities of their respective offices. As a general rule, however, most politicians in patronage-ridden systems, such as Brazil's, view public resources as a way to distribute favors and gain support at the polls.

Legislators tend to act under the assumption that their reelection will be based primarily on what they have done for the home district, not on decisions that affect the nation overall. This is especially true in countries where politics is organized around patronage rather than programmatic principles. In Brazil, despite growing numbers of people who vote on the basis of television images and ideological positions, the clientelist tradition remains strong.[5] In such systems, legislators will be more intent on applying federal funds to public works projects in their electoral districts than on promoting overarching national interests or collective goods for the whole country. The emphasis on funding divisible, local projects for which politicians can claim direct credit is especially likely to prevail among legislators from rural districts.

A conflict between attending to local and regional constituencies and granting the military higher budget shares arises in Brazil for two reasons. The first involves the difficulty of transforming military projects into "pork," that is, programs directed to specific localities. The second concerns the "zero-sum" perspective with which legislators approach the budget: by law, they can only assign more money to one ministry by subtracting it from another.

The core handicap of the Brazilian military in contending for federal funds is the dearth of resources they possess that politicians can use for electoral purposes.

To begin with, military bases yield little political capital insofar as Congress has virtually no say in their location. The absence of a direct legislative role in decisions on military bases diminishes an important electoral reason for congressional representatives to support the armed forces. The relatively small size and heavy concentration of the country's arms industry in one corner of one state (São Paulo) limits its use as political currency.[6] Few legislators, especially outside the state of São Paulo, are motivated to support the defense industry for electoral reasons. The historic insularity of defense production—the result of decades of tight military control aimed at minimizing outside interference—has also deprived the sector of vital elements of the coalition behind defense spending in the United States and Europe, including labor and the university. In this connection, one analyst notes that it is inappropriate to view the Brazilian arms industry as a "military-industrial complex."[7] In short, the Brazilian armed forces suffer from a paucity of resources that can be exchanged for votes. At the same time, certain civilian ministries—such as transportation, education, health, and agriculture— are highly suited for this purpose.

The rule that Congress can only redistribute the money assigned by the executive rather than increase total expenditures increases the barrier to the promotion of military spending among legislators seeking to win elections.[8] Having to make trade-offs, legislators calculating their political survival militate in favor of holding down the military budget. Because legislators tend to view government expenditures on defense as an outright drain on their opportunity to build political clientele, they are tempted to divert funds earmarked by the president for the armed forces away from them and to civilian ministries more conducive to political patronage.

A collective action problem skews the incentives of legislators to spend for political patronage in the pursuit of electoral victory and disregard calls for higher defense expenditures, which could placate the military and enhance political stability. Given that a military coup would diminish the powers of the Congress, if not close it altogether, legislators do indeed have an interest in the stability and survival of democracy. However, a colossal collective action dilemma usually prevents them from acting on this interest. Only if a vast majority of parliamentarians agreed to forgo patronage could they achieve the collective goal of guaranteeing political stability. Yet in this case, even those legislators who refused to cooperate in such a collective effort would enjoy the ensuing democratic stability. Since free riders can benefit without bearing any cost, no individual legislator has a rational interest to give up patronage—and risk losing the next election to a free-riding competitor who keeps applying it.[9]

In other words, the contribution of *individual* legislators to military funding (and by extension, to the collective good of safeguarding democracy) requires a sacrifice. Given that other members of Congress would be extremely unlikely to contribute to this cause as well, no legislator has an incentive to make a contribution on his or her own. The moderation of an individual politician's hunger for patronage resources would barely affect the military's budget share and the commitment of the armed forces to democracy. But by forgoing a crucial weapon in electoral competition, it might well risk that individual's political future.[10]

The organizational weakness and large number of Brazil's political parties greatly worsens this collective action dilemma. A stronger party system could commit legislators to pay greater attention to the collective goal of democratic stability and, therefore, to support higher defense expenditures as part of a policy to safeguard corporate military interests. But in the absence of the coordination that better organized and disciplined parties could provide, legislators rationally follow their own immediate political interests, for better or for worse. The desire to free ride by relentlessly pursuing patronage becomes irresistible.

The logic of political survival is somewhat varied for presidents. Chief executives are also motivated to use federal spending to please a broad range of groups and sectors and to win legislative support for their programs—incentives that are reinforced by the common practice of former Brazilian presidents reentering politics, even at lower levels.[11] However, they rationally proceed with greater caution than legislators when it comes to actions that could antagonize established national powers and jeopardize the viability of the democratic system overall. More than any other single political actor, the president is held accountable for the general state of affairs in the country and, by extension, for the failure of key collective goods to be met. In this connection, the military monitor presidential conduct more keenly than the personal actions of legislators. Since antagonizing the armed forces could lead to a major political crisis—in the extreme, to the overthrow of the government—presidents rationally exercise caution in their efforts to challenge the military. Presidential attempts to divert budget resources away from the armed forces to important civilian causes are held in check by the obvious interest they have in completing their current terms.

At the same time, presidents do not face the same collective action dilemma as legislators insofar as they, as individuals, can make a direct and appreciable contribution to the military's budget. They can counteract the reduction in defense expenditures suggested by the Congress and provide the armed forces with supplemental funds derived outside of normal budgetary procedures. That all three civilian presidents since 1985 considered it prudent to do so at the nadir of their political popularity suggests that the armed forces remain an important factor of power in the calculus of Brazilian executives. Through discretionary funding as well as other concessions, vulnerable and weak presidents still seek to remain in good standing with the armed forces. The supplemental funds that Brazilian presidents can provide, however, have difficulty compensating for the cuts that Congress makes.

The combined calculations of legislators and presidents suggest that as long as Congress retains ample decision-making powers over the budget, and as long as Brazilian executives manage to preside over fairly stable governments, defense shares will remain relatively modest and may even decline further. As the authoritarian past recedes further into the distance and fears of a military coup fade, the incentives of both legislators and presidents will militate increasingly in favor of civilian rather than military spending. Historical precedent—that is, the decline of military budget shares over the last period of democracy in Brazil—supports this expectation.

THE SEARCH FOR POLITICAL CLIENTELE DIMINISHES
MILITARY BUDGET SHARES, 1945–1964

The budgetary dynamic that transpired from 1945 to 1964 constitutes a historic parallel to what has occurred since congressional control over the budget increased with the constitution of 1988.[12] This parallel confirms my claim that democracy as such unleashes incentives for civilian politicians to reduce the military's share of public spending. The decline in recent years is not specific to the current period of history, but a systematic result of the competitive dynamic of democracy.

The demise of Getúlio Vargas's authoritarian Estado Novo and the installation of democracy in 1945–46 ushered in an era of mass politics. With the expansion of the electorate, populist and traditional politicians alike seized new opportunities to mobilize voters. This included obtaining federal funds to compete for political clientele, a prospect enhanced by the constitution of 1946, which granted Congress the power of the purse.[13] With electoral motives in mind, committees in both houses of Congress reviewed and amended the budget drawn up by the executive.[14]

In the competition for appropriations, the military lost out to ministries that lent themselves more readily to regionally based pork barrel projects. Shifts in the federal budget from 1945 to 1964 indicate that the federal funds politicians used to court voters were extracted at the military's expense. As depicted in Figure 1, the percentage of government spending devoted to the armed forces dropped from 35 percent of total expenditures in 1947 to 14 percent in 1964.[15] If the military constituted the main loser in this budgetary game, pork barrel programs were the major beneficiary. Health and education programs, directed toward the increasingly powerful middle and working classes, also grew steadily until the coup of 1964. Another programmatic factor that contributed crucially to the decline of the military budget shares between 1945 and 1964 was the increasing role of the state in economic development.

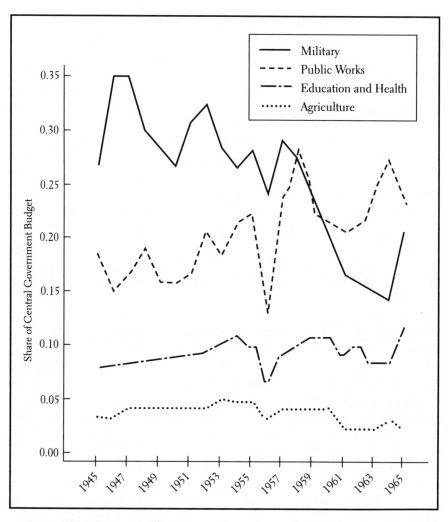

FIGURE 1. Program Shares, 1945–1965

Source: Barry Ames, *Political Survival: Politicians and Public Policy in Latin America* (Berkeley and Los Angeles: University of California Press, 1987), 110. Copyright © 1987 The Regents of the University of California.

The importance that legislators placed on influencing budgetary expenditures was also reflected in the keen competition among them for seats on the budget committee. The prevalence of congressional logrolling, whereby legislators lent mutual support to one another's pet projects, further attests to the priority that legislators placed on securing nonprogrammatic, nonuniversal benefits conducive to distribution on a regional basis.

Between 1945 and 1964, the military was a privileged budgetary recipient only in the midst and immediate aftermath of political crises.[16] Brazil's presidents were well aware that military dissatisfaction could come to haunt them. Given the country's tradition of "moderating coups," which deposed only the chief executive and replaced him with another civilian, presidents experienced far greater pressure than legislators to placate the military. Chief executives who came to power on a precarious basis and whose governments remained insecure pushed for higher military expenditures. Getúlio Vargas, for example, provided the military with a budget increase in the first year of his second government (1950–54). Juscelino Kubitschek also pumped up military allocations in order to ease the initial military opposition to his government. When executives sought to pacify the military through increased budget allocations, shares to health, welfare, and the police shrank accordingly.[17] Notably, however, even during periods of political crisis public works took precedence over military spending.[18]

The fact that military budget shares fell dramatically from 1945 to 1964, which coincided with the height of the cold war, calls into question the frequently advanced assumption that the demise of communism worldwide and the loss of a strategic rationale for Latin American militaries are the central causes of declining budgets in the current era. The defeat of communism, coupled with the virtual elimination of threats to internal security, have certainly put additional pressure on military budgets. However, the decline of military budget shares over the previous period of Brazilian democracy supports the centrality of the argument advanced here: that the armed forces' bargaining position is weak because military expenditures have little electoral value and actually present an "opportunity cost" for legislators and, to a lesser degree, executive politicians.

BUDGETARY POLITICS DURING MILITARY RULE, 1964–1985

Did the period of authoritarian governments interrupt the dynamic described above? Did the armed forces benefit financially from the tight restrictions on electoral competition in this era? The decline of congressional power over the budget, coupled with the military origins of Brazil's presidents from 1964 to 1985, might lead one to predict a marked increase in military spending during the authoritarian regime. Defense expenditures did rise from 1965 to 1970. But overall, they did not expand as much as one might expect. The military governments in Brazil did not take excessive advantage of their stay in power to boost the armed forces' narrow corporate interests. Throughout, they allocated large shares to economic development. And after the decision in 1974 to pursue a political opening, they revived clientelist practices to bolster ARENA's electoral popularity. Both of these goals cut into the military's budget share. At the same time, the military governments of 1964–85 were careful to avoid projecting the impression of enriching themselves or the military as an institution.[19] Especially compared to their counterparts in Argentina, Chile, and Peru, Brazil's uniformed presidents kept military spending relatively modest.

In the immediate aftermath of the 1964 coup, the Castello Branco government stripped Congress of many previous budgetary powers. The constitutions of 1967 and 1969 strengthened executive control over public expenditures and drastically reduced the independent capacity of legislators to cultivate clientele by manipulating federal funds.[20] Defense expenditures did increase during the first decade of military rule. But annual military budget shares in the second decade of military governments were on average one-third lower than military budget shares during the previous decade.[21] A sharp turn downward in military spending took place under the government of General Geisel (1974–79). At the same time, funds allocated to the Ministries of Agriculture, Communications, Education and Culture, and Health rose significantly over the course of the second period.[22]

Leaders of the military regime in Brazil defined their purpose in broad developmental terms. Building roads, airports, dams, telecommunication systems, nuclear power plants, and other infrastructural projects throughout the country was at least as important to them as enhancing narrow corporate interests.[23] The PND II (Plano Nacional do Desenvolvimento II) exemplified the developmental mission of the Brazilian armed forces. Begun in 1974, it promoted the capital goods sector and basic heavy industry. A costly government expense, the program undoubtedly contributed to driving down military expenditures as a share of total government spending.

Above and beyond their economic goals, the inordinate interest of regime leaders in maintaining public support led them to apply federal resources in some of the same ways as clientelist politicians, leaving the military ministries to compete with other funding priorities even under a system whose power rested ultimately on military backing. The goal of supporting programs to win support for the regime became especially important after 1974, when President Geisel decided to pursue a political opening. Notably, this coincided with the beginning of a visible turn downward in defense expenditures.

Regime leaders seeking to expand the voting base of the government party (ARENA) in order to slow down the gradual advance of the opposition MDB increased public spending systematically for patronage purposes. The major electoral defeat ARENA suffered in direct elections for the national Congress and state legislatures in 1974 increased the imperative of using public funds to build support by distributing benefits. The government's pursuit of electoral victory entailed transforming ARENA into a "gigantic patronage machine."[24] It led the very same officers who had previously denounced political clientelism to revive the practice of using public resources for electoral ends. The government targeted specific groups for gain, in addition to diffusing funds throughout the economy. President Geisel greatly increased health spending and the number of publicly provided medical treatments. To keep support in the countryside, he increased access to farm credits and established programs of industrial decentralization. His administration paid greater attention to primary education (a well-known vote-getter among the lower and middle classes) and granted higher wages to urban workers. President Figueiredo (1979–85) continued the effort to enhance the electoral competitiveness of the PDS (the new party label under which ARENA reconstituted itself) and pave a smooth exit from power. His administration granted large shares for primary education and made more funds available for public housing. It also expanded agricultural credit and land for small farmers. Only in the last year before stepping down did President Figueiredo approve military budget requests that had long gone unattended.

Toward the end of the military regime, professionally minded officers from all branches were frustrated that the armed services had not undergone greater modernization and technological advancement, especially considering the economic growth Brazil had experienced in the preceding two decades. Officers from the more technologically oriented navy and air force had grown resentful of the budgetary restrictions that the military presidents, all army generals, had imposed on their service branches. On the eve of the transition to democracy, unified support existed for bolstering the armed forces' external defense capabilities, notwithstanding differences among officers as to what political role the armed forces should play in the new democracy.

In 1985, all three branches of the armed forces revealed ambitious plans for technological modernization. The army had conceived a program of reorganization and re-equipment. Força Terrestre 1990 (Land Force 1990) called for new and improved weapons (armored cars, tanks, missile launchers, helicopters, and electronic systems), new garrisons (especially in the northern Amazon region) and a major increase in troops, from 183,000 to roughly 296,000.[25] The navy announced new initiatives as well, especially in the area of nuclear-powered submarines. Similarly, the air force revealed plans to develop new air-to-air missiles, telecommunications satellites, and a subsonic jet fighter, the AMX. Sustaining these projects would require a high level of funding. A key question on the eve of the transition to democracy was whether these funds would be forthcoming or not.

BUDGETARY CONFLICTS IN THE NEW DEMOCRACY, 1985–1993

Politicians and soldiers have clashed over the size of military budget shares in Brazil's new democracy. As in the previous period of democracy, defense spending has proven to be a low priority for most politicians, especially legislators.

Above all, heightened electoral competition has greatly reinforced politicians' incentives to use federal funds for patronage purposes. The competitive dynamic of democracy has induced them to divert funds claimed by the armed forces to spending on socioeconomic programs that could be distributed to their personal followers or to specific categories of political supporters. For this reason, the share of military expenditures in the total budget has diminished significantly under the nascent democracy.[26]

Other new developments have also hurt the military's ability to contend for appropriations. The economic crisis plaguing Brazil since the mid-1980s has intensified the competition among groups vying for federal funds. The demise of communism worldwide, the decline of serious threats to internal security, and the resolution of most of Brazil's historical border disputes weaken the military's bargaining position in this contest. These developments have put the raison d'être of the Brazilian armed forces so much in question that members of the U.S. defense establishment and international funding agencies like the World Bank and International Monetary Fund have expressed skepticism about Brazil's need for a traditional military.[27]

How in fact has the military budget fared? Defense allocations increased slightly between 1982 and 1985, but since 1985, with the exception of one year (1990), the military's share of the budget has undergone a steady contraction (see Figure 2). The armed forces lost one-quarter of their budget share between 1985 and 1993: the percentage held by the military went from 20.65 in 1985 to 14.27 in 1993.[28] The upward incline from 1982 to 1985 should be understood as an effort to stabilize the regime transition by placating the outgoing military. The trend downward thereafter reflects the proliferation of demands that have arisen within the democratic system, and the incentives that politicians have faced to support precisely those demands with the highest electoral stakes, even at the risk of antagonizing the military.[29]

Do these percentages correspond to an absolute decline in defense expenditures? The International Institute for Strategic Studies records a falloff from U.S.$1.731 billion in 1985 to U.S.$1.643 billion in 1992 (in terms of 1985 prices and exchange rates).[30] Obviously based on different definitional criteria of "defense expenditures," the U.S. Arms Control and Disarmament Agency records an overall increase from 1985 to 1993 (from U.S.$3.778 billion to U.S.$5.852 billion). But this overall increase masks a decline between 1988, when defense expenditures stood at U.S.$7.465 billion, and 1993, when they stood at U.S.$5.852 billion (in terms of constant 1993 dollars).[31] If concerns about placating the military in the early stages of the new civilian regime accounted at least partly for the initial absolute rise in expenditures, the competitive dynamic of democracy has undoubtedly contributed to the declining trend in more recent years.

To protect their budget shares, the armed forces have pursued a number of

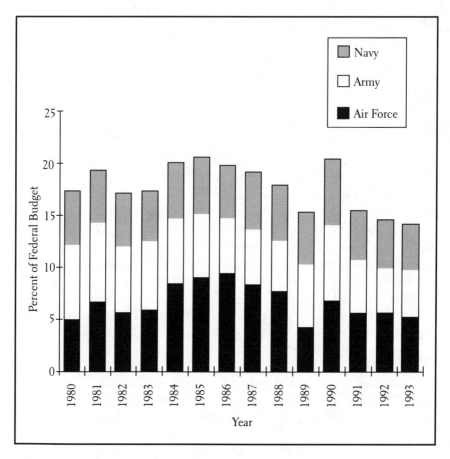

FIGURE 2. The Military's Budget Share, 1980–1993

Source: Brasil, Secretaria de Planejamento e Coordenação da Presidência da Républica, *Anuário Estatístico do Brasil* (Rio de Janeiro: Fundação Instituto Brasileiro de Geografia e Estatística-IBGE, 1982–93).

strategies. In line with the central role of Congress in the budgetary process, they have sought to build alliances among legislators across the political spectrum. Former ARENA politicians may have seemed an obvious source of backing at first. Presumably, the close ties many of them established with the military governments of 1964–85, coupled with their conservative political leanings, would dispose them favorably toward the military. However, former Arenistas and other conservatives have figured prominently among the politicians opting to back pork barrel projects over military programs in order to advance their own political fortunes. This shows that electoral incentives frequently override long-standing ideological leanings and demonstrates the powerful pull of electoral incentives.[32]

In addition to targeting individual legislators, the military lobbied successfully for the formation of a congressional committee, the Committee of National Defense (Comissão de Defesa Nacional) in the House of Deputies, as a forum for publicizing and mobilizing support for their pet projects. Beginning in 1988, a stream of military personnel have gone before its members to explain and justify the acquisition and/or development of various weapons systems.[33] The armed services have also gone to great lengths to inform committee members that the budget of the Brazilian armed forces is not high by comparative standards.[34] The Committee of National Defense provides the armed forces with some degree of visibility but lacks the stature that leading officers would like it to have. Legislators view membership on it as relatively unprestigious and unimportant politically. Attendance at presentations is conspicuously poor, and many have been canceled for lack of interest on the part of legislators.[35] This confirms military issues' low value in the electoral calculations of democratic politicians.

The armed forces have also solicited the lobbying contribution of private industry. At first glance, it would be logical to assume that businesspeople belonging to the Brazilian Association of Defense Materiel Industries (Associação Brasileira de Materiais de Defesa or ABIMDE) would be strong allies of the military.[36] Yet the potential for a united defense of the armed forces' modernization and re-equipment plans has diminished with the emergence of serious tensions between military and industrial interests within the defense sector. A central source of conflict concerns the relative importance of military versus commercial considerations in determining sectoral policy. Military and commercial interests converged in the 1960s and 1970s, when arms production concentrated on uncomplicated weapons that could be widely sold, especially in other developing countries. But since then, the private sector has been reluctant to invest in many of the more sophisticated but commercially unviable weapons programs that interest the armed forces. Another point of growing divergence between the military and private industry concerns the acceptability of continued technology dependence in certain areas. While the armed forces seek strategic independence, private business remains focused on cost-effectiveness. The severe economic difficulties facing the defense sector since the late 1980s have exacerbated these tensions.[37]

The lobbying on which the military have embarked to protect defense expenditures is generally considered acceptable within the context of democratic government. It appears, however, to be less effective than strong-arm lobbying. As the following discussion suggests, in Brazil's new democracy the armed forces have fared best on the financial front when the weakness of civilian governments has created room for military saber rattling and other forms of intimidation and led the presidents that preside over those floundering governments to seek favor with the military.

The Budget Process

In 1985, the incipient democracy inherited the budget procedures imposed by the military regime, which had greatly strengthened the executive branch at the expense of the legislature. Congress's budgetary powers had amounted essentially to ratifying the executive document. Yet the constitution of late 1988 brought important changes that greatly enhanced the role of Congress in budget deliberations. Above all, Congress can propose amendments altering the distribution of expenditures suggested in the executive's proposal. Eventually, Congress approves the budget in a plenary session. The president can veto the decision, but an absolute majority in both houses of Congress can override the president's veto in a secret vote.[38] Despite these enhanced powers, there is one restriction on Congress that transforms the allocation of federal funds into a zero-sum game: Congress cannot increase the total amount of funds specified in the executive budget.[39] Thus proposals to assign more funds to some ministries call for cuts in others.

With the new rules and procedures in place, the following dynamic has unfolded. Following the arrival in Congress of the executive's budget proposal and its examination by a joint committee of the Senate and House of Deputies (Comissão Mista do Orçamento do Congreso), legislators have inundated the budget committee with amendments. After much wheeling and dealing, this committee has typically recommended reducing the military's share of the budget and allocating more to ministries suitable for public works and other vote-getting projects. The budget that Congress eventually passes bears strong signs of its members' electoral concerns. The number of amendments added to the budget law has increased enormously, jumping from 8,000 in 1989 to 12,000 in 1990, to over 72,000 in 1991.[40] In 1993, the number of amendments reached a record 73,000.[41]

The armed forces, in response to receiving budget shares that they generally perceive as meager and insufficient, decry the low priority politicians accord them. Their discontent is unlikely to be addressed as long as the government enjoys solid public support. But if support for the government is weak, the armed forces can reasonably expect the president to find supplemental credits for them. Such a strategy of financial co-optation on the part of the president, however, faces certain technical and political constraints. The main technical restriction is one of fiscal solvency, as economists in the three postauthoritarian governments have stressed. A central political limitation concerns the president's need to reserve funds for legislators whose support is needed for government programs. Given the weakness of Brazil's political parties, the president often lacks a permanent base of congressional backing and depends on such tactics. As a result, presidential discretion has not compensated for congressional reluctance to grant the military's demands for funds.

The Sarney Presidency

Budgetary politics during the Sarney presidency bore out the general political logic of legislators and presidents described above. The actions of Congress reflected a perception of military spending as a political liability. This became clear after 1988, when Congress gained the capacity to alter executive budget proposals as part of its routine powers. President Sarney manifested greater generosity toward the armed forces than did Congress. His willingness to put them on firmer financial ground grew stronger as his own political standing deteriorated.[42]

The military's budget share did drop from 1985 to 1988 (from 20.65 percent to 18.05 percent), but the continuation of executive control over the budget in the first three years of the new democracy helped buffer the military from experiencing more severe losses. Sarney's weak mandate conditioned him to be extra careful to remain in the military's good graces. The allocations the executive awarded to the armed forces in this period were sufficient to allow them to maintain existing projects and to make progress in the development of new ones.

Beginning as early as 1988, the first year in which the legislature enjoyed expanded budgetary powers, the congressional budget committee moved quickly to decide where to cut allocations it considered excessive. The military ministries were one of the first places they looked. Under pressure from fellow legislators to support regionally based education, housing, and health projects, the head of the committee suggested shifting resources from the proposed military budget (which had few legislative defenders) to fund these other projects.[43]

Congressional interest in reducing the military budget became even more apparent in 1989, when Sarney's desperate bid for military backing led him initially to allocate a relatively large share to the military.[44] Shortly after the congressional budget committee received the executive proposal, its chair recommended reducing by 17.5 percent the funds destined for the armed forces and redistributing this amount to the Ministries of Agriculture, Transportation, Mines and Energy, and the Interior.[45] The budget committee voted to sustain the defense cuts that the chair proposed. In fact, in the stage of congressional amendment making, 90 percent of all proposals involved pork barrel projects, 70 percent of which recommended funds targeted for the military as a source of revenue.[46] The official justification was generally that public works had greater social utility than military expenditures in a country with a negligible foreign threat.[47] This position is difficult to dispute. However, the fact that legislators manifested far greater willingness to support distributive regionally based projects for which direct credit could be claimed rather than programmatic reforms favoring redistribution to the poor suggests that enhancing social welfare was not their first concern.[48]

Last-minute manipulations on the part of President Sarney in both 1988 and

1989 propped up the military's budget shares in fiscal years 1989 and 1990. In 1988, Sarney issued a decree applying a huge sum of supplemental money to the budget. The resources for this purpose came from the Merchant Marine Fund, a reserve formed by additional freight charges on imports, which under law can be applied only to the construction of ships. The military ministries were but one beneficiary of this eleventh-hour ploy designed to smooth over political conflicts by expanding the size of the pie to be divided.[49]

In 1989, the military ministers brought pressure to bear against an ever more vulnerable president to liberate supplemental credits for their priority projects.[50] Seeking to placate military opposition and gain dividends for his own political future and the political careers of his family, President Sarney suddenly announced at the end of October that he would liberate and divide among various groups an additional NCz$8.2 billion (equivalent to U.S.$1.81 billion). These credits came from the emission of government bonds, which could legally be used only in instances of "extreme emergency." Stretching the definition of their proper use, Sarney proposed that they be applied principally to the Ministries of Agriculture, Transportation, and Mines and Energy, as well as to the army, navy, and air force. The three military ministries collectively received 17 percent of the NCz$8.2 billion released. Congress possessed the powers to reject Sarney's proposal, but it did not choose to do so. Visions of what Sarney's spending spree could offer legislators tempted a sufficient number of them into approving the proposal over the protestations of a few principled legislators and the ministers of finance and planning.[51]

The events of 1988 and 1989 taught the armed forces that funding for their pet projects would be anything but assured under Brazil's democracy. It is worthy of note that in fiscal 1989 and 1990 the armed forces were not too well endowed even with the extra money Sarney diverted their way. All three branches of the armed forces were forced to cut back on their modernization projects, training, and miscellaneous operating costs. With good reason, military leaders wondered how they would fare under a president less inclined to succumb to their demands.

The Collor Government

If the military confronted difficulties under the Sarney government, their fate worsened with the Collor presidency. For most of Collor's tenure, the armed forces faced not only an unreceptive Congress, but also a president intent on charting his own course with secondary concern for the consequences of his actions on the military. The measures necessary to carry out Collor's aspiration of opening the Brazilian economy to world competition—privatization, strict austerity, and a pro-U.S. foreign policy stance—conflicted with the military's goal of bolstering defense appropriations and acquiring new high-technology weaponry.

Only when Collor's popularity took a dramatic dip—from May 1992 onward, when revelations of his involvement in corruption surfaced—did he shift course and start to take seriously the armed forces' financial demands.

Financial constraints on the armed forces during the Collor government slowed the progress they could make with respect to modernization and re-equipment. Research funds for the nuclear-powered submarine and subsonic fighter suffered cuts. The armed forces' joint project of fortifying the northern Amazon border came to a virtual standstill.[52] Finances were so tight at one point that training was scaled back dramatically in all three service branches. The army operated on a part-time basis in order to save money on meals for soldiers. Officers and soldiers alike violated institutional regulations and assumed second jobs.[53] Ironically, while it cut military expenditures, the Collor government gave tremendous rhetorical support to military professionalism and to the conventional defense mission of the armed forces. To confer prestige on combatant roles, the president himself engaged in publicity stunts such as flying in fighter aircraft and performing military maneuvers wearing army fatigues.

How did the budgetary process unfold in the brief yet important period of the Collor government? Congress proceeded for the most part in the same fashion as it did under Sarney. After receiving the budget proposal handed down by the executive, legislators submitted thousands of amendments proposing infrastructural projects within their own districts. The ministries that figured highest in this bidding were the ones conducive to pork barrel projects: Education, Health, Transportation, and Agriculture.[54]

Even in the midst of the crisis surrounding President Collor's impeachment, many legislators showed little concern about antagonizing the military at a time when the stability, if not survival, of Brazil's new democracy may have been in question. In July 1992, a group of congressional representatives spearheaded a move to withdraw appropriations intended for the navy's nuclear submarine project from the government's long-term budget plan (Plano Plurianual 1993–95). To the navy's great dismay, the congressional budget committee approved the reappropriation of these funds for other uses.[55] A further sign that Congress would persist in asserting its powers and immediate interests was the elimination in December 1992 of a budgetary category for "secret funds" and the insistence that these funds be openly associated with specific ministries.[56] Over the course of the prior two years, individual legislators had questioned and criticized the complete lack of congressional control over this fund.[57]

Notwithstanding the collective action dilemma that inhibited legislators from supporting higher shares for defense spending, after the Collor corruption scandal emerged legislators were sufficiently concerned about the armed forces' continued adherence to democratic institutions that they agreed in August 1992 to a presidential initiative aimed at redressing long-standing salary disparities between military officers and public servants in the legislative and judicial branches. Full salary equity remains far off, but the decision to gradually align military pay with the pay of personnel judged to be of equivalent status in the legislative and judicial branches represented a shift in Congress's prior treatment of the matter.[58]

What varied much more than congressional conduct across the two and a half years of the Collor administration was the president's behavior. As part of an initial determination to keep military spending in check, in December 1990 Collor decreased a scheduled military pay raise to an amount equivalent to that awarded civilians in the public administration. The message in this much publicized move was that the military should expect no special treatment from the commander in chief.[59] Another key development of this kind concerned the government's initiation, over strong military protests, of efforts to renew the lapsed U.S.-Brazilian military accord. Collor's motivation for renewing the accord included the hope that it would award Brazil's armed forces with low-cost secondhand equipment from the United States and therefore diminish their consumption of domestic finances.[60] But the clearest sign of Collor's intention to keep military spending down was the budget itself. As noted above, military expenditures in the 1991 and 1992 fiscal budgets dropped significantly from where they stood in 1990 (from 20.53 percent of the budget in 1990 to 15.64 percent in 1991 and 14.71 percent in 1992).

Serious corruption charges leveled against the president broke the Collor government's resolve to limit military spending. Immediately after news of the scandal broke in May 1992, Economy Minister Marcílio Marques Moreira promised to liberate funds for the military in order to avoid yet another crisis in the government.[61] Toward the same goal, the government made a major effort the next month to reintroduce in the multiple-year budget plan of 1993–95 (Plano Plurianual 1993–95) the military projects that the congressional budget committee proposed be canceled. Various nuclear projects figured prominently among the items the government managed to reinstate.[62] In short, while the military refrained from taking sides in the Collor impeachment affair and let the country's elected politicians decide the president's fate, the implicit threat they wielded to the government's survival, the result of decades of military interventionism, helped them to benefit financially from the crisis.

The Franco Government

The centrality of political determinants of defense spending was also evident under President Itamar Franco. Congress persisted in showing less interest than the president in placating the military's budgetary concerns, notwithstanding the armed forces' strengthened bargaining position under the Franco government. The armed forces' share of the budget continued the preexisting pattern of gradual decline. They received 14.27 percent of the federal budget in 1993, down from 15.64 percent in 1991 and 14.71 percent in 1992.[63]

Congress continued to direct large shares of the budget to projects that improve members' chances of reelection, necessarily reducing the amount available to the military. For example, after conducting negotiations over approximately seventy-five thousand amendments to the 1993 fiscal budget, Congress divided among itself close to U.S.$9 billion for public works, an amount equivalent to 16 percent of the amount spent on investments and expenditures. Compared to this, the military received 3.4 percent.[64] The unrestrained submission of amendments did not subside in 1994, even following a prolonged and much-publicized investigation of corruption among members of the congressional budgetary committee. At least seventeen legislators had accepted kickbacks from construction firms in exchange for backing projects that would provide these firms with contracts.[65] In 1994, even members of the PT, a party that generally does not engage in patronage politics, were among those who submitted amendments aimed at acquiring public works projects in their home districts.[66]

Relative to the Congress, the president's actions revealed greater preoccupation with maintaining military support for the government and for the democratic regime more broadly. Until the Cardoso stabilization plan reversed Franco's low approval ratings (only in the last few months of his tenure), weak popular support led President Franco to try to placate the military with budgetary and salary concessions whenever possible. Military saber rattling, first evident in a May 1993 *pronunciamento* decrying low military salaries and later increasing after the discovery in October 1993 of corruption within the congressional budget committee, contributed to Franco's caution toward the military. President Franco refrained from punishing the officer responsible for the May 1993 manifesto.[67] Immediately following the incident, he also promised to provide the armed forces with maximum possible salary increases and to command the liberation of special funds for re-equipment purposes.[68] In a further gesture intended to calm the military, Franco substituted the outgoing head of the Secretariat of Administration—a decisive position with respect to salary readjustments for public sector workers, including the armed forces—with a retired general, Romildo Canhim.[69]

Thus Franco's attempt to pacify the armed forces undoubtedly helped keep their appropriations higher than they would have been otherwise. But this was a temporary tactic. Should the competitive dynamic of democracy continue to be played out, the overall trend toward modest military budgets will persist. Brazil's politicians show no signs of abandoning the pursuit of patronage resources. Even during a crisis-ridden period of Franco's presidency, the government reversed a previous decision to eliminate two ministries notorious for the distribution of patronage, the Ministry of Regional Integration and the Ministry of Social Welfare.[70]

IMPLICATIONS OF BUDGETARY POLITICS FOR CIVIL-MILITARY RELATIONS

The demonstrated willingness and ability of civilians to challenge the armed forces over the federal budget has positive and negative aspects. On the positive side, the fact that elected politicians increasingly have shifted government priorities away from military spending in favor of civilian programs is a sign of civilian strength and the expansion of popular sovereignty. Insofar as the power of the purse is an essential requisite of civilian control over the military, Brazil's elected politicians are succeeding in increasing their powers over the military.

Yet the goals for which Brazil's politicians have reduced military budget shares are less than optimal from the standpoint of promoting stable civil-military relations. Instead of ensuing from a deliberate and carefully pondered policy, military budget shares have declined under the uncoordinated and often unbridled patronage interests of the country's politicians. The allocation of federal funds according to electoral imperatives has created ill will on the part of the armed forces toward elected politicians (arguably a higher degree than a more thoughtful policy of reducing military expenditures would produce), and hindered the development of efforts to depoliticize the military and turn their attention squarely to matters of external defense. The political machinations surrounding decision making over the budget have also exacerbated the military's long-standing antipathy to the rampant clientelism that characterizes Brazilian politics. The tendency of clientelist politics to create waste and corruption clashes with the positivist impulse within the Brazilian military. The military have little patience with the circuslike character of Brazilian budgetary politics.

In this vein, the armed forces have begun to express misgivings about accepting financial sacrifices imposed on them by a self-serving political class. Similarly, the officer corps has questioned the incentives that the current system provides for military subordination. Obedience to civilian authority, high-ranking officers contend, effectively impedes their capacity to gain budget shares and develop in professional directions. Conversely, conduct that includes issuing veiled threats and other forms of intimidation enhances their ability to gain finances. The correlation they note between military subordination and a loss of budgetary status is not propitious from the standpoint of inducing the military to leave politics.[71] The short-sighted political calculations that drive the actions of clientelist politicians may indeed undermine collective goals such as the development of acceptable nonpolitical roles for the military.[72]

Yet the officer corps' annoyance over obstacles to modernization and professional development would not in itself be sufficient to undermine their support for democracy. Only in conjunction with other problems that arise from short-sighted and irresponsible policy making, most notably economic deterioration,

would the military gain the motivation and public support to overthrow or severely weaken democratic political institutions.

CONCLUSION

Expectations that the military would be a privileged and unusually strong contender for federal funds in Brazil's democratic regime have failed to materialize.
Budgetary politics in the new democracy have revealed instead that the imperatives of electoral competition influence both legislators and presidents to keep
military spending at bay. After congressional budgetary powers were bolstered in
1988, electoral incentives generated strong pressure for legislators to support
patronage-yielding public works programs over military projects. Brazilian presidents also need to balance the budgetary priority they assign to the military with a
host of political and economic considerations. While they are more willing than
legislators to make allowance for defense expenditures, spending on the military
does little for their overall popularity. The likelihood that presidents will use the
privileges of their office to supply military funding increases only when the governments over which they preside grow weak.

Thus the findings of this analysis suggest that the competitive dynamic of democracy overrode the institutional prerogatives and political strength the armed
forces commanded at the inception of civilian rule. Contrary to institutionalist
arguments, continuity has not prevailed in the nascent democracy. Instead, rational politicians pursuing electoral interests have brought about an important
change.

The calculations and structure of decision making that this chapter has depicted suggest that the military's portion of the budget will remain relatively small
and may even decline further. The incentives unleashed through democratic
competition, the pattern of declining expenditures that took place over the last
period of democracy, and the diminished security threats of the post–cold war era
all support this conclusion. Good governance and the consolidation of democratic institutions in Brazil will enhance the likelihood that even presidents will
place low priority on defense expenditures.

It is possible that the impact of electoral competition on the military budget
could eventually backfire and cause the military to try to reverse their financial
losses by radically increasing their influence over civilians or even restoring authoritarian rule. But given the domestic and international condemnation that
would ensue from such an act undertaken in the current era, this is an unlikely
danger. In all probability, the military will continue to struggle for federal funds
amid keen competition.

6

CIVIL-MILITARY
CONFLICT OVER
THE AMAZON

The Brazilian armed forces have played a key role historically in guiding the course of Amazonian development. The "soft" border and lack of state infrastructure have rendered the military an important actor in the region. Their continuing ability to control the occupation and development of Amazônia hinges in large part on the political strength they can maintain. Growing international concern since the early 1980s for the rain forest and its indigenous populations, coupled with the advent of democracy in 1985, have introduced serious challenges to the military's ability to continue dominating the formulation of policies affecting Amazônia. Leading officers from all service branches have expressed concern about the defense of Amazonian borders. But it is the army's organizational interests that are most directly at stake in the occupation and development of the region. Nationalist sectors within the army have been particularly inclined to decry the region's "internationalization."

This chapter examines and analyzes military efforts to shape government policy toward Amazônia. It begins with an overview of the historical role of the Brazilian military in the region, describes the extension of the military's role in Amazônia during the governments of 1964–85, and assesses changing patterns of military influence toward the region over Brazil's first three postauthoritarian governments. The post-1985 section examines and tries to explain variations in government policy toward three issues in particular: the demarcation of Indian lands, the construction of defense bases and systems, and conservation projects financed through foreign governments and nongovernmental organizations (NGOs). These issues reflect differences among the Sarney, Collor, and Franco administrations in the extent to which they adhered to the developmentalist approach of the military versus the conservationist orientation of international actors.

President Sarney allowed the military to retain considerable sway over policies affecting Amazônia. The government of Fernando Collor was responsible for a major shift in the government's stance toward the rain forest. This shift was related to the economic success he strove to achieve, which in turn would have a critical impact on his electoral popularity. Collor's long-term popularity would depend greatly on his ability to reignite Brazil's economic growth and put the country back on the path to success. The market-oriented reforms he enacted to combat Brazil's economic crisis depended heavily on the support of Western governments and lending institutions, such as the World Bank and Inter-American Development Bank (IDB). Since these foreign actors themselves faced pressure from ecologists to hold Brazil to higher environmental standards, they could be expected to turn the screws on President Collor should he choose not to comply with the conditions they demanded with respect to loans. This constituted the main motivation for the shift in policy that Collor put in motion. It is linked to democracy insofar as President Collor, far more than military presidents before him, felt accountable for the state of economic affairs in the country. Dictators too are subject to international pressure, but do not concern themselves nearly as much with the consequences of this pressure on their domestic political standing.

What gave Collor the strength to challenge the military over Amazônia? Collor's ability to defy the powerful domestic lobby in favor of continuing to occupy and develop Amazônia in destructive ways depended on the strength of his initial electoral mandate. Especially since the grassroots environmental movement in Brazil is relatively weak, and powerful domestic groups (namely the military, regional politicians, and private business) do not support conservation, Collor's audacious challenge of establishment actors vis-à-vis the Amazon rested on the overall popular support he could command, and not the balance of political power that existed over the particular issue. International backing certainly helped strengthen Collor's position. Itamar Franco continued, in a weaker version, Collor's policy orientation. Compared to Collor, Franco was more beholden to the military for support and thus could not defy them in the way his predecessor had. Yet there was a limit to how much Franco would let military influence over policy formulation expand. Reversing the progress Collor achieved, especially in highly visible areas, would have invited international condemnation, something Franco tried hard to avoid.

THE AMAZON IN HISTORICAL PERSPECTIVE

The Brazilian armed forces view the vast and resource-rich Amazon as an essential ingredient to Brazil's ability to become a major power. Acutely aware of the many disputes over land and water rights that mark the history of Amazônia, they contend that it should be actively guarded. The river makes the region naturally penetrable by foreign forces.[1] The expanse and emptiness of the area heighten its permeability.[2] For generations, military courses and military journals have taught cadets and officers the highlights of Amazonian history and the lessons to be learned from them.

The French and Dutch challenged Portugal's claims in the Amazon in the sixteenth and seventeenth centuries. In the mid-nineteenth century, foreign powers forced Brazil to open the river to international traffic. In the early twentieth century, Brazil seized control of border areas and augmented its territory by relying on the principle of *uti possidetis*.[3] Brazil's highest achievement in a series of efforts to claim *uti possidetis* occurred when it wrested from Bolivia and Peru what is now the rubber-rich Brazilian state of Acre, an area five times the size of Belgium.[4] Although Brazil emerged triumphant in the territorial disputes of the region in the early twentieth century, the lesson in its triumph was not lost on the Brazilian military: the further occupation and development of the Amazon would be essential to maintaining control. Historical events had borne out what geopolitics predicted.

The Brazilian military took history to heart. Its role in developing Amazônia dates back to the turn of the century, when the federal army first commissioned officers to make military and scientific expeditions in the region. In the early part of the twentieth century, the army pioneered the building of roads and a telegraph system in the western section of the Amazon. In the early 1940s, the air force built a network of airstrips in remote areas of the region. These roads and runways were the first nonriver forms of access to Amazônia. To further stake Brazil's claim to the region, a number of frontier military colonies were established in the 1950s and 1960s.[5]

THE MILITARY GOVERNMENTS OF 1964–1985

The bureaucratic-authoritarian period gave rise to an unprecedented effort to penetrate Amazônia with economic growth and development. The motto of "security and development" guided the military governments' extensive and systematic policy initiatives toward the region. The rationale was that Amazonian development would contribute to national security by placing people and infrastructure in a vast, remote region where the authority of the Brazilian state was weak, and by enhancing the country's ability to build a strong and stable economy. Moreover, the establishment of infrastructure linking Amazônia to the rest of the country would reduce regional disparities and promote national integration. The growth of rural guerrilla movements in Bolivia and Peru in the 1960s, and the discovery in the early 1970s of a rural *foco* in the Araguaia-Tocantins region of the Brazilian Amazon, gave new impetus to an expansion of the military's physical presence in the region.

The military viewed their Amazon project in heroic terms: at last, human forces would cut through the dense jungle and infuse the remote region with a Brazilian presence. Officers couched their policy initiatives in strategic language. President Castello Branco announced that "Amazonian occupation would proceed as though it were a strategically conducted war." His government termed the first of a series of development initiatives Operation Amazônia. *Integrar para não entregar* (Integrate to prevent surrender), a public relations slogan used by the regime to rally support for its policies, also carried a strong military connotation.[6]

Military and civilian elites agreed that the historic transformation they envisaged depended on an integrated approach. Extensive infrastructure (roads and airstrips, energy, and communications) first needed to be established to support mining, cattle ranching, timber production, and colonization programs. But government planners failed to appreciate the extent and severity of environmental and sociopolitical disruption that would ensue from rapid, large-scale capitalist development in the rain forest. The military governments of 1964–85 did little to consult specialists (geographers, agronomists, anthropologists, etc.) on the ecological consequences of the projects they supported. The introduction of highways, mines, agribusiness, and colonization programs soon revealed the costs of such an approach.

Operation Amazônia, implemented in 1966, stressed the economic dimension of national security. It featured financial support for firms willing to invest in the Amazon, the establishment of a development agency, SUDAM (Superintendência do Desenvolvimento da Amazônia or Superintendency of Amazonian Development), and the expansion and upgrading of transportation and communication in the region. The establishment of enormous cattle ranches through federal tax exemptions was the most environmentally consequential policy of Operation Amazônia. In the view of many scientists, cattle ranching has been the single most important source of deforestation.[7] Mineral exploration and exploitation constituted another important focus of this phase. The passage of numerous decrees and laws granting mining rights to domestic and foreign companies and the technical and financial assistance made available for exploration attracted a rush of firms to the mineral-rich Amazon Basin.[8]

The next phase of Amazonian development, the Program of National Integration (Programa de Integração Nacional or PIN), began in 1970. It featured the construction of roads, including the Transamazônica, an east-west highway of five thousand kilometers connecting the northeast to the Amazon, and the settlement of approximately one hundred thousand landless peasants from other parts of Brazil alongside it.[9] The colonization project would help transfer populations from the drought-stricken and impoverished northeast into the remote regions of the Amazon. Military circles celebrated the prospect of a highway system linking key parts of the region. The PIN had important long-term consequences for the institutionalization of military influence in the Amazon. It vastly increased the military's power to intervene in the region by subjecting large areas of land to federal control. Relatedly, it formalized the military's involvement in the question of land disputes, which developers and speculators provoked with great frequency.[10]

The bureaucratic-authoritarian regime's third development project for the Amazon, Polamazônia, began in 1975. It called for the creation of primary industries in fifteen locations throughout the region. Heavily subsidized capital-intensive projects were established to produce materials for export. One of the most prominent of these development enclaves was the Grande Carajás project, known for the production of iron ore. Other projects, all grand in scale, focused on hydroelectricity production, ranching, and rubber production. Like its predecessors, the Polamazônia projects ravaged the rain forest.

THE MILITARY'S AMAZON PROJECT UNDER CHALLENGE

By the mid to late 1970s, it was evident that the military's scheme to occupy and develop the Amazon had inflicted widespread damage on flora and fauna, violated the human, cultural, and territorial rights of indigenous populations, and inflamed conflict over land and resources. To protest the regime's policies, domestic groups whose lives had been disrupted—smallholders, rubber tappers, and Indians—joined up with forces that gave them a political voice, namely the church, the emerging Workers' Party (PT), and international NGOs (National Wildlife Federation, Environmental Defense Fund, Cultural Survival, etc.) committed to protecting the environment and the rights of indigenous peoples. These groups brought to public attention the harm that intruding ranchers, mining enterprises, and gold prospectors (garimpeiros) had caused peasants, rubber tappers, and Indians.[11] By the early 1980s, the destruction of the rain forest and the plight of forest dwellers was front-page news in the advanced industrial West.

Beyond publicizing the destruction of the rain forest and forging links with like-minded groups within Brazil, environmental and indigenous rights groups based outside the country sought to pressure the Brazilian government to adopt more ecologically sensitive policies. They seized on the link between external financing and economic development as a key point of leverage. Multilateral banks, such as the World Bank (the single biggest source of finance for international development) and the IDB, had become important funding sources for Amazonian development projects. The rain forest lobby reasoned that the banks, by making financial aid contingent on sensitivity to environmental consequences, could compel the Brazilian government to begin to protect the ecosystem. By the mid-1980s, the World Bank and IDB in fact started to suspend loans to projects that failed to meet the environmental standards they demanded.[12]

The broadening scope of international protest over the destruction of the rain forest stirred up resentment among sectors of the Brazilian state, in particular the armed forces. Military commanders decried what they viewed as an infringement on sovereignty by groups seeking to "internationalize" the Amazon. Long-founded suspicions of foreign designs on the region surfaced, and officers accused Western governments of using the environment as a pretext for preventing Brazil from tapping the resource-rich region and increasing its economic strength in order to preserve resources to exploit for themselves.[13] Charging Western critics with hypocrisy, they pointed to the consumption of resources in the developed world and the fact that North Americans ran roughshod over Indians and forests in the course of their economic expansion.

Beyond reiterating previous motivations, leading officers pointed to new developments justifying the continued development and occupation of the Amazon under military auspices. They underscored the dangers posed by increased drug traffic and the growth of informal sector prospectors pilfering gold and other contraband, and the possibility that Marxist governments, like that led by Desi Bouterse in Surinam, would infiltrate the northern Amazon with subversive elements. Only by infusing the region with a strong economic and military presence, they contended, would these forces be deterred in the long run.

Domestic political factors expanded the armed forces' organizational interest in defending the region. The leading role they played in guiding development and managing conflict in the region during the military governments of 1964–85 created a bureaucratic incentive to continue in this capacity. The military had developed a significant personnel and policy presence in the subsections of the National Security Council devoted to studying and formulating policy for land and Indian issues in the Amazon, and a similar presence in the federal government's agency for Indian affairs (the Fundação Nacional do Indio or FUNAI). Shifting the course of Amazonian policy would challenge these military strongholds.

Furthermore, the departure of the armed forces from direct power prompted the institution to search for spheres in which it could remain actively involved. The intensification of international protest over Amazonian deforestation coincided roughly with the return to civilian rule. Brazil's rapprochement with its historical rival, Argentina, which began in 1980 and gathered speed after 1985, also justified the increasing attention on the Amazon by depriving Brazil of a clear and major enemy. Consideration of these broader factors is necessary to understand fully why the same institution that in the 1960s and 1970s invited tremendous multinational investment into the region later launched a feverish campaign to denounce "internationalization." In this connection, it should also be noted that Calha Norte (Northern Headwaters), the military's project to erect an extensive system of military posts and garrisons along the northern border, appeared in the same year that the armed forces left power and well after many border-related conflicts—drug traffic, Colombian guerrillas, the threat of a Cuban-backed socialist regime in Surinam, and more—had emerged.

Military leaders would not, at least privately, deny that the type of occupation and development that has taken place in Amazônia is unsustainable in the long term, or that it has caused social dislocation and conflict, which in themselves are threats to security. At the same time, however, many officers have difficulty letting go of the traditional geopolitical ideas that originally drove the armed forces to penetrate the region on such a grand scale. Moreover, they reject the interference of other countries in what they regard as Brazil's domain. Even if the military were to endorse the adoption of a more ecologically sensitive approach to development in the region, they would want Brazilian state actors, in particular themselves, to control the pace and scope of such a policy shift.

In light of all these factors, leading officers sought to retain influence over Amazon issues under the new democracy. To what extent could the military continue to dominate the debate over Amazônia? Would Brazil's democratically elected presidents experience greater pressure than the previous general-presidents to hold back the forces of development and destruction in reaction to international opinion? The following section examines changing patterns and degrees of military influence under Presidents Sarney, Collor, and Franco. It analyzes the differing responses of these presidents to military demands for increased defense of the region, as well as military-led attempts to block government policies aimed at placating international concern over the rain forest.

GOVERNMENT POLICIES TOWARD THE AMAZON SINCE 1985

The Sarney Presidency

The military, together with entrepreneurs and local political interests, prevailed upon President Sarney to sustain the developmental orientation of previous governments toward the Amazon. Even had Sarney been inclined to pursue a policy of preserving the rain forest, developments during his tenure suggested that a weak president focused on the short-term goal of political survival would find it difficult to defy this powerful pro-growth coalition.[14] For the most part, Sarney allowed the forces of occupation and development to dominate Amazonian policy. To gain influence, the politically weaker domestic forces seeking to preserve the rain forest (Brazilian NGOs, forest dwellers, and the small percentage of urban voters for whom the Amazonian ecosystem constituted an important "postmaterial" interest) forged alliances with international groups and agencies, fighting an uphill battle. President Sarney sponsored the construction of a series of military bases along the northern Amazon border, avoided setting aside stretches of land for indigenous populations, and held at arm's length foreign entities interested in promoting rain forest protection. Nevertheless, even Sarney, who showed no particular interest in conservation and who relied on the military out of his own political weakness, recognized the need to respond to international concerns. But as he softened his stance toward the international community, military actors played a strategic role in overseeing and setting the boundaries for the program embodied in this shift.

Project Calha Norte
Calha Norte, a project to fortify the northern Amazon border, emerged as the military's first major Amazonian initiative of the postauthoritarian era. In the spring of 1985, the National Security Council secretly formulated plans for the project. When announced in the fall of 1986, the news took most Amazon observers by surprise. The military's justification for Calha Norte echoed the "security and development" theme of previous policies. According to this view, guerrilla groups from neighboring countries, drug traffickers, and smugglers of other kinds constituted risks to Brazil's security along the border. Due to the weak authority of the Brazilian state in the region, securing the border would depend on an increased military presence.[15]

Calha Norte, a series of military airstrips, garrisons, and outposts, as well as roads and agricultural and colonization projects along the northern Amazon, covers a vast stretch of land: 14 percent of all national territory and 24 percent of Amazônia. The project put a total of four thousand miles under military vigilance and allowed the army to gain control over a hundred-kilometer strip along the northern border. The "national security" status of territory within Calha Norte authorizes the military to monitor the movement of foreigners into the area. On several occasions, officers have tried to prevent investigations by foreign anthropologists, environmentalists, and journalists by denying them access to the area. In addition to Calha Norte, President Sarney issued decrees in 1988 and 1989 that granted the army more than six million hectares of land for military bases and training areas, bringing to ten million hectares the total territory under direct military control.[16]

The Yanomami Indians

In the geopolitical view of its architects, Calha Norte also responded to the threat posed by the Yanomami Indians, one of the last remaining unassimilated cultures on earth. Like other indigenous groups, the Yanomami move freely across international borders in the region and have no particular loyalty to any nation-state. They inhabit an extensive area in the state of Roraima and in neighboring Venezuela. Many military statements, including the official document proposing Calha Norte, refer to the dangerous prospect of an independent state comprised of Yanomami from Brazil and Venezuela. Protection of the Yanomami Indians constitutes a central bone of contention between the Brazilian government and defenders of indigenous rights. Since the assault on their homelands began in the 1960s, the Yanomami have dwindled radically in number. The discovery of gold in their territory in the latter half of the 1980s accelerated their decline.[17]

The constitution of 1988 created momentum for protecting the cultural, territorial, and human rights of Brazil's Indians. The constitutional debates gave Indians and their main allies (namely domestic and international NGOs) a major forum for publicizing and pressuring the government to attend to the plight of Brazil's indigenous people. By recognizing officially the social organization, customs, languages, and beliefs of Indians, as well as their original rights over territories they occupied traditionally, the constitution advanced the legal status of Brazil's indigenous populations in important ways. It also made provision for the state to demarcate Indian lands and stipulated that Congress must approve any mineral or water resource developments on Indian territory, as well as any removal of indigenous peoples from their lands, which at most could be only temporary.[18] Indian rights groups within Brazil and from around the world appealed to the Sarney government to enforce these legal provisions by setting aside large tracts of land for the Yanomami and prohibiting mining on their territory. The Brazilian military reacted aggressively against such recommendations and denounced the press for exposing and inflaming the issue. The army minister contended publicly, "Brazil cannot afford to adhere to romantic notions. The Amazon must be exploited for the sake of development. Dams and roads must be built, and Indians must become Brazilians."[19] Business interests in the region, along with state politicians, concurred with these sentiments.

President Sarney did not resist fundamentally the military's rejection of international interference in the Yanomami issue. But he did take stopgap measures to try to hold international criticism at bay. In February 1989, a presidential decree assigned to the Yanomami nineteen isolated areas (or islands) equaling only 2.4 million hectares out of an original 9.4 million hectares proposed as appropriate for the tribe's survival.[20] The archipelago of nineteen reserves would be interspersed with national forests, in which gold mining would be permitted. This measure defied the argument made repeatedly by anthropologists that the long-term survival of the Yanomami depended on a continuous and uninterrupted stretch of land.[21] In the same vein, rather than taking measures to prevent the Indians from contracting life-threatening diseases, President Sarney provided resources for the installation of emergency health posts to treat sick individuals. Along similar lines, on several occasions the Sarney government ordered federal police to remove forcefully up to forty thousand gold miners who had invaded Yanomami lands.[22] Yet periodic expulsions could not be a long-term solution to protecting the Yanomami.

International Forums and Conservation Arrangements
The military used the international scope of the Amazon debate to fuel nationalist sentiment within Brazil and to convince Sarney to resist international pressures to protect the rain forest. Military officers of SADEN leaned on Sarney to withdraw from a March 1989 environmental forum at The Hague organized by the governments of Norway, France, and the Netherlands. Their objection was to a proposal that allegedly advocated transforming the Amazon into a type of "multinational territory."[23] Other government officials from Brazil attended nevertheless and signed the declaration of The Hague. Entitled "Our Country Is the Planet," the document acknowledged a willingness "to delegate a piece of national sovereignty to the common good of humanity"[24] and proposed the creation of an international entity with powers of "decision and execution" to protect the environment. Later, when *Le Monde* published the three-page document, Brazilian authorities claimed that the text did not represent the government's official position and that the Brazilian delegation was deceived into signing. Military leaders undoubtedly played a key role in forcing these disclaimers.

Similarly, during most of the Sarney government leading officers vetoed successfully any arrangements that would allow foreign parties to survey the extent of Brazil's compliance with conditions attached to outside assistance. This included a number of proposed "debt for nature swaps."[25] Under such a deal, environmental groups purchase a portion of a country's foreign debt at a discounted rate and then donate the debt titles for reinvestment in conservation projects. In many countries where they have been carried out, national as well as international organizations have collaborated in conservation activities. Under military pressure, the Sarney government announced that it would not allow foreign monitoring as a condition of financial assistance to help protect the Amazon. The minister of the army as well as the military head of SADEN echoed this point: Brazil would only accept foreign aid in the form of outright donations.[26]

The Beginning of Change under Sarney
Despite continued military influence, pressures mounted over time that led President Sarney to initiate a slight shift in the direction of government policy toward

the Amazon. Instead of denying the severity or importance of the rain forest's destruction, or telling foreign governments to stop interfering in Brazil's affairs, Sarney embarked on a public relations campaign to demonstrate Brazil's concern with preserving the Amazonian ecosystem. This modification signaled the introduction of a new element in government policy toward the region. Since roughly the last year of the Sarney presidency Brazil's governments have adopted a more cautious approach toward the rain forest. As a result of this shift, the military have been forced to tame the open and brazen stance they assumed over Amazonian affairs throughout most of the Sarney government.

What accounts for this change that was begun under President Sarney, accelerated under Fernando Collor, and maintained under Itamar Franco? Undoubtedly, part of the explanation has to do with the recognition by Brazilian government officials that the costs of the previous policy were too high. Evidence against the development model initiated under the military regime—namely, the rapid degradation of a region whose wealth might be exploited in a more sensible and sustainable fashion—could no longer be denied or ignored. At the same time, other factors came into play that further inclined Brazilian officials to pursue policies that signaled a commitment to preserving the Amazonian ecosystem. These had largely to do with Brazil's economic dependence on international powers and President Sarney's recognition that Brazil's relationship with these actors could affect the country (and consequently, the evaluation of his government) in critical ways.

The late 1980s saw a deterioration of Brazil's economy and financial situation. The country's foreign policy centered on the external debt to and relations with the United States, which affected Brazil's ability to ensure imports of technology and foreign currency to service the debt. Brazil's poor environmental record, along with the debt, nuclear issues, and its highly protective informatics policy, had become central sources of friction in Brazil-U.S. relations. The main fear was that the rain forest issue would jeopardize Brazil's ability to extract favorable terms on issues of potentially greater importance, namely finance (including debt negotiations), trade, and technology. Failure to negotiate successfully on these vital matters would have an appreciable negative impact on the government in power.[27] Adding to the concern of Brazilian authorities were the heightened environmental standards that the World Bank, IDB, and other critical funding sources began to demand in the late 1980s before loaning money to projects in Brazil.[28] In short, in order to improve Brazil's standing with foreign actors who could affect its economy in vital ways and, in turn, the electorate's assessment of the president and his government, concessions on the Amazon issue were made.

Reflecting this shift was Nossa Natureza (Our Nature), a program announced in April 1989 after a period of heightened international protest. Nossa Natureza's stated purpose was to educate the public about environmental issues, to "discipline" the exploitation of the area, and to protect Indian communities. It promised to suspend fiscal incentives for cattle ranching; prohibit the use of mercury by gold miners; create national parks and forests as well as separate reserves for gold miners, Indians, and extractors; and support research on conservation.[29] The program led to the creation of IBAMA (Instituto Brasileiro de Meio Ambiente e dos Recursos Naturais Renováveis or Brazilian Institute for the Environment and Renewable Natural Resources), an agency charged with expediting the demarcation of Indian lands, controlling deforestation and the use of mercury, establishing areas to be preserved, and enforcing environmental impact studies for all projects over one hundred hectares.[30]

Nossa Natureza, while improving on preexisting policy, did not reorient fundamentally the terms of Amazonian development.[31] The secretary-general of SADEN, General Bayma Denys, along with other SADEN officials, formulated the new program. They received contributions from six interministerial groups but consulted no relevant nongovernmental specialists or groups from civil society. The central problem with Nossa Natureza lay in the failure of its proposals to be widely implemented in practice. Limited resources did not allow IBAMA to monitor effectively the burning of the forest and the use of mercury over a region so vast. Nevertheless, IBAMA appears to have been instrumental in reducing the most egregious violations of the rain forest.[32] Some top-ranking officials of the agency have also been outspoken critics of government policy toward the region.[33]

The Sarney government also bid to have the United Nations Conference on the Environment and Development ("Earth Summit") in Rio de Janeiro. The premise of this much publicized and grand affair was that global environmental management is necessary and can work, notions that contradicted the military's rejection of foreign involvement in the Amazon. Military leaders feared that since foreign environmental lobbies had targeted Brazil as an environmental offender, and had criticized specifically the "militarization" of Amazon policy, the event would turn into a tribunal against Brazil. They spoke of the "green enemy" as the new threat facing the country. In spite of military protests at the time the idea was proposed, Rio de Janeiro hosted the 1992 conference.[34]

The political weakness of President Sarney, combined with the absence of a powerful domestic constituency for conservation, prevented him from defying strong domestic groups favoring policies that would continue the trend of rain forest destruction. As such, the military, along with business interests and state politicians, retained enormous influence over government policy toward Amazônia. While elements of continuity predominated, developments in the last year of the Sarney administration suggested that presidents with more domestic political clout might check military power more aggressively in order to increase the credibility of their governments with international actors.

The Collor Government

Seeking to win favor with the international community, and in turn boost his domestic popularity through economic success, President Collor reoriented government policy toward Amazônia in significant ways. Upon coming to power, he announced the protection of the Amazon rain forest as one of his highest priorities.[35] This policy shift necessarily led the president into confrontation with the military. Among other environmentally progressive measures, President Collor set aside huge areas for Indian reserves, slowed the growth of the military's presence in Amazônia by arresting the defense project begun under his predecessor, Calha Norte, and entered into agreements with foreign actors to stimulate conservation projects. Government rhetoric changed accordingly. From the strident nationalism of the Sarney government, reflected in the slogan "Amazônia is ours" (the implicit notion being that Brazil could do anything she wanted with it), the rhetoric became one of sustainable development.[36]

The adoption of a foreign policy of moderate internationalism, which stemmed from Collor's project of neoliberalism and the opening of Brazil to the international economy, constituted a driving force in this change of direction. Collor's economic goals would require improving relations with the advanced industrial West. Assuming a more ecologically sensitive stance toward the Amazon could only contribute positively to bettering these relations.[37] In fact, as one observer contends, "[e]nvironmental interdependence and the protection of the environment may provide the Brazilian government with one of the few sources of leverage available to it in the 1990s."[38] The change in stance with respect to Amazon issues had parallels in the nuclear and informatics areas. Collor effectively curtailed the further development of nuclear weaponry by signing an accord with Argentina to allow for joint inspections of the International Atomic Energy Agency (IAEA).[39] Similarly, he ended Brazil's attempt to build a national computer industry through protectionism, which he regarded as an example of outdated and irrational Third World nationalism. In all these spheres—the Amazon, nuclear and informatics policies—Collor expanded civilian prerogatives at the expense of the military's previously unchallenged control over policy formulation.

If economic goals constituted the driving motivation behind President Collor's endorsement of a more environmentally sensitive approach to Amazônia, an enclave of military power and privilege, what gave him the strength to face down the military? In order to push through programs that would in the long run enhance his electoral standing, Collor needed autonomy from the military. The broad and diffuse support he commanded increased his ability to remain autonomous from the institution. Challenging the military to endorse environmentalism in the Amazon was an especially formidable task given the weak domestic political support for this specific position. Only a small percentage of Brazilian voters support "green issues," even in the Amazonian states. Most politicians of the region are motivated to support business enterprises and development projects that result in destruction rather than conservation. Thus Collor would have to rely on his solid yet diffuse initial mandate to undertake bold moves against the top brass. Even in the absence of strong domestic backing for the policy shift he pursued with respect to Amazônia, the overall popular support that Collor commanded when he advanced these measures provided an important buffer against military opposition. Backing by the international community certainly helped shield Collor from a backlash by the armed forces.

What steps did President Collor take to curb ecological devastation in the region? How did he challenge the military in the process? One of Collor's first acts as president was to create a new governmental agency, a Special Secretariat of the Environment (Secretaria Especial do Meio Ambiente or SEMA). SEMA's creation was an important aspect of Collor's larger effort to wrest environmental policy making away from arenas of military power. José Lutzenberger, a committed Brazilian environmentalist, was appointed to head the agency. Lutzenberger was well known and respected in international environmental circles. He was a vocal opponent of financial subsidies for projects that hurt the rain forest, a leading voice against the extension of a highway, BR-364, to link the state of Acre to the Pacific, and an ardent advocate of removing gold prospectors from Indian lands. Upon his appointment, Lutzenberger called for an evaluation of the environmental impact of Calha Norte.[40]

Collor strengthened the resource base of IBAMA in order to increase its capacity to monitor the burning of the rain forest and the use of mercury by gold miners.[41] The Collor government did reduce the rate of deforestation appreciably, although deforestation remained high by absolute standards.[42] The termination of subsidies for large agricultural projects and the imposition of closer monitoring by IBAMA were central causes of the decline. Environmental groups applauded the creation of SEMA, the choice of Lutzenberger, and the empowerment of IBAMA, but none of these measures was well received by military leaders, whose strong sense of nationalism led them to reject any policies that could be construed as gestures for the sake of international consumption.

The Yanomami Indians

Over protests from the military and regional politicians, President Collor reserved 9.4 million hectares—an area equivalent to 1 percent of Brazil's territory—for approximately nine thousand Yanomami Indians. Collor came to power promising to protect Brazil's unassimilated Indians mainly by taking steps to prevent gold prospectors from invading their lands. As a first step, explosives experts from the army, with help from the air force, the federal police, FUNAI, and IBAMA, dynamited 110 illegal airstrips built by gold miners in Indian lands, mainly in the northern state of Roraima. These strips, which proliferated during the Sarney government, provided access to remote gold-rich Indian lands. Forced removal of gold miners from Yanomami territory in the first year of the Collor administration combined with the explosion of illegal airstrips did reduce the number of miners appreciably, from about forty thousand in 1989 to approximately seven thousand in June 1991.[43]

President Collor revoked the decrees issued by Sarney that distributed Yanomami territory over nineteen scattered areas and turned the rest of their land into state parks, forests, and areas for gold mining. He also abolished another Sarney decree, signed in January 1990, which opened up a virgin forest to forty thousand prospectors bordering the Yanomami reserve in the state of Roraima.[44] Indian rights activists applauded these moves but held back final judgment until Collor signed a decree formalizing the Yanomami's possession of the land. The moment that Yanomami defenders had struggled twenty years to achieve arrived on November 15, 1991, when Collor took legal action to reserve an uninterrupted stretch of homeland (9.4 million hectares) over which the Yanomami Indians could roam freely.[45] Yanomami defenders rejoiced, agreeing that it was a crucial step in aiding the cultural survival of the tribe. A few days later, Congress approved a supplementary appropriation of approximately U.S.$2.7 million to pay for the physical demarcation of the Yanomami reserve.[46]

In making the decision, Collor overrode strong opposition by military leaders, mining interests, and the governors of Amazonas and Roraima, the two states that the reserve covers. Collor relied on his justice minister, Jarbas Passarinho, to meet with military commanders and other concerned parties to quell opposition to the measure. Passarinho, a former army colonel, Arenista politician, and minister under the authoritarian regime, enjoyed close ties to the military and other conservative interests.[47] Military leaders had tried to convince the president to reserve a twenty-kilometer strip on the border to separate Brazil's Yanomami from the Yanomami of Venezuela (who since 1991 had a large reserve of their own). This would, in their view, help prevent the development of an Indian nation at the expense of Brazil's sovereignty, but their request was not granted.[48] Passarinho tried to assure them that Brazilian sovereignty would not be at risk. At the signing ceremony for the reserve, Army Minister General Carlos Tinoco hung his head and refrained from applause.

The decree establishing a vast, uninterrupted reserve for the Yanomami was evidence of the extent to which Collor was prepared to challenge the armed forces in order to win international favor. While the reserve President Collor guaranteed the Yanomami was a necessary step in the preservation of their culture, whether he would take additional measures to keep the territory free from illegal gold miners and other intruders would form the real test of his government's commitment to preserving the tribe. Any reasonable hope of effective protection would depend on securing the compliance of the military and federal police. Collor would have to bring the military on board in order to implement his new Amazon policy. One way of appealing to them was to underscore the link between security and the environment, that is, to present as threats to security the plundering of resources by nonstate actors and the social conflict produced by large-scale development. More specifically, it would be crucial to appoint regional commanders who would not merely look the other way or drag their feet when, for example, Indian territories or ecological reserves were being invaded.

The appointment by Collor of a new commander to head the Amazon military command, General Carlos Annibal Pacheco, represented a step forward in making sure that the military would enforce judicial decisions. General Annibal Pacheco maintained that he did not believe in the "internationalization" of the Amazon and that he favored a joint effort by the armed forces and ecologists to preserve the Amazonian ecosystem. These views stood in stark contrast to those held by his predecessor, who aligned himself with the governor of Amazonas state, Gilberto Mestrinho, a notorious adversary of ecologists.[49] Even if Annibal Pacheco was personally uneasy with his position, his obedience to President Collor, the commander in chief, was a sign of military subordination to civilian control.

Debt-for-Nature Swaps

President Collor also shifted Brazil's stance vis-à-vis conservation efforts involving foreign actors. In this connection, he challenged directly the notion that Brazil alone should decide the fate of the Amazon region within its borders and endorsed innovative bilateral and multilateral solutions to conserve the rain forest.[50] With Collor's assumption of office, the Brazilian government reversed its earlier opposition to "debt-for-nature" arrangements. In 1990, Brazilian environmentalists drew up a list of projects to be financed by such means. In 1991, concrete plans were approved to exchange debt for nature. Approximately U.S.$100 million of Brazil's debt would be exchanged every year for environmental protection projects. In May 1992, officials from the Economy Ministry formally approved Brazil's first debt-for-nature swap. This would allow environmental groups to purchase portions of Brazil's U.S.$121 billion foreign debt at a discount rate and donate the debt titles to local NGOs.

Calha Norte

President Collor also announced from the outset that the Calha Norte defense system would have to be reassessed from the standpoint of its impact on the ecology of the northern border region, and that his government would try to orient the project to take into consideration environmental issues.[51] In fact, due to lack of funding, the advancement of Calha Norte practically came to a halt under the Collor presidency. Calha Norte's expansion depended not only on the commitment of the military ministries but also on the cooperation of civilian ministries to fulfill nonmilitary dimensions of the project (e.g., roads and communications). While the military maintained Calha Norte as a priority, participating civilian ministries did not, and failed to allocate sufficient appropriations to uphold their end of the deal.[52] For the most part, President Collor did not intervene and award extra funds to compensate for their abandonment of the program. As a result, the expansion of the new defense system lagged. By 1993, Strategic Affairs Secretary Mário César Flores announced that the Calha Norte project had essentially ceased to exist.[53]

Thus President Collor challenged the armed forces and other powerful interests over the fate of the rain forest, dashing the military's aspiration to make Amazônia a repository of their influence. To create an institutional basis for the protection of the Amazon, Collor established a special agency for the environment (SEMA), strengthened the powers and resources of IBAMA, arrested the growth of Calha Norte, advanced the protection of the Yanomami Indians, and accepted arrangements with foreign powers to finance conservation. In response, international praise as well as financial assistance were forthcoming.

Collor depended on economic success to maintain his electoral chances. Due to his economic program of neoliberalism and the need to improve Brazil's relations with governments, banks, and NGOs of the First World, President Collor tried to break out of the constraints to environmental protection imposed by a coalition of powerful domestic actors: the military as well as business elites and regional politicians. The boldness of Collor's environmental measures is especially noteworthy in light of the weak immediate domestic support for this position. The diffuse yet powerful support that Brazilian voters initially conferred on Collor was the main source of political strength that enabled the president to advance such striking changes and prevail.

The assertive role that President Collor played with respect to the Amazon diminished significantly the military's voice in the region but did not eliminate their influence altogether. For example, Collor assigned the SAE with responsibility for specific border projects, including Calha Norte. This was one sign that the president, while taking steps to preserve Amazônia, did not abandon entirely the national security dimension of previous policy. Yet even Sydney Possuelo, a long-standing critic of military influence over indigenous policy and one of the directors of FUNAI during the Collor government, contended that SAE did not exercise nearly the strength of the CSN or SADEN before it. Not only did residual military voices have to compete for influence among civilians within the SAE, but the agency itself had to share decision-making power with agencies like SEMA and IBAMA and ministries whose primary interests diverged from those of the military.[54] Some also charged President Collor with being more concerned with publicity than substantive change. For example, indigenous rights groups were quick to point to the health problems that remained among the Yanomami[55] and the president's failure to demarcate other Indian lands besides the Yanomami territory.[56] Yet it is important to recognize that a myriad of factors other than military influence account for these omissions.

On balance, the Collor government set the tone for a new, more environmentally friendly stance toward Amazônia. This shift entailed unprecedented challenges to military interests. Under the Collor administration, the grassroots environmental movement gained momentum. Brazilian schools introduced ecology to the curriculum. Ecotourism became the rage. Caring about the environment became a way to appear modern and cosmopolitan. As Collor left office, Amazon observers all wondered whether the policies he put in motion would form the beginning of a longer-lasting trend, or whether his successor, Itamar Franco, would return the country to the situation that existed under President Sarney, when the military exercised tight restrictions over government policy toward Amazônia.

The Government of Itamar Franco

Whereas Sarney mostly gave way to military preferences and Collor staged a frontal attack on policies the military promoted, Franco tried to strike a balance between permitting the military to expand their mission in Amazônia and keeping international criticism at bay. The armed forces' physical presence in the region increased under Franco, who endorsed their efforts to fortify border defenses and extend state control and supervision through a system known as SIVAM (Sistema de Vigilância da Amazônia or Amazon Surveillance System). At the same time, however, other developments (and nondevelopments) suggest that even President Franco held the line on certain fronts. This is especially significant given his otherwise nationalist leanings. Franco steered clear of efforts to enlist his help in rolling back the demarcation of Indian lands. Joint efforts between the army and regional politicians to reduce Indian territories all came to naught under his administration. Similarly, Franco did not return to the Sarney government's practice of rejecting foreign assistance for conservation efforts. In accordance with accommodating international interests, when it came time to appoint the first minister to the newly created Amazon Ministry the post went to a diplomat with extensive international experience. In short, notwithstanding the endorsement of SIVAM, President Franco did not permit the military to resume the preeminent position they enjoyed over Amazon policies under the Sarney government.

What explains Franco's conduct vis-à-vis the Amazon issue? Why did he concede to the armed forces in some ways, but prevent them from exercising a dominant voice in policy formulation and impede their policy preferences in others? Clearly Franco was more beholden to the armed forces than his predecessor and for this reason permitted the institution to expand its role somewhat in Amazônia. But at the same time, reversing policies that had won his predecessor great international applause would have provoked condemnation abroad. Franco was not in a position to offend the international community in light of the continued need for foreign assistance. Hence he tried to straddle the fence and adopted a weaker version of Collor's policies.

Military Defense: SIPAM/SIVAM

Since the beginning of 1993, Brazil's armed forces have transferred troops to the Amazon as one way of expanding the state's presence in the strategic region. The military units relocated to the north came from states of the center-south, for example, Rio de Janeiro and Rio Grande do Sul.[57] The intensification of military efforts to occupy the northern border forms a central aspect of a broader mission that officers are trying to stake out in Amazônia. Their marginalization from other spheres of political life since 1985 has rendered their Amazon claims especially important. Without denying that the border is vulnerable—it is indeed ill defined physically and unguarded—it is also the case that the military have felt pressured to come up with a threat credible enough to persuade Congress that they need generous budget allocations. So far, the only new threat that the Escola Superior de Guerra has defined is the "internationalization of the Amazon." Border incidents of recent years have consistently been followed by military demands to fortify defenses of the strategic region.[58] Wide-ranging political currents have supported the movement of military units to the Amazon border, if only to remove them from highly populated urban areas of the center-south, where their main practical role would remain one of internal security, almost by default.[59]

By the time Itamar Franco came to power, the military's northern border project, Calha Norte, had virtually stalled. Under Franco's weak leadership, top commanders tried to persuade the president to revive Calha Norte, as well as undertake a new project, SIPAM (Sistema de Proteção da Amazônia or Amazon Protection System).[60] The rhetoric of SIPAM is mainly one of sustainable development. The goals for SIPAM listed in an official government document include environmental protection, supervision of occupation and use of soil, prevention and disease control, protection of Indian lands, and identification of punishable illegal activities (such as drug trafficking, weapons smuggling, and the invasion of borders and Indian settlements).[61]

To realize these goals, Franco promised to implement SIVAM, a surveillance system intended to be put in place over five to eight years at the cost of U.S.$600 to $800 million. SIVAM consists of satellites, weather sensors, environmental data collection platforms, and radars capable of monitoring invasions of airspace by planes and missiles and tracking the movement of ships and ground troops. SIVAM also makes possible an integrated communications system between various government agencies involved in the region. While environmental goals predominate in the justification of the surveillance system, internal security and geopolitical aspects are also highly evident. The fact that the SAE coordinates the multiministry project reflects the strategic element of SIVAM, The surveillance system responds to the new strategic environment presented by the end of the cold war, in which new threats such as drug trafficking and ethnic-nationalistic-indigenous conflicts have come to the fore. Although SIVAM has potential use for environmental protection, in essence it appears to be a military project aimed principally at nonstate and subnational threats.[62]

SIVAM was clearly a concession by President Franco to the military. Approved officially on August 10, 1993, the go-ahead came in the wake of extensive military saber rattling. A much publicized manifesto issued by Air Force Commander Ivan Frota in May of that year focused on low budgets and salaries but hastened to mention the feeble nature of government efforts to defend the Amazon against "internationalization." The endorsement of SIVAM, along with the spate of military appointments to civilian positions in the bureaucracy, was an important aspect of the government's strategy to appease disgruntled elements within the institution.

It should be noted, however, that the armed forces are not the only group that benefits from the program. Other state actors seek to combat illegal extraction, environmental degradation, drug smuggling, and related problems that SIVAM is designed to address. International and domestic business groups supplying the infrastructure for SIVAM provide strong backing for the project as well. Finally, regional politicians support the protection system because it does not call for a radical halt to development, but rather, represents an approach that balances environmental protection and economic growth and development.

Finances will determine whether SIVAM is effectively realized. Despite the strong coalition of interests backing the surveillance project (the military, regional politicians, and private sector firms, domestic and international), it has experienced problems getting off the ground due to financial shortages and, more recently, charges of corruption surrounding the contracting of firms for the project.[63] The Brazilian government has announced that it cannot pay for SIVAM without major international assistance. The U.S. and Japanese governments have expressed reluctance to grant financial aid, partly because they perceive SIVAM as mainly a military and not environmental project. For similar reasons, it is not yet clear whether the World Bank and IDB will be forthcoming with funds. Anticipating concerns of this type, President Franco rejected the armed forces' request to coordinate the multiministry project and assigned this role to SAE instead.[64]

Indian Reserves

The demarcation of the Yanomami reserve took place in 1992, cause for celebration among Indian rights advocates and environmentalists in London, Washington, and other capitals of the developed world. In 1993, the United Nations sponsored the Year of the World's Indigenous People, further directing focus on the question of Indian rights. Reversing progress on this front, especially with respect to the much publicized Yanomami reserve, would undoubtedly have drawn negative international attention to Brazil. Although President Franco never became an advocate of Indian rights, he took no action to aid the various efforts by regional politicians and military actors to roll back the demarcation of Indian lands. The negative publicity Brazil suffered in the summer of 1993 after the killing of twenty-odd Yanomami Indians by informal sector gold miners was but a sign of what would happen if Brazil began to reverse legal protections for Indians.[65]

Efforts to reduce the Yanomami reserve began soon after the November 1991 decision. In fact, President Collor allegedly promised to "review" the decision in his desperate and unsuccessful attempt to win support to stay in office when he faced corruption charges in 1992. The scheduled constitutional revision was seen as a golden opportunity by Amazonian politicians, the military, and miscellaneous private interests to restrict the demarcation of Indian lands. A total of 230 amendments was put forth to reduce some of the demarcations already made and to prevent additional ones from taking place.[66] One proposal that enjoyed special support among local politicians was to subject all federally planned demarcations to review by individual states. If enacted, this measure would prove enormously deleterious to the protection of Indians. It could be expected that state politicians would be less subject to international sanctions because they did not associate their fate with overarching national issues, like the Brazilian economy as a whole. At the same time, they would be more affected by immediate electoral incentives to spur development in the region. The armed forces were especially interested in modifying constitutional Article 231 to prevent the reservation of land for Indians on the border.[67] The specific demand was to prohibit demarcation within an area of 150 kilometers from the border. Indian rights groups objected to this demand too. The jettisoning of the constitutional revision (explained in Chapter 3) deprived interested parties of the opportunity to pass legislation with greater ease. None of the other legislative attempts to restrict Indian lands has succeeded either. One of the main obstacles involved the failure of these proposals to receive priority on the congressional agenda.[68] Like all bills that fail to receive congressional approval in a given legislative session, the bills (*projetos de lei*) to restrict Indian lands proposed under the Itamar Franco period would be shelved.

The creation of a new Amazon Ministry and the appointment of a diplomat with close ties to the West was further testimony of Franco's recognition of the need to remain on good terms with international actors over Amazon issues. This necessarily meant keeping the military at arm's length. Rubens Ricúpero, former ambassador to the United States, was asked to head the Ministry of the Environment and Legal Amazon (Ministério do Meio Ambiente e da Amazônia Legal), designed to put all agencies involved with the Amazon and the environment under one umbrella. His appointment came shortly after the Yanomami murders of August 1993 and the resulting international outcry, which helped create new momentum for the protection of Indians. The military preferred someone who would take a stronger nationalist stance. They also regarded Ricúpero's institutional origins (Brazil's Foreign Ministry) with some suspicion. In recent years, Itamaraty (the foreign ministry) and the military have experienced quite some conflict over competing policy preferences for Amazônia. The Foreign Ministry, more interested than the military in Brazil's overall international profile, has assumed a more flexible, less intransigent and nationalistic stance than the military ministries. Upon assuming the post, Ricúpero announced that while he defended the intensification of border defense by the military, he did not believe that a plot was underway to "internationalize" the Amazon. He contended that environmental and Indian protections were valuable goals that should be reconciled with development, and that he would try to use his ties with the World Bank and IDB to gain resources for projects to preserve the ecosystem in Amazônia.[69] Ricúpero's status as one of Brazil's most able diplomats shows the importance that the Franco government placed on international concerns about the region.

Although President Franco did not take aggressive measures to demilitarize policy making over Amazônia or continue the pace of change that Collor put in motion, he did not allow the military to dominate government decision making toward the region. To the extent that President Franco permitted military influence to expand from the level that existed under Collor, it was mainly in areas related to strategic defense or that could be construed under the rubric of environmental protection. SIVAM fits both these bills. The military's increased physical presence in the region and measures to extend state surveillance stemmed largely from Franco's weak ability to counter the strong domestic forces in favor of these measures. The timing of his endorsement of SIVAM—after a period of rumblings in the barracks—suggests this to be the case. Clearly, even had Franco wanted to radically reduce military influence and pursue a more environmentally sensitive stance toward the region, his weak political capacity would probably have made it prohibitively difficult for him to do so.

It is telling, however, that even a president sympathetic to the nationalist sentiments of the military and who, moreover, was not in a strong position to defy powerful domestic interests placed limits on the resurgence and advance of the coalition for development and occupation. Accountability for the general state of affairs in the country, rather than to the interests of a few (albeit powerful) actors, compelled Franco to look beyond short-term considerations and take seriously Brazil's relations with international actors who could affect the country's economic standing in crucial ways. The motivations unleashed by democratic accountability, even if unaccompanied by the capacity that democratic elections confer, prompted Franco to look beyond the short-term goal of placating the armed forces.

CONCLUSION

A "greening" of Brazilian policies toward the Amazon has transpired since 1985. Even critics of Brazil's treatment of the rain forest have had to admit that a policy shift has taken place since the end of the Sarney government. To the great surprise of many observers, President Collor took the unprecedented step of contesting the armed forces in one of the areas they value most dearly. This achievement was noteworthy not only because the Brazilian military place special claims on the Amazon, but also because most other powerful domestic political actors share the military's pro-development stance toward the region.

The motivation and capacity of democratically elected executives to extend their control over an issue like the Amazon rain forest suggests that the competitive dynamic of democracy has far-reaching implications. Democratization empowered otherwise weak domestic groups to bring visibility to their cause, at home and abroad. Moreover, it compelled government leaders to be accountable to a broader set of actors, through indirect pressures that could affect their standing (in this case, international public opinion) as well as more direct means.

Greater than Sarney's and Franco's, President Collor's ability to challenge the military suggests that presidents need a certain degree of strength and autonomy to act on the overarching incentive of running a successful government and economy. This strength can come from generalized support, not only through backing for the particular policy at hand. Having to pay constant attention to pacifying a powerful and meddlesome military can certainly interfere with an executive's ability to pursue broad long-term goals of the kind to which President Collor aspired. In light of the political incentives and resources that appear to be important in leading Brazilian executives to challenge the military over the fate of Amazônia, the new government of Fernando Henrique Cardoso provides hope for preserving Amazonian ecology. Cardoso's highly internationalist posture and stunning electoral victory would appear to be a winning combination in this regard.

CONCLUSION

SUMMARY OF THE CENTRAL ARGUMENT AND CASES

This book has analyzed the changing balance of civil-military power in Brazil since the return to civilian government in 1985. Using an explanatory framework rooted in the principles of rational choice, it has underscored the conflicting interests between democratically elected politicians and military leaders; most importantly, the tendency of politicians to try to undermine the armed forces' influence over wide-ranging policy decisions. The picture I portray challenges the conventional wisdom of the regime transitions literature, which regards the military's institutional powers at the outset of civilian rule as a virtually impenetrable shield against the impact of democratic politics. The institutionalist premises that underlie this conventional view lead to an emphasis on continuity over change. Institutional guarantees doubtless provide postauthoritarian militaries with more protection than they would otherwise enjoy, but their effect is much shorter-lived and less decisive than previously imagined. My findings suggest that long-term military rule (during which military prerogatives expanded) and the transition to democracy (whose negotiated manner allowed for their survival) will not have as strong and lasting an imprint on Brazil's new democracy as once thought.

Chapter 1 laid out the analytical issues the study addresses. It juxtaposed rational choice to historical institutionalism and suggested that the former approach was better able than the latter to explain the reduction of military prerogatives and the diminution of the military's ability to sway specific policy decisions over time. The chapter presented three ways electoral competition has led politicians to contest the military and contract their sphere of influence: by compelling them to endorse populist measures in order to appeal to Brazil's large number of poor and increasingly mobilized voters; by stimulating them to extend their control over public resources to distribute as political patronage; and by motivating them to expand their political autonomy so that they can enact popularity-enhancing public policies of a more strictly programmatic nature. Politicians acted on these incentives even though the armed forces entered the new democracy from a particularly strong position, according to institutionalist considerations.

Chapter 2 explained and analyzed how the armed forces managed to achieve such a seemingly favorable position and what it augured for Brazil's new democracy. The military's impressive unity and entrenchment in the state after twenty-one years of direct rule promised not only to insulate the institution from outside direction of defense issues but also to allow its leaders to exercise undue influence in nonmilitary spheres. The negotiated nature of the transition seemed to cement these prospects.

Chapter 3 described the mixed success of the military lobby in the constitutional debates of 1987–88, the first major opportunity for civilians to test the staying power of the armed forces' institutionally based prerogatives. Politicians downgraded or eliminated military privileges and institutional structures where powerful electoral interests were perceived to be at stake. Where the military succeeded in retaining their prerogatives, it was mainly because the specific provisions in question did not directly or immediately impair the political standing of constitutional delegates, and/or because assembly members could not overcome collective action problems in trying to dismantle them. President Fernando Collor de Mello picked up where the Constituent Assembly left off and restructured two organs—the intelligence service and security council—in order to diminish military influence and thereby extend his own power and reach. He did little to reduce those military prerogatives whose impact on electoral politics he judged to be negligible.

Chapters 4–6 showed the limits of military influence under Brazil's new democracy through an analysis of decision making in diverse policy areas. Each of these three issue areas involves one of the three incentives (explained in Chapter 1 and summarized above) through which democracy leads politicians to try to roll back military influence. Chapter 4 examined the emergence of conflict between politicians and their inclination to appeal to large and mobilized popular sectors and the military's desire to contain popular mobilization. It showed that the occupation by uniformed officers of numerous positions within the state did not prevent vote-seeking politicians from supporting pro-labor legislation against the expressed preferences and lobbying efforts of the officer corps for tighter restrictions on labor. Even the pressure that military leaders exerted on the president, who in turn tried to use his influence with legislators, proved to be in vain.

Chapter 5 illustrated the civil-military tension that has arisen over the allocation of public resources. It demonstrated how electoral incentives to distribute political patronage pit politicians against the armed forces over the federal budget. The military's institutional prerogatives could not prevent defense expenditures from being cut for the sake of budgetary categories more conducive to political patronage, the lifeblood of a majority of Brazilian politicians. The prerogatives possessed by the Brazilian military proved feeble currency in a game defined by logrolling and other machinations to which only politicians are privy.

.The Amazon case, presented in Chapter 6, showed that politicians (especially executives) will try to prevail against the military when programmatic policies that can improve the country's prospects and thus enhance their own political standing are at stake. This can occur even when the weight of domestic opinion is not on their side in the particular issue. Whether a president can hold his ground in this situation depends largely on the strength of his electoral mandate. Presidents who are generally popular are more likely to undertake such a course and stick to it. The buffer that overall domestic support gives these presidents allows them to withstand military discontent and to adhere to policies that will advance their political standing in the long run.

The findings I present suggest that democracy generates strong pressures for politicians to assert civilian interests and diminish military influence. Rational politicians following the incentives unleashed by electoral competition will indeed be tempted to undermine the expanded level of military prerogatives that resulted from long-term military rule and that survived the transition. Electoral mandates serve to protect them in the process. Divisions among officers increase politicians' capacity to challenge the military. My perspective thus emphasizes human action and its potential for change over the emphasis of historical institutionalism on the enduring weight of institutional constraints. Power structures and institutional mechanisms established or reaffirmed during regime transitions are not immutable. Rather, they can be successfully challenged and modified by actors pursuing their own goals in the competitive setting of a democracy. The dynamic, expansive view of democracy I advance justifies a more hopeful outlook on Latin America's fledgling civilian regimes than the established wisdom suggests.

AREAS OF REMAINING INFLUENCE

It is not the contention of this book that civilians in Brazil have succeeded entirely in cutting out all pockets of military autonomy or in subordinating the institution to their control. The baseline for my analysis of declining military influence in postauthoritarian Brazil is the level of military influence that existed in 1985, the first year of the civilian regime. The point of comparison is not the precedent of civilian authority established in the industrialized West, or an ideal of civil-military relations in a democratic polity and society. By the standard I have used, civilians have indeed made progress in reducing military interference in politics. To use a simple metaphor, rather than seeing the glass as still half empty, the perspective I adopt tries to account for why it has become half full.

Civilian moves to reduce the political and economic space the military occupy are an important step in asserting civilian control, but they are not the only one. Serious gaps in civilian authority remain. Civilians have taken impressive steps to downgrade military prerogatives, but the armed forces are still a factor of power that enters into the calculations of major political actors, especially during crises. Elected public officials in Brazil have a long way to go before attaining the level of supremacy over the defense establishment that exists in advanced Western democracies. Until now they have challenged the armed forces and reduced their influence mainly for tactical purposes. Reduced military influence is not equivalent to democratic control of the armed forces.

Two policy strategies could enhance democratic control of the armed forces: if public officials were to extend their influence into policy spheres where the armed services still enjoy considerable autonomy, and if they did more to encourage officers to "control themselves" by adopting credible nonpolitical roles and internalizing the norm of subordination to civilians. The former involves regulation of the military institution from outside. The latter entails generating impulses from within the armed forces to become and remain focused on a narrow sphere of professional responsibilities.

Civilian authority remains underdeveloped in a number of substantive policy areas. Active-duty officers dominate discussion and decisions on most corporate concerns as well as issues involving warfare and defense. The tacit pact seems to be to allow the military a high degree of institutional autonomy and control over security issues provided they do not clash with important civilian interests. Military education, training, and doctrine, the system of military justice, defense organization, force levels and the nature of weaponry are almost entirely within the armed forces' purview. These issues remain the reserve of the armed services for the obverse reason that civilians have tried to remove other issues from their domain. Politicians have confronted the armed forces mainly when they have expected direct gains for their own political strategies. When they have not, military prerogatives have tended to persist. Civilian politicians would gain little electorally by trying to reduce the military's command over most corporate and defense issues. The vast majority of Brazilian voters has much more pressing concerns on which politicians rationally focus their attention and energy. Thus lack of civilian initiative due to indifference rather than military resistance is largely responsible for military autonomy in these areas. Notably, civilian politicians constrain the defense establishment's freedom to operate at will with respect to force levels and weapons systems more than the other issues noted above because of the public financing involved. The interest that public officials take in these two matters is confined mainly to their budgetary implications. Another exception to the hands-off attitude of elected public officials vis-à-vis military weaponry occurs when international governments that can exert economic leverage object to the military's production of sophisticated military technology, for example, in the nuclear area.

By neglecting issues like the numbers and location of troops in the country and the kinds of weapons they have at their disposal, civilians give up a crucial opportunity to influence the role definition and orientation of the armed forces, for example, whether they focus their attention on internal or external conflicts and retain a "guardian mission" or not. Similarly, by leaving issues like military education, socialization, and doctrine in the hands of uniformed officers—who are undoubtedly steeped in the ideas and traditions of the Brazilian military—civilians abdicate the possibility of reshaping the attitudes of an institution that could have a critical impact on the future of democracy in the country.

In addition to regulating and overseeing the military institution, civilians should enact policies that encourage leading officers to refrain from political interference on their own accord. This strategy, known as objective control, essentially involves "militarizing the military"[1] or establishing areas where the armed forces can exercise professional (strictly military) prerogatives. Although this strategy does not guarantee a politically neutral military, it enhances the prospects for political subordination by conferring a sense of prestige and an alternative mission on the institution, creating a climate that renders political intrusiveness less likely.[2] By inducing the armed forces to restrain themselves, objective control is a critical complement to methods that emphasize oversight and regulation, which depend on civilians possessing sufficient will to enforce them. Brazilian history has suggested repeatedly that poor government performance can sap this will and actually lead civilians to expand the role of the military in the pursuit of political stability. By putting the armed forces "out of reach" or at least diminishing their availability when civilians appeal to them for support, objective control helps guard against reversal of civilian predominance.

Just as many civilians have contributed to reducing military influence out of political self-interest (a motivation that has both favored and limited the assertion of civilian power), many members of the military itself accept the institution's declining status only conditionally. Instrumental calculations and not an underlying commitment to political neutrality induce such officers to comply with the reduction of their powers in the current period. Before overplaying their hand in trying to resist such measures, the military consider factors such as the need to gain credibility and preserve amicable relations with political and civil society, as well as the relatively minor threats to political stability and corporate viability in the current era.

The Brazilian military's failure to internalize the norm of political subordination has numerous manifestations. Substantial segments of the officer corps, especially within the army, maintain a belief in the legitimacy of the institution's historically arrogated right to define "permanent national objectives" and make pronouncements on and oversee developments of broad political and social significance. For example, since mid-1992, leading army officials have spoken out strongly against the rising tide of corruption in Brazil's new democracy,[3] criticized the country's public school teachers for imparting leftist political leanings to their students, denounced a Brazilian television series (telenovela) for depicting the repression of young militants under the authoritarian regime,[4] and taken President Franco and the minister of justice to task for indiscreet public behavior during celebrations of Carnaval.[5] These actions suggest that the army has not lost interest in acting as a watchdog of the government as well as defender of the nation.

In this vein, many (but not all) officers frequently express impatience and disillusionment with the importance that civilian politicians give to partisan and electoral considerations, rather than the "national interest." They denigrate politicians for being self-serving and short-sighted and decry the related lack of coherence and efficiency in government decision making under Brazil's new democracy. The frequency of such criticisms is disturbing insofar as accountability to voters and the playing out of conflicting interests and ideals are part and parcel of democratic politics. These criticisms suggest an organic statist ideal rather than a fundamental acceptance of democratic pluralism and the dynamics of democracy.[6]

Army education, a good indicator of how the service defines its role, reflects an institution committed to more than defending national borders. The 1994 curriculum for the Army Staff and General Command School (ECEME), a training ground for all officers aspiring to the rank of general, included 219 hours of instruction (out of a total of 3,280) devoted to segurança interna (internal security). As listed in the course description, this section included treatment of the doctrine of national security, the communist movement of Brazil (Movimento Comunista do Brasil) and other revolutionary groups and forças adversas (adverse forces) in the domestic and international arena. Interestingly, however, the course outline also suggested the need to distinguish where the military's legal right to interfere in internal security begins and ends.[7]

Finally, when popular support for the president is weak, the military have proven willing to seize the opportunity to expand their visibility and make demands on the government. This dynamic was evident during low points of the Itamar Franco administration, especially from mid-1993 until mid-1994. Indications of widespread political corruption, coupled with budgetary and salary restrictions on the armed forces, prompted a number of high-ranking active-duty officers to make veiled threats about the future of Brazilian democracy. Franco reacted to rumblings in the barracks by granting salary concessions to the armed forces and appointing officers to civilian positions in the cabinet.[8] He also put two generals on an official commission to investigate corruption.[9]

In short, although civilians have taken impressive steps to reduce military influence, more needs to be done to reorient the armed forces away from politics and to subordinate them to civilian authority. Whether Brazilian politicians will make the commitment to enact and maintain strategies to achieve these goals remains to be seen. Two related factors—stronger, more encompassing political institutions and improved governing capabilities—would greatly enhance the chances of this happening.

Better institutionalized political parties would have the effect of inducing individual members to identify and act more in line with long-term overarching goals. This would render individual members more likely to cooperate to supply the collective good of civilian control over the military. As noted previously, the institutionalization of civilian supremacy poses a collective action dilemma that politicians in Brazil, with its multitude of weak political parties, have faced difficulties overcoming. Even when a shared interest in checking military power has existed, individual legislators have often been reluctant to expend political capital to advance this interest. Collective backing is necessary whether the strategy of civilian control involves actively monitoring the military (for example, through congressional committees dedicated to routine analysis and oversight) or diminishing the military's volition for political involvement (for example, by providing funding for the development of robust external defense roles).

It is indeed a conundrum that the very incentives that drive politicians to rationally oppose military interests may also preclude them from ultimately establishing the conditions for civilian control. Unfortunately, there is no sign of an immediate solution to this problem. As long as Brazil's political parties remain weak and their leaders unable to lengthen the time horizons of members, self-interest will prevail rather than foresight in safeguarding democracy. A shift in the system of government (from presidentialism to parliamentarism) and changes in electoral rules to promote stronger parties would help alleviate the pernicious effects of the current system, but modifications of this kind are not high on the current agenda. Thus, while civilians may successfully reduce the political and economic space the military occupy, in the absence of additional steps to enhance civilian control a degree of continued civil-military tension and conflict can be expected.

More effective governance would also help lead the military out of internal roles. In periods of political and economic stability, Brazil's presidents do not face pressures to expand military influence in order to guarantee governability. Effective maintenance of public security by civilian officials helps prevent incidents like the use of military troops to stamp out drug trafficking and other illegal activities in Brazil's major cities, and limit the subsequent threat of "mission creep." In this connection, civilian attitudes can reinforce nondemocratic inclinations within the army. When the public opinion project Latinobarómetro asked Brazilians what was most important to them—maintaining order, combating inflation, expanding citizen participation, or protecting free expression—nearly one-third of all respondents chose "maintaining order." Similarly, when asked to rank-order the importance placed on combating crime versus stabilizing the economy versus creating a more humane and personal society where ideas count more than money, 49.3 percent of Brazilian respondents listed "combating crime" as their first priority.[10]

COMPARATIVE APPLICABILITY

Since rational choice posits universal interests, analyses couched in such a framework should be able to "travel" across cases. In other words, electoral competition everywhere should impose pressures on civilian politicians to roll back military influence, and likewise, popular support should boost their confidence to do so. Yet while the basic outline of my framework should be broadly applicable, there will of course be some variation among cases. Extant political institutions, broader power alignments, and the general effectiveness of civilian governments will cause politicians' behavior to differ somewhat from country to country.

Chile

The Chilean case is similar to the Brazilian insofar as the transition to democracy was highly constrained by authoritarian incumbents and thus upheld many military prerogatives. The extraordinary privileges that General Pinochet secured for the armed forces and codified in the 1980 constitution in fact create higher legal barriers to the restoration of civilian powers in Chile than in Brazil. Chile differs from Brazil in having well-institutionalized programmatic political parties. A comparison between the two cases, which aside from this difference share many important similarities, is useful for assessing the impact of this factor on civilian conduct toward the military.

As in Brazil and in line with my theoretical expectations, public officials in Chile have taken steps to diminish the armed forces' institutional powers and actually made policy decisions against military preferences. However small and gradual these measures, they constitute an impressive achievement in light of the extensive military prerogatives codified in the 1980 charter created under General Pinochet, and in a series of laws passed between the plebiscite of 1988 (in which voters rejected a continuation of the authoritarian regime) and the presidential election of December 1989. The programmatic commitment to popular sovereignty and social reform, more pervasive among Chilean politicians than Brazilian, figures prominently alongside more pragmatic calculations for weakening the military politically. The organizational strength of political parties, much higher in Chile than in Brazil, has allowed the center-left to coordinate its members around a strategy of reducing military influence that is deliberate and assertive, yet at the same time careful to uphold the collective interest in democracy's survival by not pushing the military beyond their tolerance.

Political Prerogatives

Once it became clear that a permanent state of authoritarian rule would not be possible, General Pinochet drew up plans for a "protected democracy" consisting of a strong political right and a military with ample political powers. Both had been allies since the advance of leftist radicalism in the early 1970s and were expected to support each other against the inevitable reemergence of the center-left in a new democracy. The 1980 constitution formed the basis of Chile's "protected democracy." The Ley Orgánica Constitucional de las Fuerzas Armadas (Organic Constitutional Law of the Armed Forces), drawn up in the last year of military rule, would bind the hands of Pinochet's civilian successors even tighter.[11] Legal provisions enshrined in these documents had a greater likelihood of persisting than the military prerogatives retained in Brazil through more informal agreements.[12] The Pinochet regime also showed a high level of foresight in securing advantages for conservative *electoral* forces and not just the military. Efforts to mold the Chilean Congress, whose expanded powers under democracy include making decisions that affect the status of the armed forces, have helped indirectly to protect military prerogatives.

Provisions for designated senators, fewer representatives in the Senate and Chamber, and a binomial electoral system benefited the political right. Nine seats in the Senate were reserved for nonelected officials, whose selection was made by the outgoing military regime. The provision of designated senators, coupled with a reduction of elected representatives overall (from 150 to 120 in the lower house and from 60 to 26 in the Senate), meant that in the first postauthoritarian civilian government slightly over a third of the Senate would be comprised of nonelected officials who in all probability would be sympathetic to the conservative ideas embraced by the major rightist parties, Renovación Nacional (National Renovation or RN) and Unión Democrática Independiente (Independent Democratic Union or UDI).

The "binomial majoritarian system," introduced by the regime in its final year, further overrepresents the right. The rules provide for two seats per district, for which each party can present two candidates. Voters choose one candidate on one party list. The list that receives the highest number of votes earns the first seat. In order for one party to gain both seats, it must obtain more than twice as many votes as those cast for the competing list. Thus, a party (alliance) commanding a little more than 33 percent of the vote will end up with half of the seats. Designed under the assumption that the center-left opposition coalition would have a majority and that the right would have slightly more than one-third of the vote, this system has served its intended purpose of limiting the predominance of the former opposition and guaranteeing the military's conservative supporters a disproportionate share of legislative influence.

Alongside measures favoring the electoral right, the Pinochet regime instituted provisions to undermine the advance of the left. Among these was a constitutional article that in effect banned all Marxist parties and revolutionary movements. Another article prohibited simultaneous membership in political parties and intermediate groups, such as labor unions. This was instituted with the explicit purpose of impeding popular sector mobilization by leftist parties.

As for military prerogatives, two provisions of political consequence deserve particular mention. The Pinochet charter called for a powerful and military-dominated National Security Council, whose powers extended beyond advising the president to exercising veto power over policies affecting national security.[13] The military were granted majority voting status on this council. Voting members consisted of the chiefs of staff of the armed services, the director general of the national police (carabineros), and the presidents of the Senate and supreme court. The Pinochet regime enhanced military autonomy further by placing legal constraints on the chief executive's ability to dismiss the chiefs of the army, navy, and air force, and carabineros. By law, the president cannot order the departure of any of these commanders. This safeguard assures the continuation of General Pinochet as army commander until 1998, a position he has used to keep a watchful eye over the new democracy.

Above and beyond these specific provisions, the charter put in place by the Pinochet regime sought to impede change by establishing barriers to amending the constitution that would be nearly impossible to overcome, especially given the above-mentioned measures to strengthen the political right: three-fifths approval by both legislative houses in two consecutive Congresses. In short, the outgoing authoritarian regime covered its bases well. It conferred constitutional guarantees on the armed forces directly. And it passed legislation to boost the electoral chances of conservative politicians, who would presumably support the military in return for their own protected status. These achievements contributed to General Pinochet's depiction of his stay in power as a misión cumplida (mission accomplished).[14]

Whether democratic forces could undo these "safeguards" installed by the outgoing authoritarian regime would form a crucial test of the resilience of Chilean democracy. The effort has been led by the Concertación de Partidos por la Democracia (CPD or Coalition of Parties for Democracy), the coalition of Christian Democratic, Socialist, Partido por la Democracia (PPD or Party for Democracy), and other center and center-left parties that mobilized citizens to vote against the regime in the 1988 plebiscite and went on to form the foundation of the two postauthoritarian governments.

The rejection of the regime by a majority of Chilean citizens in 1988 augured well for the reform effort.[15] In fact, it empowered members of the coalition to demand major constitutional reforms against the will of General Pinochet even before the election of the new government. Negotiations that included leaders of the major parties and top-ranking military officers yielded a package of reforms that voters approved overwhelmingly in a referendum held on July 30, 1989. Voter turnout was impressive (over 93 percent of the electorate), and 85.7 percent ratified the changes. The results of the referendum increased the size of the Senate (from twenty-six to thirty-eight) as partial compensation for the designated members; reduced the previous prohibition on Marxist parties to a ban on groups that advocated and used violence; eliminated the prohibition against joint membership in political parties and labor unions; limited the National Security Council to playing a strictly advisory role, and eliminated the military's majority voting status on the council by balancing the representation between civilians and military personnel. Now at least one civilian must side with the armed forces if their opinion is to prevail. One of the most significant changes resulting from the referendum was that it made the constitution easier to amend, thus increasing the possibility of further change. The requirement that three-fifths of the members of both houses in two consecutive Congresses ratify an amendment was reduced to a stipulation that a one-time, two-thirds legislative quorum be required for most changes.

The referendum of July 1989 was indeed a major step in democratizing the authoritarian order established by the previous regime. Notably, even parties of the right supported a number of the changes enacted. For example, the right-wing UDI advocated eliminating the article prohibiting simultaneous membership in parties and intermediate associations for fear that such a ban would hinder its own efforts to mobilize voters. UDI's opposition to this article, which was intended originally to sever links between labor unions and leftist parties but resulted in impeding the electoral strategies of right-wing parties as well, exemplifies one of the inherent conflicts of interest between democratically elected politicians, for whom popular mobilization for electoral purposes is a central goal, and the armed forces, which strive to contain activation of the mass citizenry.

Notwithstanding the important democratizing impact of the constitutional reforms passed in the referendum, several articles that limit popular sovereignty and civilian control have remained in place, including the designated senatorial seats, the binomial electoral system, and the president's inability to dismiss the top military commanders. Patricio Aylwin's substantial margin of victory in the 1989 presidential election against the candidate supported by General Pinochet and the political right, Hernán Büchi, gave him confidence to undertake further constitutional reforms.[16] But would a Congress that was highly skewed to the right approve the proposed reforms?

The same opportunism that inspired right-wing parties to oppose aspects of the authoritarian constitution hindering their own advancement motivated them under the Aylwin government to defend arrangements that enhance their electoral standing, such as the designated senators and the binomial electoral system. Following the 1989 election, the right commanded a majority in the Senate due to the designated senators as well as the electoral system.[17] This put the Concertación in the position of needing to gain the support of some segment of the right in order to pass legislation. Understandably, rightist parties would have little interest in altering a system that confers such advantage on them. So far, they have managed to block reform efforts to transform the electoral system into one based on proportional representation.

Interestingly, on one occasion under the Aylwin government three members of the right (from the RN, specifically) switched over to the opposition and cast the decisive votes to dismiss a supreme court justice. The issue at hand was the court's human rights record during the dictatorship. Since the supreme court and military had been in close alliance under authoritarian rule, a vote against a justice symbolized a vote against the military.[18] Prompting the defections was a scandal in which army intelligence was revealed to be spying on politicians of the Renovación Nacional, ultimately ruining two members' presidential aspirations.[19] Military justice handled the case and deemed that no specific offense had been committed under existing law. After the scandal broke, the president of the party announced a new receptiveness to constitutional changes aimed at weakening military prerogatives.[20] The demonstrated willingness of (some) rightist politicians on this and other occasions to challenge military-related prerogatives that impede their own autonomy, in contrast to their defensive stance toward military-initiated provisions that protect their narrower electoral interests, suggests the existence of multiple political "games."[21] In the larger game at stake—involving politicians against military elites—even conservative politicians will contest the latter in order to expand the playing field for politicians as a whole. But when military-designed institutional arrangements work in their favor, these same politicians are willing to protect and use them to their own advantage.

Important assertions of civilian authority did take place under the Aylwin presidency despite the paucity of constitutional reforms. These developments, though crucial indicators of a shifting balance of power between civilians and the military, have not received the attention that examples of residual military power have, or the attention they deserve. Surprising to many observers was the fact that

President Aylwin used his constitutional powers as commander in chief to successfully reject several of General Pinochet's proposals for army promotions. The officers who Aylwin vetoed tended to have records marred by financial irregularities or were known as political articulators within the army. By blocking the ascent of these officers, President Aylwin effectively helped shape the composition of the high command.[22]

The Aylwin government also made organizational changes to weaken the military's role in internal security. In its first year of office the government returned the *carabineros* to the Interior Ministry after a seventeen-year period under the Ministry of Defense. This transfer underscores internal security as the preserve of the police and not the military. Under the preexisting arrangement, the defense minister could call out either the police or the army to respond to domestic disturbances. The removal of the *carabineros* from under the Defense Ministry should also help restore public trust in the force. Most Chileans still associate the *carabineros* with the political repression of the Pinochet era. Beyond the concrete impact of strengthening the role of the police (over the military) in the sphere of internal security, the loss of military status for the *carabineros* has symbolic importance insofar as it restores the situation that existed before the 1973 coup.[23]

The Aylwin government maintained its resolve to keep the army out of internal security by rejecting the army's demand to participate in the newly created Oficina Coordinadora de Seguridad Pública (Coordinating Agency of Public Security or OCSP) in the first quarter of 1991. The OCSP is charged with coordinating the antiterrorist program waged by the *carabineros* and the investigative police. The national security council proposed the creation of this antiterrorist unit after the murder of Senator Jaime Guzmán, leader of the UDI. Committed to cracking down on terrorism, President Aylwin agreed to its formation but on the condition that the army not be allowed to participate.[24]

In sum, President Aylwin made some progress in asserting the authority of the presidency, but failed to break through many important constraints of General Pinochet's legacy. For example, he never succeeded in restoring the presidential prerogative to dismiss a commander in chief.[25] It would be up to his successor, Christian Democrat Eduardo Frei, to press on with reforms.

President Eduardo Frei assumed office in March 1994 intent on preserving political stability while enacting reforms to diminish military prerogatives and make the electoral system more representative. In October 1995, the Frei government submitted to the Senate a package consisting of thirty-one proposed constitutional reforms. Proposals in this package included the elimination of the designated senators, the restructuring of the national security council to allow for greater civilian authority, and the granting of greater oversight powers to Congress. Excluded from the package were proposals to reform the Ley Orgánica Constitucional de las Fuerzas Armadas,[26] which would have restored further powers to the presidency over the military. Although amendments targeting the Ley Orgánica were excluded, the reform package, if approved, will go a considerable way toward expanding Chilean democracy.

What are the prospects that the Congress will pass this package of constitutional reforms? The economic prosperity and stable political situation that Frei inherited, combined with an impressive electoral mandate for change (58 percent of the vote), will provide crucial backing for efforts of this kind. Interestingly, in late October 1995 the Concertación managed to garner the endorsement of the more progressive wing of the Renovación Nacional for these reforms. Led by party president Andrés Allamand, this faction of the party defends the economic model inherited from the dictatorship but calls for greater political democracy and social reform. It is acutely aware of the need to move to the center and distance itself from the military government in order to capture more electoral support.[27] It should be noted that advocating the elimination of the institution of the designated senators is based at least in part on narrow self-interest. Were the institution to remain intact, the political right would be subject to the risk of losing its superiority in the Senate since it is the existing government that has the right to appoint the new group of *designados*.

The more ideologically conservative UDI and the more conservative members of the RN reject the proposed amendments, consistent with their repeated obstruction of efforts to restore the president's power to remove the service chiefs and director of the national police. An underlying fear of a return to the instability that erupted during the Allende years (1970–73) inhibits these rightist politicians from fully endorsing measures that would decrease the military's presence and autonomy within the state. This stands in contrast to the Brazilian right, whose greater sense of security about the socioeconomic order makes its members more willing to challenge the military. Occasional terrorism from the far left keeps alive concerns about stability in Chile. In the right's view, a powerful military and political right can perform a valuable function in deterring popular sector mobilization.

Support from the Allamand faction of the Renovación Nacional renders probable the reform package's approval. The departure of the (current) designated senators in 1997, together with General Pinochet's departure as army commander in 1998, will make additional reforms likely.

Human Rights

Following the death and disappearance of over two thousand people during the dictatorship, moral principles, a concern for deterring future abuses, public opinion, and a host of other political calculations demanded that President Aylwin address the problem of accountability for human rights violations. The Chilean case bears out the universal difficulties that resolution of this issue poses following an era of extensive abuses. For the military, having to account for past conduct strikes a raw nerve. They are willing to expend precious political capital to resist prosecution. For people who suffered the loss of family members, bringing the military to justice is more important than any other aspect of civil-military relations in the new era.

In the first year of his administration, President Aylwin set up the Comisión por la Verdad y la Reconciliación (Commission for Truth and Reconciliation) to investigate the most flagrant breaches of human rights committed between September 1973 and March 1990. The truth commission (or Rettig commission, named after chair Raúl Rettig) was charged with compiling a record of the victims—not the offenders—and recommending forms of moral and material reparation. The report's imminent release, along with investigations of corruption involving the Pinochet family and high-ranking military officials, prompted the army to make threatening gestures in December 1990. Even though the president did not call for prosecution of the guilty parties, the inquest compromised the military's authority and reputation by exposing the brutality and extent of their crimes.[28] It also provoked military leaders, who feared that the Rettig report might lead down a slippery slope to a repeal of the amnesty that the institution granted itself for abuses committed between 1973 and 1978. President Aylwin himself contended that amnesty could only be conceded after the legal establishment of guilt. The Aylwin government did not open the way for official trials to be held, but it did invite the families of victims to work through the judicial system and conduct their own trials, in which information gathered by the Rettig commission could be submitted as evidence. Many observers were surprised that Aylwin was willing to press the military even this far.

But nearing the end of his presidential mandate, President Aylwin wanted to leave office with all of the trials resolved, putting closure on a conflictual issue. In early August 1993 he announced a proposed solution to bring the trials to a speedy conclusion, known as the Ley Aylwin. This represented a compromise with the military, who wanted to see the court cases, some eight hundred, put to rest. The formula proposed by Aylwin stipulated that special judges try the military in ways conducive to rapid judgment (the standard procedures in civilian courts were invariably time consuming), that the proceedings take place in secret, and that amnesty be applied automatically for abuses committed before 1978. Whereas the president was willing to compromise with the military—especially after an army show of force in May 1993, which was motivated partially by the government's handling of human rights issues—members of his coalition in the Congress were not prepared to go so far. In late August 1993 the Socialists and the PPD blocked the proposal out of objection to the secrecy clause.[29] They argued that citizens had a right to know what took place in the trials, and that secrecy would allow the judiciary, a close ally of the military during the dictatorship, to abdicate its responsibilities once again. Human rights groups had worked hard to generate congressional objections to the Ley Aylwin. They reminded the Socialist Party, not a single member of whom broke ranks, of its long-standing commitment to defending human rights. Above and beyond their own principled commitment to human rights, politicians on the left were undoubtedly uneasy about how their constituents would react to their support for what many regarded as a *punto final* (an end point to court proceedings) in order to resolve a festering issue with the military.

Partisan interests also led the political right to block the bill. Although its members had signaled earlier that the condition of secrecy was precisely what they sought,[30] they used the occasion to deprive the president of a victory and embarrass the administration. One analysis states, "[H]aving lost to the *Concertación* in municipal elections the year before, and under pressure to coalesce as an effective oppositional force, the right wing was in no mood for compromise."[31] They refused to support a bill that would accelerate the trials, even though the military had expressed a desire to see them brought to a speedy conclusion. Unable to orchestrate conciliation, President Aylwin withdrew the bill.

Under the Frei government, the issue of accelerating the court proceedings has emerged once again. At this time, it is not yet clear how the question will be resolved. The immediate catalyst putting the trials back in the public eye was the supreme court conviction and subsequent imprisonment of retired general Manuel Contreras, former chief of Chile's secret police (Dirección de Inteligencia Nacional or DINA), and second in command General Pédro Espinoza. The two were charged with ordering the 1976 assassination of Orlando Letelier, foreign minister and ambassador to the United States under the Allende government, and his assistant. The U.S. government had put considerable pressure on Chile to pursue the case. Chilean public opinion strongly supported the imprisonment of Contreras and Espinoza. An opinion poll taken in July 1995 suggested that 65.8 percent of Chileans wanted to see the two generals go to jail.[32]

On May 30, 1995, Chile's supreme court upheld a lower court conviction of June 1994 that sentenced Contreras and Espinoza to seven and six years, respectively. This decision marked the first conviction of high-ranking Chilean officers for human rights violations and hence assumed monumental symbolic significance. Public opinion (65.8 percent of all Chileans polled) strongly supported the imprisonment of Contreras and Espinoza.[33]

Yet hours before the court issued arrest warrants on June 13, 1995, Espinoza sought refuge in an army barracks, and Contreras absconded to a naval hospital with the help of officers from the army and navy. Elements within the army and navy had seized the opportunity of withholding Espinoza and Contreras to engage in tactical bargaining maneuvers aimed at deterring prosecutions of other military men. The intention was to impede the imprisonment of Contreras and Espinoza in exchange for government concessions on the trials, such as an extension of the amnesty until March 1990 or a *punto final* law to put an end to court actions against officers charged with human rights offenses. While authorities managed to imprison General Espinoza on June 21, 1995, former Pinochet confidante Contreras eluded arrest for months.[34] Finally, in late October 1995, Contreras went to prison.

On the one hand, many regarded the imprisonment of Contreras—who had averred that he would never spend "a single day in jail"—as a victory for human rights. On the other hand, it appears that President Frei was able to enforce the sentence against Contreras only by offering concessions to the military, including a pay hike and a commitment to propose legislation to put closure on remaining court cases. (The proposed legislation does not, however, include the military's demand to extend the amnesty law to 1990.) The Senate will soon vote on a new government draft bill to speed up pending human rights cases.

The military's human rights record has been arguably the most sensitive and contentious issue facing Chile's new democracy. Civilians have made progress in this area, but it has been gradual and mixed. By exposing human rights abuses in the Rettig report, President Aylwin went further in challenging the military than many observers initially expected. But like all presidents, he sought to moderate conflict and was thus willing to adopt shortcuts to wind down the trials. Yet, similar to the case of Argentina, legislators of the president's own coalition were not so amenable to sacrificing principle in order to appease the military. They were willing to hold the armed forces to a higher standard of accountability. It remains to be seen how long they will be able to stand their ground against Chile's second postauthoritarian president, who, like his predecessor, faces military pressures to bring the trials to closure.

Budgetary Prerogatives
To ensure that their fortunes were not tied to the whims and electoral interests of civilian politicians, General Pinochet took measures to guarantee the military's fiscal autonomy before leaving power. The Ley Orgánica Constitucional de las Fuerzas Armadas guarantees that the budget of Chile's armed forces will not fall below the absolute amount they received in 1989. The armed forces have also continued to enjoy a long-standing legal entitlement to revenues from the state-owned copper company, CODELCO. During the Pinochet regime, provisions of the original law giving the military a cut of CODELCO sales were expanded. Since 1986, the armed forces have enjoyed the right to 10 percent of all copper profits, with a "floor" (minimum amount) of U.S.$180 million. In recent years, the armed forces have extracted upwards of U.S.$400 million per year from this extrabudgetary source.[35] The resources channeled to the military through the copper fund are divided equally among the three forces and designated expressly for the purchase of equipment. Because it pays for new weaponry, money from

copper has indirectly expanded the military's ability to increase the numbers and salaries of personnel.

Despite what these guarantees might suggest about the insulation of the Chilean military from civilian influences, the armed services are indeed subject to budgetary pressures that democratization has intensified. As in Brazil, military expenditures in Chile have faced heightened competition from other interests. The pressures on politicians to increase the share of nonmilitary funds may be especially immediate where political parties are weak and clientelism is strong, as in Brazil, but they are also compelling where more programmatic and better organized parties exist, as in Chile. In Chile, defense shares have declined while social expenditures have risen since the transition to democracy occurred. Defense expenditures fell steadily from 12.82 to 9.49 as a percentage of the national budget in the years between 1989 and 1993.[36] During the same period, the share of the budget devoted to social spending, such as health, housing, social security, and education, rose from 62.13 percent to 66.14 percent.[37] Civilians have tended to regard the level of (real) military expenditures of 1989, a figure they are legally required to match, as more of a ceiling than a floor.[38] From time to time, civilian politicians have also proposed reallocating money from the copper fund for education, health, and other social programs.[39]

Both of Chile's postauthoritarian governments have made equity-enhancing social programs a priority.[40] Enhancing the welfare of the underprivileged has long been a central programmatic goal of the Christian Democrats, Socialists, and other center and center-left parties of the Concertación. Beyond seeking to strengthen its own support base through public policy advances, the governing coalition sees social reforms as necessary for maintaining sociopolitical stability. Its centrist members are especially intent on preventing pent-up social demands from exploding into a populist upsurge or *desborde*.[41] Motivated by these various factors, the Aylwin government enacted reforms in taxation, health care, social security, education, and labor policy. Similarly, the Frei government has targeted health care, education, and housing as key areas for further reform.

Reforms in these areas are especially urgent in view of the neglect that Chile's poor suffered during the Pinochet era. From 1969 to 1988, the poorest 40 percent of Santiago's residents saw their income share contract from 19.4 percent to 12.6 percent.[42] This increasing inequality meant impoverishment since economic growth per capita was not impressive on average. In 1987, it was estimated that 44.4 percent of all Chileans lived in poverty.[43] Exacerbating the problem of shrinking income levels was the privatization of services in areas like health care, which effectively reduced funds available for public services. Medical facilities and services deteriorated, depriving large numbers of citizens of regular access to quality medical treatment.

Thus military spending in Chile has been subject to competition from public policies designed to address social needs, build political support, and strengthen the prospects for stability. The course of reform leading to contracting military budget shares has been gradual, reflecting a recognition of the need to maintain economic viability, as encapsulated in the government slogan "growth with equity."[44] This prudence is made possible by the organizational cohesion of Chilean political parties and the ability of party leaders to uphold long-term collective interests instead of pander to immediate popular demands.[45] It contrasts markedly with the practice that Brazil's clientelist politicians engage in of shelling out benefits in order to outdo their competitors, with little regard for long-term economic viability. Thus, even though the enactment of social reforms in Chile has worked against the armed forces in the immediate sense of lowering their budget shares, the soundness of these policies is something military leaders cannot fault. Thus, although the reforms wrought by political institutions in Chile may come about only gradually, the judicious manner in which they are enacted makes it unlikely that they will be reversed. By contrast, the military in Brazil is highly critical of the way the country's politicians choose to distribute government re sources. Not only does rampant clientelism hurt their corporate interest in higher budget shares; it also creates broader economic problems of the kind that, in combination with political fragmentation and instability, could ultimately provoke the military to step back into power.

Even in the most bounded of Latin American transitions from authoritarianism, democracy has reemerged with more vigor and resilience than an institutionalist perspective would predict. Elected civilians have managed to enact some democratizing political reforms, conduct an inquest of human rights abuses rather than accept the military's self-granted amnesty uncritically, and successfully shift the government's priorities away from military spending and toward civilian programs. The fact that these changes occurred in the first postauthoritarian civilian government and with General Pinochet at the helm of the army suggests that there will be strong and enduring pressures against residual pockets of military power. The persistence that politicians of the center and left have shown in trying to recapture Chilean democracy is impressive and bodes well for future reforms. If the center-left can gain more seats and eliminate provisions that skew the electoral system to the right, the resulting legislative composition will undoubtedly favor the further reduction of military privileges. If economic growth continues and the social order remains unpolarized, some members of the more moderate right may even let down their guard and vote with the center and center-left to ensure this result.

Indeed, the governing capabilities of civilians will ultimately be critical in determining the fate of remaining military prerogatives. So far, governance under the new democracy has militated in favor of the gradual and irreversible reduction of military power. During the Aylwin administration, economic growth averaged slightly over 6 percent per year. Annual inflation declined every year and was on average just under 18 percent. The population living below the poverty line declined from 40 percent to only 33 percent in just two years (1990–92) and most probably diminished further thereafter. Moreover, civilian consensus and demonstrations of electoral support for mainstream politicians have marked Chile's new democracy. The country appears to have avoided a regional tendency of rejecting established political parties for neopopulist leaders with authoritarian leanings.[46] If this consensual pattern continues, and there is every reason to believe it will, Chilean politicians may eventually succeed in restoring civil-military relations to their pre-1973 form.

Argentina

If my argument about electoral incentives and the capacity of elected politicians to reduce military influence applies to cases of constrained transitions like Brazil's and Chile's, it should apply a fortiori to a less constrained case like Argentina's. The balance of power that existed between civilians and the military at the inception of the new democratic regime positioned President Alfonsín (December 1983–July 1989) to pursue a tough line toward the armed forces. Because Argentine society so overwhelming repudiated the dictatorship, sensitivity to public opinion for the sake of electoral success alone pointed in this direction.[47] The sudden collapse of the military government in Argentina left the armed forces with few noncoercive mechanisms to shield themselves from civilian pressures. Moreover, many officers recognized the need to rebuild the corporation's image. These factors set Argentina apart from Chile, where a not insignificant portion of the population continues to look favorably on the Pinochet regime's accomplishments and where the political right prevents a radical dismantlement of military prerogatives. They help account for the fact that the Argentine armed forces (relative to their counterparts in Brazil and Chile) have lost the most standing since the return to civilian rule in 1983.

The Argentine military's weak bargaining position at the inception of the new democracy, compared to the military in Brazil or Chile, stemmed from the failures of the self-styled Proceso de Reorganización Nacional (Process of National Reorganization) from 1976 to 1983 and the unspeakable human rights atrocities committed by the military during that era. The junta was responsible for policies that weakened Argentine industry and produced high levels of unemployment.[48] State repression and terror led to the "disappearance" of at least nine thousand individuals. In a desperate attempt to salvage the regime, the Galtieri government undermined its image even further in a reckless decision to initiate a war with Great Britain over the Malvinas/Falkland Islands.

Radical candidate Raúl Alfonsín focused his presidential campaign on restoring the rule of law, tolerance, and human rights. Alfonsín had been a defender of human rights even before his bid for the presidency. Public opinion and electoral incentives contributed to his advocacy of democracy and constitutional liberties. Once he was elected, the need to gain autonomy from the armed forces—partly in order to make policy decisions in accordance with the needs and demands of other groups—reinforced the impulse to weaken the military politically. By emphasizing basic democratic values, the Radicals were able to "widen significantly their traditional support base, inject a level of popular mobilization unprecedented in contemporary Radical history, and finally, make the question of democracy the crucial issue."[49] By contrast, rumors of a military-union pact, on which the Unión Cívica Radical (URC) seized, hurt Peronist presidential candidate Italo Luder. General Cristino Nicolaides, commander in chief of the army during the interim government of Reynaldo Bignone, had apparently struck a deal with Peronist union leaders to respect the military's conditions for a negotiated transition. Public statements by Alfonsín's Peronist challenger that he would honor the amnesty that the military had granted to themselves gave further credibility to the charges of an alleged pact.[50]

President Raúl Alfonsín did use the favorable conjuncture he inherited, coupled with his own impressive electoral mandate, to push the military harder than attempted in any other South American country.[51] The Alfonsín government severely undercut the armed forces' political prerogatives, challenged corporate autonomy in trials against officers accused of human rights abuses, and drastically reduced defense spending. The subsequent government of Peronist Carlos Saúl Menem (July 1989–present) has basically upheld Alfonsín's efforts to curb the political involvement of the military and to keep defense expenditures in check, although it did relent on the prosecution of officers for abuses committed in the "dirty war."

Political Prerogatives

The Alfonsín administration instituted numerous organizational changes to reduce the military's political autonomy and influence.[52] Laws passed during this period transferred decision making over important policy areas—such as the military budget, defense production, logistics, and national defense policy—from the heads of the three branches of the military (downgraded from commanders to "chiefs of staff") to a civilian-led Ministry of Defense. The Alfonsín government also took away the right of the individual military services to control various defense industries and charged the Ministry of Defense with assigning civilians to supervise them. The transfer of these issues from the purview of the armed forces to civilians established an important sphere of civilian authority.

The Radical government also succeeded in passing legislation limiting the armed forces' influence over internal security. The National Defense Law, passed in 1988, forms the cornerstone of this effort. Two aspects of this law deserve mention. The first is the position it takes on impeding military participation in internal security affairs. The National Defense Law legislated a separation of the areas of national defense (defined as external defense) and internal security, putting the military in charge of the former, and making police forces and border patrols primarily responsible for the latter.[53] The new law banned the military from planning hypotheses for internal conflict and from using military intelligence for domestic purposes.

A second key aspect of the National Defense Law is its denial of a seat for the military on the Consejo de Defensa Nacional (National Defense Council). Intended to put civilians in a position to set defense priorities free of military interference, this provision prevents the armed forces from having an institutionalized role in the formulation of national defense policy. The Alfonsín government and its allies in the Congress managed to negotiate a final version of the bill that was very close to the original. Broad nonpartisan support for the basic sentiments of the proposal was important in keeping military objections in check. While possible in Argentina, the mustering of broad political support for narrowing the sphere of military influence has been difficult to achieve in Chile, where civil-military relations remain a more partisan subject.

While managing to project a more conciliatory image, President Carlos Menem has upheld most of the measures to reduce the military's political influence undertaken by the previous administration.[54] Institutional prerogatives transferred from the military to the civilian-led Ministry of Defense under Alfonsín's presidency have stayed within the Defense Ministry's purview. Provisions limiting military participation in internal security remain intact. President Menem went a step further and in 1994 eliminated obligatory military service, long esteemed by the military as a method of inculcating Argentine youth of wide-ranging social and class backgrounds with the values of the institution. The elimination of the draft came in the wake of negative publicity about hazing practices within the army, youth protests, and discussions within the Peronist party about how to attract the support of young Argentines.[55] In a March 1995 address to Congress, President Menem mentioned among his accomplishments the termination of conscription, "in line with the desire of successive generations."[56]

Relative to President Alfonsín, Menem's reasons for following this course appear to be more pragmatic than moral. Intent on enhancing his own personal power and autonomy, he does not want the military in his way. Menem seeks direct support from the electorate and tries to marginalize established power centers, including the military, trade unions, and even some powerful business sectors, similar in many ways to Fernando Collor's efforts in Brazil. Menem's combination of a populist political style and a neoliberal economic program compel him to undermine these pillars of the *patria corporativa*, the organic-corporatist organization of society envisioned by traditional Peronism.

Human Rights

The prosecution of military officers drew more attention than any other aspect of the Alfonsín government's policies toward the armed forces. As encapsulated by one observer, "The trials of the *ex-comandantes* made political and moral sense."[57] While the human rights trials would undoubtedly provoke some currents within the military, to not hold them seemed morally indefensible as well as risky politically. In the campaign, Alfonsín had announced his intention to punish junta leaders for their extensive misdeeds. Many Argentines would not easily forgive the president if this promise were broken. Moreover, many officers wanted to see the ignominious commanders of the dictatorship disassociated from the military as an institution. The absence of a figure of General Pinochet's stature facilitated the decision to prosecute.

These factors augured well for government efforts to prosecute the top brass. What impaired the success of the trials was the manner in which they were conducted. Rather than being executed quickly and stopping with junta members, the trials were prolonged and extended to unit commanders. This implicated scores of junior officers, leading many to wonder where retribution would end. Notably, members of Congress—thirty deputies from the Radical Party and the entire Renovador wing of the Peronists—wanted the trials to affect officers beyond the former junta members. The more vulnerable and hence more cautious Alfonsín sought to restrict the numbers of officers facing prosecution by passing legislation in December 1986 calling for a sixty-day limit on new indictments. But the prospect of an end point or *punto final* only led human rights groups and lawyers to drive a horde of new cases into the courts.[58] The extension of the trials downward into the ranks exacerbated civil-military conflict. Tensions came to a head in the rebellion of junior officers during Easter week of 1987. Aldo Rico, the leader of the rebellion, demanded a termination to the trials in exchange for ending the rebellion. In response, Alfonsín submitted to Congress a bill that eventually acquitted all officers at the rank of lieutenant colonel and below. The Easter week revolt and two subsequent rebellions under Alfonsín served as a reminder that even in the most favorable context for the assertion of civilian control, there are limits to how far civilians can go in confronting the armed forces without provoking a backlash.[59] But it is also important to bear in mind that had the trials not been mishandled—that is, had they been brought to a speedy close in December 1985 after the prosecution of former junta members—civilians may well have accomplished their essential and original goal.

Human rights policy constitutes the main area in which the Menem government relented on his predecessor's stance toward the military. In order to advance his own government's agenda, Menem needed to ease the civil-military tensions that erupted in the latter half of the Alfonsín administration. But he was unwilling to concede greater expenditures for defense and did not wish to grant the military greater political autonomy. Instead, President Menem sought reconciliation with the armed forces by pardoning the imprisoned leaders of the dictatorship and those who led uprisings under the Alfonsín government. Although Menem knew he would pay a political price for this gesture—since countless citizens, human rights groups, and politicians could be expected to assail it—he proceeded nevertheless. His main goal was to eliminate a festering wound in order to focus on new problems, namely, the country's severe economic crisis. Coupled with a host of symbolic measures to enhance the military's prestige, the presidential pardons did indeed have this effect. At the same time, Menem also managed to send the message that he would stand firm against military insubordination in the future by taking swift and harsh measures against a military revolt in December 1990, the only major act of insubordination launched under his tenure.

Defense Spending

Both of Argentina's presidents since 1983 have kept defense spending low. The Alfonsín government drastically reduced the military budget in relative and absolute terms. As a share of public sector expenditures, the armed forces occupied 32.3 percent in 1982, compared to 18.4 percent in 1990.[60] In 1982, defense expenditures equaled U.S.$2.203 billion. By 1991, they had fallen to $1.244 billion (in constant 1982 U.S. dollars).[61] Economic motivations, as well as political incentives, were undoubtedly part of the reason for the decline in defense spending under the Alfonsín government. Upon coming to power in 1983, Alfonsín inherited an economy wracked by foreign debt, inflation, and unemployment. But the new president was also driven to cut defense spending as part of an overall plan to diminish the standing of the armed forces, as most of Argentine public opinion demanded. The drastic reductions he imposed did severely weaken their operational capacity. By the late 1980s, finances were so tight that the work week was shortened and the capacity for training was severely undermined by insufficient resources like fuel for planes and bullets for rifles.[62]

Driven by pragmatic economic goals and electoral motivations, the Menem government has continued the trend toward lower military budgets begun under Alfonsín. The priority of the Menem government on economic adjustment and neoliberal restructuring has kept defense spending low and led to the privatization of military industries and a foreign policy stance that precludes the development or purchase of sophisticated technology to which the United States and other major powers object. When pressured by international lending institutions like the International Monetary Fund and World Bank to cut public spending, the government has tended to regard military expenditures as one of the most expendable items in the budget. Notwithstanding his less confrontational posture, Menem has done little to reverse the material losses suffered by the armed forces under his predecessor. While expanding the budget for paramilitary forces, he has continued to restrict finances for the traditional armed services. Whereas total military expenditures equaled 2.6 percent of GDP in 1989, they fell to 1.7 percent of GDP in 1993.[63] The Menem government has persisted in reducing force levels (from ninety-five thousand men in 1989 to sixty-five thousand in 1993),[64] privatizing military assets, and paring down operations. Financial constraints, coupled with international pressure, also compelled the government to jettison the Condor missile project. Some countervailing measures have been enacted to conciliate the military, such as pay raises and the diversion of revenues from the privatization of defense industries. But all in all, the Menem government has continued to restrict military spending as part of its program of restoring economic growth and stability.[65]

The economic record of the Menem government has indeed been impressive. From a rate of nearly 5,000 percent in 1989, inflation was brought down to 8 percent in 1993. High inflation, first between 1983 and 1985 and later from 1989 to 1990, had forced the majority of Argentines to live at a lower standard. From 1990 to 1993, Argentina experienced an average growth rate of nearly 8 percent per year.[66] This economic recovery in a country that had suffered through serious economic problems for at least two decades was critical in strengthening Menem's ability to gather support for a constitutional change that would allow sitting Argentine presidents to run for immediate reelection.[67] In May 1995, he was elected to a second term.

The Argentine case lends further evidence to the thesis that elected civilians can challenge a previously unwieldy military and prevail. The Alfonsín government's strategy of pushing the military to the wall, especially vis-à-vis human rights, did exceed the tolerance of an important segment of officers. But the fact that President Menem could rein in the military politically and contain defense spending—even after a group of officers had reminded civilians of their institution's coercive potential—suggests that presidents who play their cards right and preside over successful governments can hold their ground and extend civilian control in important ways. The greater involvement of civilians from various institutions in defense issues and an increasing acceptance within the military of restricted budgets and the need for military reform are sure signs of progress.[68] Many Argentine observers of civil-military relations are optimistic that civilians can keep the armed forces subordinate politically but at the same time integrate them more successfully into Argentina's constitutional order.[69]

Peru

The case of Peru since the return to civilian rule in 1980 confirms the finding that elected civilian governments can downgrade military autonomy and influence. But it also suggests that the absence of effective political institutions greatly compromises such a government's willingness and ability to check military power when serious problems develop, such as a severe economic crisis and a formidable terrorist threat. Peru's second postauthoritarian president, Alan García, took impressive steps to assert control over the military in the wake of a landslide electoral victory in 1985. García's successor, Alberto Fujimori, inherited a deep economic and political crisis, which included the expansion of the guerrilla insurgency, Sendero Luminoso (Shining Path). Fujimori has given the army a freer hand in the campaign against subversion. This has compromised his own independence vis-à-vis the military and strained the government's relationship with Washington and other international powers.

The Belaúnde Administration (1980–1985)
The Peruvian military left their governing role (1968–80) with many institutional prerogatives intact. Their standing was favorable compared to the Argentine military, though not as secure as that of the Chilean armed forces. Much of the institutional framework that developed during the military regime remained in place under Peru's first postauthoritarian president, Fernando Belaúnde (1980–85). This structure included the involvement of the Joint Command of the Armed Forces in state planning and intelligence agencies, and military participation on the National Defense Council, which had the power to define national objectives. Belaúnde also allowed the military to retain substantial autonomy in their internal affairs.[70] Since state repression during the governments of Generals Juan Velasco Alvarado (1968–75) and Francisco Morales Bermúdez (1975–80) had been limited, especially in comparison with contemporary authoritarian regimes on the continent, the new civilian government was not under pressure to take the military to task for past human rights violations.[71]

Between 1980 and 1985 there was a notable reduction in the *exercise* of the military's institutional powers even though President Belaúnde did not undertake an aggressive policy of limiting the military's role. Military influence in politics was effectively confined. Moreover, among officers themselves a professional or institutionalist position predominated, favoring a withdrawal of involvement in political and economic decision making after the divisive effects of twelve years of military rule.[72]

Defense expenditures also began to contract under the Belaúnde government, before taking a precipitous plunge under the García presidency. Whereas military spending constituted on average 24.3 percent of public sector outlays from

1969 to 1979, between 1980 and 1985 they represented an average of only 18.6 percent.[73] As a percentage of gross domestic product, defense spending began a slight decline under Belaúnde. From 1980 to 1985, military expenditures averaged only 4.19 as a percentage of GDP, down from an average of 4.73 between 1969 and 1979.[74]

The Government of Alan García (1980–1985)
If the Belaúnde government trod lightly vis-à-vis the armed forces and refrained from intervening in their internal affairs, the García administration contested them openly and tried actively to subordinate them to civilian command. Alan García won the 1985 election by a wide margin. Military leaders recognized the mandate this gave him.[75] A politician with a typical populist style, García's dynamism and personal communication skills helped him gain widespread electoral support by reaching beyond traditional APRA (Alianza Popular Revolucionaria Americana) voters. Taking advantage of Peru's weak party system, García used all means to attract electoral support, including populist appeals and large-scale patronage. His unrestrained political tactics made him highly popular in the first half of his term but soon exacerbated Peru's economic and political crisis. Whereas García initially succeeded in pushing back military influence, concern for minimal stability soon forced him to give the armed forces a freer hand. Thus, Peru's weak party system made García's early populist success possible, but also made it difficult for civilian politicians to resolve the country's severe problems, inviting a resurgence of military influence.

Like Fernando Collor in Brazil, García promised a "new beginning" in Peruvian politics. Making a break with the past included establishing civilian supremacy over the military. A confident García set out to reduce the military's institutional powers, stand up to top commanders over human rights abuses, and cut defense expenditures. The García government transferred several functions away from the military-dominated National Defense Council to the civilian Council of Ministers. This diminished the military's ability to influence decisions of broad political, social, and economic scope. García also took measures to reshape the structure of authority in the defense sector. Without negotiating or even consulting much with leading officers beforehand, the president announced in March 1987 a proposal (later approved) to create a Ministry of Defense to replace the separate service ministries. García managed to overcome military resistance—including a show of force on the part of the air force—and inaugurate the ministry. This was a celebrated accomplishment even if the appointment of an army general as the first minister diminished it somewhat.[76] In short, under García the military lost considerable capacity to exercise influence from within the Peruvian state.[77]

President García also insisted on improving human rights standards, a point of serious tension between his government and the military. Although initial plans for a developmental approach to counterinsurgency proved overly optimistic, the commitment to curbing abuses persisted. In the first year of his presidency, García conducted numerous meetings with military leaders in which the need to respect human rights was a central theme.[78] He underscored his seriousness about the matter by summarily dismissing the president of the Armed Forces' Joint Command (the nation's highest-ranking military official) and two other high-ranking army commanders after the discovery of a massacre of peasants by army soldiers in the village of Accomarca. Such a dramatic assertion of the commander in chief's authority, never seen before in Peru, was not lost on the security forces. The gesture set an important precedent. The numbers of dead and disappeared recorded from mid-1985 through 1987 were one-third the levels of the 1983–84 period, suggesting that the president's efforts had a positive effect, even though some abuses did continue to take place.[79]

President García also made sizable cuts in defense spending. As a percentage of gross domestic product, military expenditures constituted an average of 2.40 under the García presidency, down from 4.19 under his predecessor's government.[80] Similarly, as a share of public sector outlays, defense spending equaled on average 16 percent under García, compared to the 18.6 percent under his predecessor.[81] The García government kept officers' salaries at modest levels and also cut back on big-ticket items, for example, canceling an order of twenty-six Mirage 2000 fighter jets from France.[82]

García's ability to stand firm against the military and other potential challengers rested on the popularity of his government. The return to growth and the increase in real incomes that many Peruvians experienced in the first two years of the administration added to the initial electoral support the president had received. Until early 1987, the public granted García high approval ratings.[83] But his populist support was fickle. Because a sizable share of Peruvians had no underlying affinity to APRA, the durability of their support would depend on continued performance. With the reemergence of serious economic problems and the advance of Sendero Luminoso in the last two years of the García government, public support deteriorated badly, causing García to lose the upper hand he had previously enjoyed vis-à-vis the military. The government's reaction to another massacre, this time at Cayara, reflected this changing balance of power. García did not even attempt to cashier the commanders under whom the atrocities took place, as he had done two and a half years earlier.[84]

Notwithstanding signs of backtracking after mid-1987, the advances President García made to assert civilian control over the military should not be underestimated. As one prominent observer of Peru noted in 1989, "Peru's democracy—at eight years of age, extraordinarily open, inclusive, and seemingly resilient—defies the conventional social science wisdom."[85] An important contribution to democratizing Peru was García's success in weakening the military's participation over decisions of broad-ranging scope, breaking their previous monopoly over the defense sector, and holding them to higher human rights standards.

The Presidency of Alberto Fujimori (1990–present)
The failure of Peru's party and state institutions to meet the simultaneous challenges of economic crisis and guerrilla insurgency led to the victory of political outsider Alberto Fujimori in the 1990 presidential election. In April 1992, President Fujimori derailed constitutional democracy in a coup by his own hand. Political and economic conditions had deteriorated to such a point that the majority of Peruvians supported the *autogolpe* (self-coup).[86] Without organized political parties or cohesive state institutions to back the kinds of policies necessary to return the country to normalcy, President Fujimori looked to a small number of civilian technocrats and the military. In this connection, it should be emphasized that the president sought out the military as a power base, and not vice versa.[87]

As far as the structure of decision making in the defense sector is concerned, President Fujimori has not reversed or diminished much of what García achieved to extend civilian control.[88] Yet de facto and de jure military autonomy have expanded with respect to counterinsurgency, resulting in the violation of civil liberties and human rights. Due to decrees issued by Fujimori, local army commanders saw their authority extend beyond policing functions to all government activities in the emergency zones, which cover almost two-thirds of the country. Military units have the right to enter prisons and universities, strongholds of Sendero Luminoso. One decree law even declares that all Peruvian citizens may be drafted into the military or have their property and other assets seized.[89]

How did the suspension of constitutional rule and invocation of military power affect President Fujimori's standing with the Peruvian public and international community? On the one hand, the self-styled Government of Emergency and National Reconstruction is widely recognized for having made considerable progress with respect to economic problems and the guerrilla insurgency. These achievements gave President Fujimori clout to lobby for a constitutional change allowing for immediate presidential reelection, and later to win reelection. In April 1995, Peruvian voters elected Fujimori to a second term with nearly 64 percent of the vote. This reflects the great emphasis the electorate placed on political and economic stability, even though efforts to stabilize the system in Peru led to expanding military influence. Notwithstanding President Fujimori's achievements, reliance on the military as a foundation of personal rule since April 1992 has entailed political costs.

Many citizens are uneasy with the authoritarianism of the Fujimori government. Public reaction to the government's handling of a high-profile human rights case, La Cantuta, reflected concern about the degree of military impunity that has existed since the 1992 coup. This case involved a secret military court's decision in February 1994 to exonerate the military high command and mete out lenient sentences to the nine military personnel found guilty of abducting and executing nine university students and a lecturer in July 1992. The fact that a secret military court tried those accused of the killings had already produced an outpouring of public criticism. An impartial civilian investigation would almost certainly have also implicated the president's two closest military advisors, intelligence chief Vladimiro Montesinos and army commander General Nicolás de Bari Hermoza. In a poll conducted in September 1994, 48 percent of those questioned objected to Fujimori's dictatorial tendencies.[90]

Popular protests over the government's decision of June 16, 1995, to issue an amnesty to violators of human rights—liberating those military personnel in jail for the La Cantuta murders, along with anyone else implicated in the seventy-some human rights cases still pending in military courts at the time—sparked the biggest antigovernment demonstration in years and led to an immediate drop in Fujimori's popularity, from 76 to (an albeit still high) 68 percent between June 12 and 17.[91]

President Fujimori's heavy reliance on the military has also strained relations between Peru and the international community. The president is very much aware that much-needed aid and economic support depend on controlling human rights abuses. In the immediate aftermath of the April 1992 *autogolpe*, the United States, Canada, and Spain suspended most nonhumanitarian aid to Peru. International financial institutions also closed the door to the country. Although this initial posture has been relaxed, human rights remain a central condition for Peru's full reinsertion into the international financial community. Washington expressed its disapproval of the way the amnesty was handled. Fujimori is indeed caught "between the sword and the wall": he faces an army command whose members insist that "excesses" are inevitable in a war against internal subversion, yet he must minimize human rights abuses in order to receive the financial aid necessary for making the economic improvements so crucial for sustaining his standing with the electorate.

While President Fujimori has granted the military greater autonomy in the struggle against insurgency, he has kept the armed forces under relatively tight personal control overall. Drawing on his intelligence connections, intelligence chief Vladimiro Montesinos has helped subordinate the military to his will. While less concerned that President García to confine the military's sphere of influence, Fujimori seems to have more actual influence over the military than his predecessors. At present, the armed forces are subject to considerable civilian control, but this control is vested in President Fujimori as an individual, not in the presidency as an institution. Whether it can outlast the incumbent is therefore unclear.

Since 1980 Peru has gone from President Belaúnde, who did little to actively rein in the armed forces, to García, who took bold steps to reduce their autonomy, to Fujimori, who has used them as a foundation of personal rule. This variation cannot be explained by the terms of the transition away from authoritarianism or the military prerogatives in existence at the outset of civilian rule. Especially after the first postauthoritarian government, electoral institutions and the incentives and constraints they created, coupled with the broader political and economic climate, were paramount in shaping presidential conduct toward the military. Alan García, like Fernando Collor, wanted nothing to come between himself and the electorate. The highly fluid but not polarized state of Peruvian politics created incentives for García to push back the military upon coming to power. He succeeded in subordinating the military as long as his government presided over a relatively positive political and economic situation. But the actions of García's successor, Alberto Fujimori, suggest that if political and economic crises become severe enough, populist presidents in weakly institutionalized political systems find themselves hard-pressed not to knock on the barracks door, despite the complications resulting from such a course of action. A comparison between the García and Fujimori governments thus supports the argument that weakly institutionalized political systems cut both ways: under noncrisis conditions they generate especially strong incentives for elected politicians to downgrade challengers to their autonomy, including the military; yet because such systems are also highly prone to political and economic instability, politicians who once faced irresistible incentives to remove the military from political roles may well find themselves tempted to rely on the institution for support.

Conclusions on the Comparison among Cases

Figure 3 offers a rough graphic depiction of the changing status of the armed forces in the postauthoritarian contexts of Chile, Brazil, Peru, and Argentina. For simplification's sake, it refers to "levels" of military influence: this shorthand label encompasses the *range* of issues in which the armed forces interfere, the amount of influence they have on these issues, and the status of their formal prerogatives. What conclusions can be drawn from this picture?

Above all, a comparison of the four cases confirms the existence of a downward trend of military influence after the transfer of power to civilians, with the Fujimori period in Peru constituting a deviation (at least temporary) from this course. The starting point of the downward trend does have an impact on where

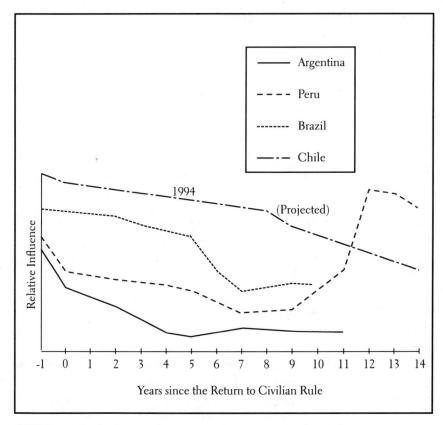

FIGURE 3. Levels of Military Influence since the Return to Civilian Rule.

the military stand a decade or so under the new civilian system. Thus for a short to medium period of time the terms of the transition from authoritarianism are an important determinant of military influence. Relative to Argentina and Brazil, countries that returned to civilian rule within two years of each other, the Brazilian military continue to enjoy higher standing than the Argentine armed forces. This accords with the relative status of the two militaries at the beginning of the civilian period.

Figure 3 also suggests, however, that initial institutional constraints do not create permanent limits to the expansion of democracy. Even where the terms of the transition from authoritarianism could not have been more advantageous to the military, as in Chile, civilians have managed to reduce the institution's influence and prerogatives. Over time, factors other than the initial level of military prerogatives gain importance and shift the institution's position. The strength of civilian institutions, and the impressive governing capabilities they confer on Chilean politicians, will help civilians overcome the disadvantages they faced vis-à-vis the military at the outset of the democratic regime. Civilian control in Chile could eventually surpass the levels attained elsewhere despite the unmatched level of institutional guarantees the country's armed forces extracted before leaving power. Conversely, after undergoing a steep decline under President Collor, military influence rose slightly under President Franco. This rise reflected the president's low public approval and inability to govern—a situation the military nearly always use to their advantage—more than it did a resurgence of the armed forces' initial strength. In short, the more distant the transition from authoritarianism becomes, the less the military's standing at the outset of the new regime affects the civil-military balance.

Two additional observations deserve mention. First, in Argentina and Brazil, two of the three cases where the military experienced some recovery after a period of decline, the upward turn in military influence appears to have been short-lived. Military influence leveled off rather quickly and then began to drop back down. Second, in the same two cases, even though the armed forces' position improved somewhat following notable losses, their standing remained far below that enjoyed in the initial postauthoritarian period. In Argentina, President Alfonsín responded to restiveness in the barracks by allowing military autonomy to expand in de facto ways toward the end of his term. Yet this expansion could not begin to make up for the armed forces' overall weakening since 1983. Following this brief period of concession, President Menem reinstated the previous policy of checking military power and curbing defense spending. Similarly, in Brazil, the height of the military's political involvement under Itamar Franco did not compare to the level of military activity under President Sarney. The range of issues in which the military interfered became visibly narrower. Under Sarney, military interference in civilian decision making extended to wide-ranging social, economic, and political matters, such as strike activity in urban areas and social mobilization in the countryside. Under Franco, leading officers focused their efforts squarely on extracting higher salaries and budgets from the government. Moreover, the window of opportunity that allowed for the application of strong-arm lobbying was brief. In roughly the last six months of Franco's presidency, the successful unfolding of the government's economic stabilization plan (Plano Real) and a corresponding rise in public support led to the cessation of saber rattling and the subsequent concessions that had marked the previous year.

Among the four cases in question, Peru constitutes the only major reversal in the diminution of military power. Peru defies the pattern displayed in Argentina, Brazil, and Chile toward a general reduction of military influence over time. The armed forces have a broader, more active and visible role under President Fujimori than under President Belaúnde. In this respect, Peru under Fujimori is an anomaly in the region. Until the Fujimori presidency, civil-military relations in Peru bore a rough similarity to the trajectory experienced in Brazil. In both countries, the first postauthoritarian governments were careful to avoid provoking the military, who had succeeded in retaining numerous prerogatives. Popular disaffection in the context of weakly institutionalized political systems created the foundation for young neopopulists to emerge (Collor and García), whose popularity rested on a platform of change, including the downgrading of military privileges. In Peru, however, the depth of the economic crisis and the unparalleled violence wrought by Sendero Luminoso led the successor government of Alberto Fujimori to reverse the process of demilitarization that García sponsored. In Brazil, although Franco did not continue Collor's campaign to advance civilian predominance, nor did he invoke military power in the way that Fujimori has. The comparison between Peru and Brazil thus suggests that a minimal level of political and economic stability is necessary for the competitive dynamic of democracy to result in the diminution of military power over time. The examples offered by Argentina and Brazil suggest that because the Fujimori government has contained the guerrilla threat, put the Peruvian economy on more solid footing, and tried to relegitimate itself through new elections, strong pressures to reduce the military's role in politics will surely arise. The clear downward slope manifested in the other cases under examination—Argentina, Brazil, and Chile— suggests that the natural tendency under stable democracy is toward an extension of civilian power. In the current era, a major challenge to the established sociopolitical order would seem to be the only condition that would prompt many politicians to sacrifice their electoral interests and expand military power in order to preserve their more fundamental stake in sociopolitical stability. Given the collapse of communism on a world scale and the rarity of large-scale domestic subversion, the emergence of such a threat is unlikely in most of the region today. Thus, there is good reason to expect that the dynamic of democracy will yield a general convergence downward in the military's stature over time.

CONCLUSION

The dynamic and expansive view of democracy advanced in this book departs from the general inclination in the recent literature on transitions to democracy to stress the limits that the military impose on democracy and underscores instead the limits that democracy places on the military. The advent of formal political democracy—that is, the introduction of democratic rules and procedures—has yielded important substantive changes in the balance of power between civilians and the military. Despite the deeply conservative tendencies of Brazilian politics and the extensive military prerogatives that survived the transition from authoritarianism, electoral incentives and popular mandates have led politicians to oppose the high command successfully over specific policy decisions and to reduce its members' ability to interfere in politics in general. The ascendance of politicians over soldiers and the advance of popular sovereignty has had consequences even for social and economic policy making, as the expansion of labor rights and the decline of defense budget shares suggest. The rolling back of military influence since 1985 has proceeded gradually and amidst countervailing forces that have temporarily checked or arrested the process. The erosion of military power has also occurred unevenly over different issues. But overall, military leaders have narrowed their political efforts from trying openly to influence broad-ranging civilian decisions to protecting preexisting corporate benefits. Indeed, they have assumed an increasingly defensive stance. Between the inception of civilian rule in 1985 and the end of the third postauthoritarian government in 1994, the decline of military influence is the overriding and most persistent tendency that has emerged in civil-military relations.

In his famous analysis of the first modern, representative democracy, the United States, Alexis de Tocqueville depicted the advance of democracy as irresistible. Democracy itself would reinforce the passion for political and civic equality, one of democracy's basic principles, which would spread to ever new spheres of the polity and erode the privileges of the old ranks and orders.[92] That the advance of democracy will be equally unstoppable in Brazil—a country characterized by profound status distinctions and burdened with the crises of development—is doubtful. Yet as this study has shown, democracy has a tendency to expand even in such unfavorable contexts and under a relatively weak democratic regime. If democracy remains a minimally viable system of governance, the competitive dynamic it unleashes can be expected to drive the military to retreat further before an emerging and advancing civil and political society.

NOTES

INTRODUCTION

1. Numerous authors have addressed these questions, including Stepan, *Rethinking Military Politics*; Agüero, "The Military and the Limits to Democratization"; Fitch, "Democracy, Human Rights, and the Armed Forces"; Loveman, " 'Protected Democracies' and Military Guardianship"; Pion-Berlin, "Military Autonomy and Emerging Democracies"; Varas, *La Autonomía Militar*; Zagorski, *Democracy vs. National Security*; and Zaverucha, *Rumor de Sabres*.

2. See Stepan, *Rethinking Military Politics*; Baretta and Markoff, "Brazil's Abertura"; Dreifuss, "Nova República"; Hagopian, " 'Democracy by Undemocratic Means'?"; Karl, "Dilemmas of Democratization"; Eliézer Rizzo de Oliveira, "Constituinte, Forças Armadas"; Zaverucha, "The Degree of Military Political Autonomy"; and O'Donnell, "Challenges to Democratization," and "Transições, Continuidades." More recently, O'Donnell observes that the mode of transition has little impact on what occurs after the first democratically elected government, and that factors unrelated to the transition process are more decisive in shaping the kind of democracy that develops in a country. See O'Donnell, "On the State, Democratization, and Some Conceptual Problems," and "Delegative Democracy."

3. A "most likely" case study is especially suited to the invalidation of a theory since a "most likely" case ought to confirm a theory if any case can be expected to. See Eckstein, "Case Study and Theory," for an explanation of how to use case studies in this way.

CHAPTER 1

1. "Military" will be used to refer primarily but not exclusively to the army, the most politically active branch of the armed forces in Brazil, historically and currently.

2. Schmitter and Karl address important aspects of this debate in "What Democracy Is and Is Not."

3. See Dahl, *Polyarchy*, 7–8; and *Dilemmas of Pluralist Democracy*, 11.

4. See Stepan, *Rethinking Military Politics*; Hagopian, " 'Democracy by Undemocratic

Means'?," 149; O'Donnell, "Challenges to Democratization," 282; and Karl, "Dilemmas of Democratization," 14, who first used the term "birth defect" in this way.

5. Other analysts who focus on the transition process in shaping the subsequent regime include Bruszt and Stark, "Paths of Extrication"; Fishman, "Rethinking State and Regime"; Karl and Schmitter, "Modes of Transition"; and Stepan, "Paths toward Redemocratization."

6. O'Donnell, "Challenges to Democratization," 282.

7. Hagopian, " 'Democracy by Undemocratic Means'?," 148, 154.

8. O'Donnell, 282.

9. See March and Olsen, "The New Institutionalism," and Thelen and Steinmo, "Historical Institutionalism in Comparative Politics," for excellent discussions of this approach.

10. Krasner, "Punctuated Equilibrium," and "Sovereignty." Another classic example of a branching-tree approach is Lipset and Rokkan, "Cleavage Structures, Party Systems, and Voter Alignments."

11. For examples of military interference in this period, see Stepan, *Rethinking Military Politics*, 103–14; and Zaverucha, *Rumor de Sabres*, 169–208.

12. The term "rational choice institutionalism" (as opposed to historical institutionalism) is sometimes used to describe the application of rational choice principles to explain how institutions develop and how they affect political and economic outcomes in turn. To avoid confusion, I will refer to this approach simply as "rational choice" instead of "the rational choice variant of new institutionalism." Examples of such work include: North, *Institutions, Institutional Change, and Economic Performance*; Shepsle, "Studying Institutions"; Cook and Levi, *The Limits of Rationality*, pt. 3; Bates, *Beyond the Miracle of the Market*; Levi, *Of Rule and Revenue*; and all the books edited by James Alt and Douglass North in the Cambridge University Press series, The Political Economy of Institutions and Decisions.

13. Ames, *Political Survival*; Geddes, *Politician's Dilemma*.

14. Chalmers, "The Politicized State."

15. Hagopian, "The Politics of Oligarchy," is an excellent analysis of the persistence of clientelism even during the authoritarian period. Mainwaring, in "Clientelism, Patrimonialism, and Economic Crisis," examines the resurgence of clientelism since the early 1980s.

16. This impulse led junior officers in 1930 to challenge the Old Republic (1889–1930) and the oligarchic elites that upheld it. It also constituted a major source of the military's opposition to the democratic political order that existed in Brazil from 1945 to 1964, in which clientelistic politicians figured prominently. The economic deterioration that clientelism produced over this period was important in leading military elites to question the viability of civilian rule and to support a leading role for technocrats in the subsequent regime. In the current period, in which the need for austerity is widely recognized, military elites often decry the squandering of state resources by self-interested civilian politicians.

17. Souza, "The Contemporary Faces of the Brazilian Right," 117–18, discusses new rhetoric and populist styles among rightist politicians in Brazil.

18. The value that Brazilian politicians place on satisfying popular opinion was demonstrated in the impeachment of President Fernando Collor. Collor's removal was a foregone conclusion once public opinion swung decisively against him and the decision was made to record legislators' votes publicly. The economic austerity that the president's neoliberal policies had imposed on the poor and middle class caused these sectors to be especially unforgiving of the president. Also fueling citizen mobilization was the public's increasing intolerance of elite impunity, a long-standing Brazilian tradition. See Weyland, "The Rise and Fall of President Collor," 5.

19. While Brazil's system of proportional representation with open party lists limits the degree to which voters can hold legislative politicians accountable, legislators do exert themselves to improve their chances of congressional reelection and prepare for executive positions (such as city mayors and state governors), which many of them avidly seek. In 1988, for example, more than one in every five legislators was willing to leave Congress for a mayoralty in his or her home state. See Power, "Politicized Democracy," 82.

20. The latitude Collor enjoyed vis-à-vis the armed forces was made more ample by the fact that he defeated a socialist-leaning candidate, Luis Inácio (Lula) da Silva, who was feared by large sectors of Brazil's civilian as well as military elite.

21. This finding is reported in "Are Brazil's Military Getting Restive?," *Latin American Weekly Report* (April 25, 1991): 6.

22. Fernando Collor received his initiation into politics in the late 1970s as an appointed mayor (*prefeito biônico*) of Maceió, the capital of the state of Alagoas.

23. See Geddes, *Politician's Dilemma*, 132.

24. Opinion surveys conducted in the last year and a half of the Franco government suggested the importance Brazilians placed on economic stabilization, even if it meant undergoing austerity in the short term. See "O Brasil Quer Paulada," *IstoÉ* (September 22, 1993): 24–28.

25. This point is noted by Ames, *Political Survival*, 44–47, 81, and 98; and Geddes, *Politician's Dilemma*, 21–23, 44, and 134.

26. Successful reelection to the Brazilian Congress is actually quite low, averaging about 40 percent. But many Brazilian legislators use their congressional positions as launching pads for executive offices (the presidency, state governors, city mayors). Building clientelist networks is important for reelection to the Congress as well as election to these other positions. The uncertainty of reelection correlates positively with the pursuit by individual politicians of patronage resources. On the calculations and strategies of Brazilian legislators, see Ames, "Electoral Strategy under Open-List Proportional Representation," and "Electoral Rules, Constituency Pressures, and Pork Barrel"; and Power, "Politicized Democracy."

27. The classic work by Mancur Olson, *The Logic of Collective Action*, contends convincingly that large groups with common interests often do not engage in collective action in the absence of individual incentives or sanctions.

28. This discussion of the weakness of Brazil's party system is based especially on Mainwaring and Scully, "Parties and Democracy in Latin America," and Mainwaring, "Brazilian Party Underdevelopment."

29. Broad socioeconomic factors certainly contribute to the weakness of Brazil's party system. Such factors include high levels of poverty, which render a large segment of the population responsive to politicians offering populist promises and limit the viability of parties that focus on ideologically driven programmatic goals. The growth of the electronic media, which enables politicians (especially chief executives) to circumvent organized politics and appeal directly to the mass citizenry has further weakened the role that political parties play in structuring Brazilian politics.

30. Informal bailiwicks (*redutos*) help legislators claim credit for the traditional and categorical patronage they distribute. This is discussed by Ames, *Political Survival*, 113; and Shugart and Carey, *Presidents and Assemblies*, 183.

31. See Ames, "Wheeling, Dealing, Stealing and Appealing," 10.

32. Ibid., 12.

33. Power uses this term in "Politicized Democracy," 81.

34. Murillo Santos, air force general, interview by author, August 14, 1989, Brasília. See also Flores, "A Sociedade e as Forças Armadas"; "Meta é Profissionalizar," *Estado de São Paulo*, August 11, 1985; and "Professor Vê Divisão das Forças," *Folha de São Paulo*, September 7, 1986.

35. This terminology is used by Anderson, *Politics and Economic Change*, 91.

36. Huntington, *Political Order*, 217.

37. A number of scholars conceptualize power in this way, including Baldwin, "Power Analysis and World Politics"; March, "The Power of Power"; and Keohane and Nye, *Power and Interdependence*.

38. O'Donnell and Schmitter, *Transitions from Authoritarian Rule*, 67.

39. In *The Military in Politics*, chap. 5, Stepan compares the dynamics of military interventions in Brazil between 1945 and 1964 and finds that the support of a significant segment of the political elite was essential in the making of a successful coup. The importance of public opinion on the military's political conduct from 1945 to 1964 is a pervasive theme in Skidmore, *Politics in Brazil*.

40. The following authors suggest the extent of public support the regime managed to orchestrate for itself: Cohen, *The Manipulation of Consent*; Geddes and Zaller, "Sources of Popular Support"; Mettenheim, "The Brazilian Voter"; and Skidmore, *The Politics of Military Rule*, 110–12. An interview I conducted in July 1992 with Octávio Costa, retired general and head of the public relations organ under the Médici government (1969–74), confirmed that even the most authoritarian of Brazil's general-presidents sought to govern through consensus as well as coercion. See Linz, "The Future of an Authoritarian Situation," for an interesting discussion about the pervasiveness of the democratic ethos in the contemporary world, a fact that leaders of authoritarian regimes recognize and devise means to cope with.

41. Most militaries, including the Brazilian, consider popular support to be critical not only for the seizure of domestic power but also for victory in war. Even when warfare is not imminent, good relations with the Congress help the military build up their arsenal.

42. Agüero examines the effect on the military of the 1989 Venezuelan riots in "Debilitating Democracy." The toll that the bloodshed of the May 1992 riots took on the Thai military is reported in "Order in the Ranks," *Far Eastern Economic Review* (August 13,

1992): 8–9. See also "March of Democracy," *Far Eastern Economic Review* (August 13, 1992): 9–10.

43. See Needler, "Military Motivations," 69–70; and Nordlinger, *Soldiers in Politics*, 65–78, for informative discussions about the institutional interests that motivate the military to seize power.

44. The literature on the 1964 coup is extensive. See Cohen, "Democracy from Above"; Dreifuss, *A Conquista do Estado*; O'Donnell, *Modernization and Bureaucratic-Authoritarianism*; Parker, *Brazil*; Santos, *The Calculus of Conflict*; Sodré, *A História Militar*; Stepan, "The New Professionalism"; and Wallerstein, "The Collapse of Democracy." See also D'Araujo, Soares, and Castro, *Visões do Golpe*.

45. Payne, *Brazilian Industrialists and Democratic Change*, 95. Only 24 percent of the industrialists Payne surveyed said they felt threatened by the left.

46. Ibid.

47. Ibid., 87.

48. During the crisis of the Collor government military leaders clarified repeatedly that they would neither advocate the president's resignation nor defend him against charges leveled by the congressional investigative committee. Collor was unable to persuade the military to repress public demonstrations in which protesters wore the color black to symbolize the demand for his resignation. See "Os Militares e o Presidente," *Estado de São Paulo*, September 3, 1992; "Longe do Barulho," *IstoÉ* (September 9, 1992): 23.

49. Data from a research project entitled "Strategic Elites, Political Culture, and Dilemmas of Development," carried out by IUPERJ illustrates this point well. Interviews conducted in Brazil between October 1993 and June 1994 of 320 individuals from four elite sectors—top public officials, elected politicians, business leaders, and union leaders—suggested virtual unanimity on the inconceivability of a return to military rule. When asked about what factors constitute the main obstacles to democracy in Brazil, not a single person chose "the threat of military intervention." The most reported answers were "low educational level of the population" (24.1 percent) and "high levels of poverty and social inequality" (23.4 percent). Reis and Cheibub report this finding in "Political Values of Elites," 12.

CHAPTER 2

1. This does not mean that differences of opinion within the officer corps do not exist. Some groups are more liberal, narrowly professionalist, and willing to leave behind the state and nation-building roles that the institution played historically. Other officers are more hard-line, conservative, and even nationalist. But it is rare that these divisions become articulated publicly. There are visible differences among groups of retired officers, some of whom are notorious for their authoritarian leanings.

2. Among the authors who note this achievement are Bacchus, *Mission in Mufti*, 43; Bruneau, "Consolidating Civilian Brazil," 982; and Skidmore, *The Politics of Military Rule*, 109. For further commentary on this issue, see "Demonstração de Unidade do Exército," *Jornal do Brasil*, August 22, 1989, p. 2.

3. The following authors emphasize these divisions: Stepan, *The Military in Politics*, especially 229–66, and *Rethinking Military Politics*, 13–29; Chagas, *A Guerra das Estrelas*; and Stumpf and Pereira, *A Segunda Guerra*.

4. Skidmore, *The Politics of Military Rule*, 109.

5. For a more in-depth discussion of these factors and the divisive impact they had on the army from 1945 to 1964, see Hunter, "Back to the Barracks?," especially 70–106; Benevides, *O Governo Kubitschek*; Flynn, *Brazil*; Peixoto, "O Clube Militar"; and Skidmore, *Politics in Brazil*.

6. Not all high-ranking officers belonged to one group or the other. Many, while sympathizing with President Vargas's attempt to institute social reforms and an economic program favoring national industry, feared the tolerance that Vargas and his allies seemed to have for the left. The *legalistas*, another group of officers, were characterized by a respect for electoral results.

7. Leading these cliques were officers such as Oswaldo Cordeiro de Farias, Juárez Távora, Eduardo Gomes, and Pedro Góes Monteiro. According to several senior officers I interviewed, the average middle-class Brazilian in this era knew of the leading personalities within the army. By contrast, their contemporary counterparts find it difficult to name anyone beyond one or two officers in the highest institutional positions of leadership.

8. For a biography on this figure, see Camargo and Góes, *Meio Século de Combate*.

9. An examination of military biographies reveals the extent of this phenomenon. An excellent source where condensed biographical information of this kind can be found is the *Dicionário-Histórico Biográfico Brasileiro, 1930–1983*, compiled and published by the Fundação Getúlio Vargas.

10. Barros, "The Brazilian Military: Professional Socialization," 404.

11. See Coelho, *Em Busca da Identidade*, 118.

12. See Bacchus, *Mission in Mufti*, xiii. Officers holding cabinet posts other than the Ministry of the Army, Navy, Air Force, and EMFA were also prohibited from active duty and appearance in uniform.

13. Linz discusses the military's concern about the emergence of a charismatic leader in "The Future of an Authoritarian Situation," 240–41.

14. For further details on the selection process, see Alves, *State and Opposition*, 106.

15. Some accounts stress ideological divergences (rather than the defiance of organizational norms) in explaining the failure of Albuquerque Lima and Sílvio Frota to reach the presidency. For example, Flynn emphasizes the fact that the former's reputation as an "authoritarian nationalist" was at odds with the internationalist leanings of the regime (*Brazil*, 425–44). Similarly, Skidmore underscores the idea that Frota's authoritarian tendencies posed a threat to Geisel's project of political opening (*The Politics of Military Rule*, 197–99). These factors undoubtedly played a role in the defeat of the two generals. The Brazilian officers I interviewed on the subject, however, tended to place greater explanatory weight on the military hierarchy's concern that Albuquerque Lima and Sílvio Frota were potential caudillos intent on defying the norm of bureaucratic leadership. A written account of this interpretation is Kucinski, *Abertura*, 67.

16. In this respect, the bureaucratic nature of the Brazilian regime contrasts sharply with the regime led by General Pinochet in Chile, who exempted junta members from

the rules of compulsory retirement. For an excellent discussion of the exceptions Pinochet made for his followers and the impact of such a policy on the army at large, see Arriagada, "The Legal and Institutional Framework," 117–43.

17. The routine capacity to remove officers selectively became especially important when President Geisel tried to rein in the intelligence community. The use of retirement regulations to rid the ranks of unsavory individuals is discussed by Kucinski, *Abertura*, 69; Skidmore, *The Politics of Military Rule*, 243; and Zirker, "Democracy and the Military," especially 599. See also "Newton Cruz na Reserva Sem a Quarta Estrela," *Jornal de Brasília*, March 28, 1985; and "Exército Exclui Ustra da Lista para Promoções," *Correio Braziliense*, July 24, 1987.

18. For a discussion of this ruling, see Viana Filho, *O Governo Castelo Branco*, 207.

19. See Wesson, *The Latin American Military Institution*, 65.

20. Oliveiros Ferreira, interview by author, December 1989, São Paulo.

21. Bacchus, *Mission in Mufti*, 101. See also Skidmore, *The Politics of Military Rule*, 151.

22. See Kucinski, *Abertura*, 49–50. There were, of course, incidents that eluded the control of the president and military leadership, the most notable being the Rio Centro affair. On the night of April 30, 1981, a bomb exploded inside a car occupied by an army sergeant and captain from the security apparatus in Rio. It was intended to detonate at a rock concert in Rio Centro; had it done so, it would have killed or injured scores of innocent bystanders. Although the general who commanded the region was dismissed, the event ended in a cover-up, which disturbed a large portion of the officer corps, including General Golbery do Couto e Silva. He responded by resigning as head of the civilian cabinet.

23. See "Militar Não Pode Falar de Política," *Jornal de Brasília*, April 20, 1979. Unless otherwise noted, all translations are the author's.

24. Excellent summaries of the doctrine of national security and its pervasive influence on officers include Stepan, *The Military in Politics*, 172–87; and Ronald M. Schneider, *The Political System of Brazil*, especially 242–53. A review of the major Brazilian military journals, such as *A Defesa Nacional* and *Revista Militar Brasileira*, quickly reveals the importance placed on this doctrine.

25. Military curricula continue to reflect the weight of this doctrine. See Brasil, Ministério do Exército, *AMAN: Plano do Ensino*; and Brasil, Ministério do Exército, *ECEME: Curso de Comando e Estado-Maior: Currículo*.

26. Comparative evidence suggests that the armed forces are able to remain more unified under regimes that perform relatively well. See Pion-Berlin, "Military Autonomy and Emerging Democracies," especially 92.

27. Military prerogatives in Brazil extend to control over activities such as civilian aviation, navigation, and the space program. For a more extensive list of military prerogatives than I cover here, see Eliézer Rizzo de Oliveira, *De Geisel a Collor*, chap. 6; Stepan, *Rethinking Military Politics*, chap. 7; and Zaverucha, "The Degree of Military Political Autonomy."

28. Santos, "Fronteiras do Estado Mínimo," 52.

29. This section on the CSN is based largely on Góes, *O Brasil do General Geisel*; Miyamoto, "Conselho de Segurança Nacional"; "Conselho de Segurança Nacional: O

Poder Deconhecido," *Visão* (August 1, 1983): 18–21; and a September 1989 interview I conducted in Brasília with General Danilo Venturini, secretary-general of the CSN under President João Figueiredo (1979–85).

30. During the Figueiredo government, the entire collegial body did not even meet once. See "Sigla Esconde Entidade com Mais Poderes," *Jornal do Brasil*, April 5, 1988.

31. The following authors discuss at length the role of the secret service under the military governments of 1964–85: Bitencourt, "O Poder Legislativo e os Serviços Secretos"; Lagoa, *O SNI*; Góes, "Militares e Política"; and Stepan, *Rethinking Military Politics*, chap. 2.

32. Decree Law 4341, of June 13, 1964, created the SNI. For a brief and informative description of Brazil's intelligence system before this, see Bitencourt, "The 'Abertura' in Brazil"; and "Inteligência Teve Início Durante o Governo Vargas," *Correio Braziliense*, July 5, 1992.

33. This came about through Decree 60.940 of July 4, 1967.

34. A minister could defy an SNI veto if he or she had the backing of the president.

35. For an elucidating chart of the intelligence and security apparatus of the military regime, see Alves, *State and Opposition*, 130.

36. For an excellent history of the militarized state police in Brazil, see Fernandes, "O Militar Como Categoria Social." See also Barros, "The Brazilian Military: Professional Socialization," 353–55.

37. The Inspetoria was created by Decree Law 317, issued on March 31, 1967.

38. See "Após 64, PMs Subordinam-se ao Exército," *Folha de São Paulo*, February 24, 1985.

39. In these elections, the opposition MDB (Movimento Democrático Brasileiro or Brazilian Democratic Movement) made important gains especially in states with large urban electorates. It almost doubled its representation in the lower house, substantially increased its numbers in the Senate, and won control over several state legislatures. Specifically, the MDB won 16 of 22 Senate seats open for dispute and increased its numbers in the assembly from 87 to 160. For details, see Skidmore, *The Politics of Military Rule*, 173; and Bruneau, "Brazil's Political Transition," 260.

40. From the time it was imposed in December 1968 until its repeal in 1978, AI-5 was responsible for the punishment of more than 1,607 Brazilians. An excellent description of executive powers under AI-5 is presented in Alves, *State and Opposition*, 80–100.

41. For a full description of this law, see Alencar, *Segurança Nacional*. The Lei de Segurança Nacional allowed military courts to prosecute civilians accused of "crimes against state security." The regime sometimes included activities like union organizing and criticizing the government in this category. Brazil entered the democratic period in 1985 with the Lei de Segurança Nacional still in existence. See Zaverucha, "The Degree of Military Political Autonomy," 285.

42. September 2, 1961, was the date of the last amnesty in Brazil.

43. Other schemes for choosing the president (besides direct elections and the electoral college option) included the selection of a "consensus candidate," and the institution of a parliamentary government from which a prime minister and president would emerge.

44. Bruneau, "Brazil's Political Transition," 263.

45. My inquiries on this subject in personal interviews with civilian elites closely involved in the transition met with reticence and evasion.

46. See Hagopian, "'Democracy by Undemocratic Means'?," 155; Eliézer Rizzo de Oliveira, "Constituinte, Forças Armadas e Autonomia Militar," 174; Stepan, *Rethinking Military Politics*, 64–65; and Zaverucha, *Rumor de Sabres*, 167.

47. Sources that affirm this include Eliézer Rizzo de Oliveira, "Constituinte, Forças Armadas e Autonomia Militar," 159; Zaverucha, *Rumor de Sabres*, 167–68; "Forças Armadas Temiam Mudanças, Diz Cardoso," *Folha de São Paulo*, May 20, 1986; and "Cardoso Diz Que Notícia do Pacto com Militares é um 'Mal-Entendido,'" *Folha de São Paulo*, May 22, 1986.

48. Of the deputies who participated in the making of the new constitution 217 had been members of ARENA in 1977. This fact is reported in Bruneau, "Brazil's Political Transition," 271, who credits Fleischer, "From Non-competitive to Competitive Elections."

49. See Eliézer Rizzo de Oliveira, "Constituinte, Forças Armadas e Autonomia Militar," 174–75.

50. See Stepan, *Rethinking Military Politics*, 65.

51. For further speculation, see Eliézer Rizzo de Oliveira, "Constituinte, Forças Armadas e Autonomia Militar," 159, 174–75.

52. See Conca, "Third World Military Industrialization," 241–42; Proença, "Tecnologia Militar"; and Centro Ecumênico de Documentação e Informação, *De Angra a Aramar*.

CHAPTER 3

1. For a biographical sketch of all Constituent Assembly members, see Rodrigues, *Quem é Quem*.

2. In response to critics, however, Sarney appointed an independent fifty-member commission, the Provisional Commission on Constitutional Studies, to prepare a draft constitution as a basis for deliberations of the Constituent Assembly beginning in February 1987. Headed by distinguished jurist and veteran politician Afonso Arinos de Mello Franco, the body became more commonly known as the Arinos Commission. Its decisions had no official bearing on the Constituent Assembly, and, in fact, the assembly disregarded many of the recommendations the commission made. For a systematic treatment of how the Arinos Commission dealt with the military prerogatives under examination here, see Hunter, "Back to the Barracks?," chap. 3.

3. "Aprendendo a Fazer Lobby no Congresso," *Relatório Reservado* (September 16–22, 1985); and "Militares Podem Selecionar Mais Seis Oficiais para Assessoria Parlamentar," *Folha de São Paulo*, March 4, 1987. It is interesting to note that the army did not even have a formal lobby until 1962. This is discussed in "Militares na Revisão Constitucional," *Correio Braziliense*, October 25, 1993. The central and expanded role that military lobbyists have played since 1985 constitutes an adaptation to the increased importance of Congress in making decisions that affect the armed forces.

4. The three army lobbyists I interviewed in Brasília between 1989 and 1992, Colonels Luiz Reis de Mello, Gilberto Serra, and José Benedito de Barros Moreira, all underscored

the importance of developing and maintaining a positive public image for the institution. Barros, "The Brazilian Military in the Late 1980s," 185, attests to the professional character of the military lobby.

5. See Brasil, Ministério do Exército, Centro de Comunicação Social do Exército, *Temas Constitucionais: Subsídios* (hereafter referred to as *Temas Constitucionais: Subsídios*). In order of appearance, this booklet addresses the internal security prerogative of the armed forces, ministerial status for the three service branches, the national security council, military justice, military control over the police, military service, and the political rights of military officers. See also "Lobistas à Paisana," *Jornal do Brasil*, April 26, 1987.

6. Sources that convey the military's position include a special issue of *Relatório Reservado* devoted to a debate among prominent military officers and academic political scientists and journalists. The encounter was sponsored by the Núcleo de Estudos Estratégicos at the Universidade Estadual de Campinas (UNICAMP). See "Os Militares e a Nova Constituição," *Relatório Reservado* (December 1986). Carvalho, "Militares e Civis," and Fortes and Nascimento, *A Constituinte em Debate*, also reveal civilian and military positions toward military provisions in the constitution.

7. See "As Forças Armadas e a Constituinte," *Jornal do Brasil*, June 18, 1987.

8. For a systematic comparison of the status of numerous military provisions at various stages before the final vote, see Brasil, Assembléia Nacional Constituinte, *Quadro Comparativo*.

9. For a list of these participants, see Brasil, Assembléia Nacional Constituinte, Comissão da Organização Eleitoral, Partidária e Garantias das Instituições and Subcomissão da Defesa do Estado, da Sociedade e de Sua Segurança, *Anteprojeto*, 3 (hereafter cited as Comissão da Organização Eleitoral, *Anteprojeto*.

10. See "Militares Não Querem Ministério da Defesa," *Correio Braziliense*, December 31, 1986; and "A Teoria do Abacaxí," *Jornal do Brasil*, May 18, 1987.

11. In fact, many officers I interviewed admitted privately that EMFA does not in fact coordinate defense functions among the branches, which remain quite independent. In recent years, EMFA has played a leading role in the joint effort among the services to pressure the government for higher salaries.

12. *Temas Constitucionais: Subsídios*, 8–10.

13. Power, "Perfil dos Ex-Arenistas," tables 24 and 25, p. 13.

14. This rationale is presented in Comissão da Organização Eleitoral, *Anteprojeto*, 28–29.

15. "As Forças Armadas e a Constituinte," *Jornal do Brasil*, June 18, 1987; "Sem Xenofobia nem Emoção," *Estado de São Paulo*, May 16, 1987.

16. For a comparison of the military's fundamental attributions over the course of Brazil's various constitutions, see Vita, *Constituição, Constituinte*.

17. See "Defesa da Ordem," *Veja* (February 4, 1987): 24. A survey of congressional attitudes conducted in 1990 suggests a relatively strong correlation between members' views on this issue and past party affiliations. Whereas 72.5 percent of all respondents affiliated with the PDS at the time of the survey or with ARENA at some point favored a constitutionally sanctioned internal security role for the military, only 38.4 percent of respondents with no association with the PDS or ARENA supported such an attribution. See Power,

"Perfil dos Ex-Arenistas." Much of this information was later published by the same author in "The Political Right and Democratization in Brazil."

18. See Hunter, "The Brazilian Military," 34, on this point.

19. Admiral Mario César Flores, military representative in the Arinos Commission, interview by author, February 17, 1989.

20. *Temas Constitucionais: Subsídios*, 6.

21. Ibid. In this connection, several Brazilian army officers I interviewed in June and July of 1992 commented on the participation of the U.S. Army in riot control after the upheavals in Los Angeles following the Rodney King decision. Many inquired about who ordered the army to act and, subsequently, who assumed direct command of the force.

22. PT deputy José Genoino spearheaded the effort to eliminate an internal security role for the armed forces. For a description of his and other legislators' amendments, see Brasil, Assembléia Nacional Constituinte, Comissão da Organização Eleitoral, Partidária e Garantias das Instituições, *Emendas Oferecidas ao Substitutivo*. See also "Sem Xenofobia nem Emoção," *Estado de São Paulo*, May 16, 1987; and "Dois pra Lá, Dois pra Cá," *Senhor* (June 23, 1987): 43–46.

23. As this author learned from a well-placed confidential source, Deputy Ricardo Fiúza invited army lobbyists to his Brasília apartment in order to draft and/or revise his subcommittee report. Thus, the similarity between the army's position and the text that emerged is not surprising. The committee's version read: "The Armed Forces, comprised of the Navy, the Army, and the Air Force, are permanent and regular national institutions, organized on the basis of hierarchy and discipline, under the supreme authority of the President of the Republic. The Armed Forces are intended for the defense of the country, for the guarantee of the constitutional powers, and for law and order" (reprinted in "As Forças Armadas e a Constituinte," *Jornal do Brasil*, June 18, 1987).

24. See "Quem Dá as Ordens? Ninguém Responde," *Jornal do Brasil*, September 6, 1987.

25. This information was received in a confidential interview in Brasília on September 1, 1989. The following article hints at this meeting and what transpired during it. See "Commissão Mantem Forças Armadas Defendendo Lei e Ordem," *Folha de São Paulo*, November 7, 1989.

26. For articles on the military's reaction, see "Forças Armadas Advertem Partidos," *Gazeta Mercantil*, August 28, 1987; "Políticos Acompanham a Reação," *Gazeta Mercantil*, August 28, 1987, p. 9; "Leônidas Rejeita Anteprojeto," *Jornal do Brasil*, August 28, 1987; and "Ameaça de Impasse Militar," *Jornal do Brasil*, August 21, 1987.

27. "Militares Mantêm Poder Sobre a Ordem Interna," *Jornal do Brasil*, November 7, 1987.

28. This is discussed in "Militares Mantêm a Garantia da Ordem," *Estado de São Paulo*, August 27, 1988.

29. See "Inalterado Papel do Militar," *Jornal de Brasília*, August 27, 1988.

30. *Constitution of the Federative Republic of Brazil 1988*.

31. Some observers have noted, however, that the constitution does not provide a precise set of procedures for civilians to mobilize the military in internal affairs. For example, Article 137, which concerns the declaration of a state of siege, a situation in which "law

and order" are presumably at risk, requires that the president gain congressional authorization. If Congress refuses, the president ("one of the constitutional powers") can circumvent the requirements of Article 137 and call in the military by invoking Article 142 on the grounds that "law and order" are at stake. Zaverucha discusses this absence of a clear command structure in "The 1988 Brazilian Constitution," 12–13.

32. Both Brizola and Franco Montoro were presidential hopefuls.

33. In a confidential interview with the author in December 1989, a former aide to Franco Montoro revealed that the SNI had put pressure on the governor to clamp down on social protest. This same source also stated that information gathered from the intelligence service of the *polícia militar* was often transferred directly to the army and SNI without passing through the hands of civilian authorities. Articles describing meetings between Governor Franco Montoro and SNI director General Ivan de Souza Mendes include "SNI: Preocupação: A Solidez da Nova República," *Jornal da Tarde*, May 21, 1985; and "A Polícia Vai Agir com Mais Rigor," *Jornal da Tarde*, May 22, 1985.

34. For example, see the campaign brochure Comitê PMDB: Candidatura pró Ulysses e Waldir, Informativo especial, "Segurança: Uma Nova Polícia Militar," July 1989.

35. This legal change (Decreto-Lei 2.010 of January 12, 1983) was published in *Diário Oficial* (January 13, 1983): 761–63. The other qualifications it imposed on gubernatorial control of the *polícia militar* were that EMFA would assume command of the *polícia militar* in case of external war or "grave disturbance" of order, and that the army could intervene in the training and preparation of the *polícia militar*. For a discussion of these changes, see "Brizola Pesou na Decisão do Governo," *Folha de São Paulo*, January 14, 1983; and "PMs Têm Controle Mais Rígido do Governo," *Estado de São Paulo*, January 14, 1983.

36. This decree was number 88.540. It was put into effect on July 20, 1983. See "Presidente Poderá Convocar as PM," *Gazeta Mercantil*, July 21, 1983.

37. This de facto system of dual command is discussed in ibid.

38. *Temas Constitucionais: Subsídios*, 18–20.

39. Subcomissão da Defesa do Estado, *Anteprojeto*. Brasília: Centro Gráfico do Senado Federal, June 1987.

40. See "PM Continua 'Força Auxiliar,'" *Jornal do Brasil*, November 7, 1987.

41. See "Tutela Sobre as PMs Irrita Governadores," *Jornal do Brasil*, September 17, 1987.

42. See "Substitutivo Prevê Desvinculação entre PM e Exército," *Folha de São Paulo*, August 16, 1987.

43. I am grateful to Bernardo Cabral's aide, António Carlos Pogo de Rego, for bringing this compromise to my attention.

44. See Brasil, Câmara dos Deputados, *Projeto de Lei no. 2.146 de 1989* (do Poder Executivo), Mensagem no. 177/89.

45. Like most sessions of the Committee for National Defense in the Chamber of Deputies, the meeting to debate this bill was open to the public. Of the many sessions I attended, this was the most acrimonious. Two informative articles on this episode are "Deputado Acusa o Exército de Querer Controlar as PMs," *Jornal do Brasil*, May 11, 1989; and "Genoino Susta Aprovação de Texto sobre PM," *Folha de São Paulo*, May 11, 1989.

46. This agency and its appropriation of congressional powers is treated in Teixeira and Vianna, *A Administração do "Milagre."*

47. The proposed composition was: the president of the republic, the presidents of the Senate and the Chamber of Deputies, the majority and minority leaders in the national Congress, one military representative (chosen by an annual rotation among the three armed forces), six representatives from civil society, two indicated by the president of the republic and four elected by the Chamber of Deputies and the Senate, and, in the event of a decision to install parliamentarism, the prime minister.

48. See Comissão da Organização Eleitoral, *Anteprojeto*, 25-26; and Comissão da Organização Eleitoral, Partidária e Garantias das Instituições, *Relatório Preliminar e Substitutivo*, 4. The committee proposals are also discussed in "As Forças Armadas e a Constituinte," *Jornal do Brasil*, June 18, 1987; and "Dois pra Lá, Dois pra Cá," *Senhor* (June 23, 1987): 43-46.

49. See "O Fim do Conselho de Segurança?," *Jornal da Tarde*, June 25, 1987; and "Conselho da República é a Inovação de Cabral," *Jornal de Brasília*, June 25, 1987.

50. Given the inclusion of military members, the National Defense Council was the more controversial of the two councils among the left. While most leftist legislators supported the National Defense Council's creation, noting it as a vast improvement over the former CSN, the PT and PC do B rejected it. See "Constituinte Extingue Conselho de Segurança," *Jornal do Brasil*, April 15, 1988.

51. Its members are the vice president, president of the Chamber of Deputies, president of the Federal Senate, majority and minority leaders in the Chamber of Deputies and the Federal Senate, the minister of justice, and six native-born Brazilians (two appointed by the president, two elected by the Federal Senate, and two elected by the Chamber of Deputies).

52. The civilians are the vice president of the republic, president of the Chamber of Deputies, president of the Federal Senate, minister of justice, minister of external relations, and minister of planning.

53. In "Um Governo Renovador," 154, Dreifuss describes the legal measure Sarney used for this purpose.

54. Informative articles on the transformation of the CSN into SADEN include "Muda o Conselho de Segurança, Mas Só de Nome," *Correio Braziliense*, September 29, 1988; and "Sarney Transforma Conselho de Segurança em Secretaria," *Folha de São Paulo*, September 30, 1988.

55. See "Para Senador, é Golpe Branco," *Estado de São Paulo*, September 30, 1988.

56. See "Instituto Pode Passar ao Ministério de Saúde," *Folha de São Paulo*, March 9, 1988; "SNI Veta a Nomeação de Angarita para Secretário da Receita Federal," *Folha de São Paulo*, February 27, 1986; "Uma Aula de Pintura e Bordado," *Senhor*, February 18, 1986.

57. Articles that reveal the far-reaching activities of the SNI under Sarney include "SNI e Pazzianotto Intermediam," *Correio Braziliense*, July 23, 1988; "General Ivan Evitou que Crise Fosse Maior," *Jornal do Brasil*, August 8, 1989.

58. In this connection, senior officers close to president-elect Tancredo Neves had indicated in early 1985 that they wanted him to contract the jurisdiction of the SNI and to re-

move the military's presence in the agency. See "Militares Querem que Tancredo Reduza Poder do SNI," *Relatório Reservado* (December 31–January 6, 1985). Also notable is the absence of any mention of the SNI in *Temas Constitucionais*, the booklet the army lobby distributed.

59. See "No SNI, Civis Ganham Menos que Militares," *Estado de São Paulo*, September 16, 1988; and "Muitos Funcionários para Pouco Serviço," *Estado de São Paulo*, September 16, 1988.

60. Bitencourt, "O Poder Legislativo e os Serviços Secretos," 112. This master's thesis, written by a prominent civilian official within the intelligence community, is the single most informative source on the ANC's treatment of the SNI. By the same author, see also "The 'Abertura' in Brazil."

61. In the absence of control over the agency, however, there is no guarantee that all personal files are revealed.

62. See "SNI Deve Mudar e Vigiar Mais Ameaças Externas," *O Globo*, November 5, 1986; and "SNI Pede Ajuda a Cientistas Políticos," *Jornal do Brasil*, July 22, 1988.

63. Individuals associated with Brazil's intelligence community, including General Agnaldo del Nero Augusto and Luis Bitencourt, have noted in personal communication with the author the need to break the automatic association many Brazilians make between information gathering by the state and military repression.

64. Genoíno participated in an attempt by the Communist Party of Brazil to establish a rural *foco* in Araguaia, a remote region of the Amazon. In 1972, the army discovered the guerrillas and then proceeded to liquidate them. By 1975, all of the guerrillas were either dead or in jail. Genoíno was imprisoned for five years.

65. "Collor Anuncia os Três Futuros Ministros Militares," *Folha de São Paulo*, January 18, 1990; and "Professor Elogia Futuros Ministros Militares," *Folha de São Paulo*, January 19, 1990.

66. Weyland, "The Rise and Fall of President Collor," 10.

67. "Secretaria Reduz em 25% o Aparato do SNI," *Folha de São Paulo*, March 28, 1990, claims that the agency was downsized from four thousand to eight hundred. "Congresso Vai Fiscalizar Atividades de Espionagem," *Jornal do Brasil*, March 15, 1992, states that it was reduced from four thousand to about two thousand. "Outro Vôo de Arapongas?," *Visão* (March 11, 1992): 10–13, estimates that 20 percent of all agency personnel were eliminated. Another report (without a comparative reference) states that Collor employed only three hundred people in intelligence functions. See "Espião de Collor," *IstoÉ Senhor* (June 12, 1991): 14–15. Many civilians employed by the SNI with less than five years in the federal bureaucracy lost their jobs altogether. Others with more seniority went to other government agencies.

68. See "Collor Decreta Fim do 'Sistema,'" *Estado de São Paulo*, April 29, 1990. According to this report, the 350 employees of the SADEN fell to 51 in the corresponding division within the SAE.

69. Ibid.

70. See, for example, "Crítica Atinge Criação de Rede no Exterior," *Estado de São Paulo*, February, 23, 1992.

71. Duarte's background is discussed in "Tensão Marca Relação entre Collor e Mili-

tares," *Folha de São Paulo*, May 11, 1990; and "Congresso Deve Fiscalizar Lado Secreto do Governo," *Jornal do Brasil*, August 5, 1991.

72. "Secretaria Reduz em 25% o Aparato do SNI," *Folha de São Paulo*, March 28, 1990.

73. See Eliézer Rizzo de Oliveira, *De Geisel a Collor*, 196; Zirker, "The Military Ministers."

74. "Como Funciona o SNI do Governo Collor," *Jornal do Brasil*, August 5, 1991.

75. Zirker, "The Military Ministries."

76. "Documento Revela Uso do Dinheiro," *Jornal do Brasil*, August 7, 1991.

77. See Krasno, "Brazil's Secret Nuclear Program," 428; "Deputado Pede Investigação de Verbas Secretas da SAE," *Jornal do Brasil*, August 5, 1991; "PT e PDT Querem Fiscalizar Verbas Nucleares Secretas," *Folha de São Paulo*, August 6, 1991; "Senado Quer Fim de Verba Secreta," *Jornal do Brasil*, April 12, 1992.

78. Brasil, Câmara dos Deputados, *Projeto de Lei no. 1.862 de 1991* (do Poder Executivo), Mensagem no. 504/91.

79. An analysis of the executive proposal by two legislators, José Dirceu and Marcelo Barbieri, expresses this opposition. Dirceu and Barbieri also maintain that Congress should be able to make inquiries about intelligence on a regular, not case-by-case basis, and that no one party or political current should dominate the legislative committee on intelligence. See Brasil, Câmara dos Deputados, *Análise do Projeto de Lei no. 1862 de 1991* (do Poder Executivo). A published source that raises some of these same points is "Outro Vôo de Arapongas?," *Visão* (March 11, 1992): 10–13.

80. See "Hoje, só Militares Têm Informações," *Jornal da Tarde*, May 31, 1991.

81. Brasil, Câmara dos Deputados, *Projeto de Lei no. 1.887 de 1991*.

82. "Eliezer Transfere Ao Seu Adjunto Ex-agentes do SNI," *Jornal de Brasília*, April 28, 1992; and "Conselho Ministerial Ficará com Funções do Antigo SNI," *Estado de São Paulo*, May 19, 1992.

83. Admiral Flores did, however, represent the most professional, nonpolitical current within the Brazilian armed forces.

84. Many of the organization's concerns are revealed in a daily internal publication, *Coletânea de Assuntos de Especial Interesse da SAE*. This consists of open source material culled for SAE analysts and policymakers. The seventeen editions I obtained were from May 1993. The domestic issues they covered included governmental corruption; relations between various presidential candidates and the military; movements for land reform; the problems of federalism; attitudes of Brazilian citizens toward politicians; inadequacies in the country's transportation system; poverty in the northeast and its effect on the rest of Brazil; restiveness within the armed forces; and reform proposals vis-à-vis the intelligence system. Over three-quarters of the articles featured topics of a more international character, including global nuclear developments; Brazil's economic relations with Argentina and Chile; U.S. interference in the Brazilian Amazon; laws about industrial property rights; defense programs of the Brazilian armed forces; Brazil's status in the United Nations; and drug trafficking in Brazil and other South American countries.

85. In fact, army leaders concerned that public sentiment might turn against the army expressed reservations about the institution's direct and prolonged involvement in the operation. See "Militares Defendem 'Intervenção Branca' no Rio," *Jornal do Brasil*, October

24, 1994; "Zenildo Promote Investigar Denuncia de Tortura," *Jornal de Brasília*, December 1, 1994; and "Exército Enfrenta Oposição para Sair do Rio," *Folha de São Paulo*, December 2, 1994.

86. The operation required the creation of a special juridical formula securing the agreement of the state (Rio de Janeiro) to federal intervention, because in principle the operation constituted an illegal intervention in state affairs. The gravity of the situation induced state authorities to endorse the use of federal troops.

87. The vast majority of Rio's residents supported the military's intervention. One poll indicated that 86 percent favored it. See "População Aprova Operação do Exército," *Correio Braziliense*, November 13, 1994.

88. President Franco also convoked the Council of the Republic and the National Defense Council in October 1994 to decide whether to decree a state of emergency and deploy army troops to combat violence and organized crime in Rio de Janeiro. Thus, Franco used the mechanisms called for in the constitution of 1988 to reduce the role of the military in deciding such matters. See "Itamar Precisa Ouvir Conselhos antes de Decidir," *Jornal do Brasil*, October 26, 1994; and "Estado de Defesa," *Folha de São Paulo*, October 30, 1994.

89. This bill was Projeto de Lei no. 4349 de 1993.

90. The entire seminar was transcribed. See Brasil, Câmara dos Deputados, Comissão da Defesa Nacional, *O Público e o Privado: As Razões e os Segredos de Estado e as Liberdades Individuais* [Seminar: Intelligence Activities in a Democratic State—The Case of Brazil], May 18, 1994; *Serviço de Inteligência em Outros Países*, May 18, 1994; *O Papel do Legislativo Brasileiro nas Questões de Inteligência*, May 19, 1994; *Serviços de Inteligência no Brasil*, May 19, 1994; *As Atividades de Inteligência Civil para o Brasil: A Perspectiva do Ministério das Relações Exteriores*, May 25, 1994; *As Atividades de Inteligência Civil para o Brasil: A Perspectiva do Ministério das da Justiça*, May 25, 1994; *As Atividades de Inteligência no Brasil: Um Breve Retrospecto Histórico*, May 26, 1994. An informative newspaper article on the conference is "Uma Lei para a Inteligência," *Jornal do Brasil*, May 30, 1994.

91. These included Congressmen José Genoino and Marcelo Barbieri, Professor Jorge Zaverucha, journalist Márcio Moreira Alves, and retired colonel Geraldo Cavagnari. Cavagnari helped found Brazil's first civilian research institute on military affairs, the Núcleo de Estudos Estratégicos at the University of Campinas. He is also the primary advisor to the PT on military issues.

92. Normally, support by three-fifths of parliament in two consecutive votes is needed to amend the constitution. During the constitutional revision, this threshold was lowered to 50 percent of members present in a single vote.

93. Several proposals, worded slightly differently, were advanced to this effect. Among them were proposals by Deputy Roberto Freire and Deputy Maurício Najar. See Brasil, Congreso Nacional, Revisão da Constituição Federal, *Apresentacão de Proposta Revisional Brasília*, numbers 014252-4 and 015065-5.

94. Ibid., number 014266-3.

95. Ibid., numbers 010289-8, 010329-6, 011014-3, 011021-7, 011489-5, and 011827-2.

96. Ibid., numbers 007694-3 and 014648-3.

97. Ibid., number 014257-2. Interestingly, a survey conducted in 1993 showed that 76

percent of legislators polled supported the creation of a unified Ministry of Defense. In 1990, the same survey was carried out and only 67 percent of legislators favored a Ministry of Defense. This change is reported in "FHC e o Ministério da Defesa," *Jornal do Brasil*, November 9, 1994. Both leading presidential candidates in 1994, Luis Inácio (Lula) da Silva and Fernando Henrique Cardoso, also expressed their support for the creation of a Ministry of Defense. See Partido dos Trabalhadores, *Lula Presidente*, 52–53; and "FHC Planeja Reduzir Ministérios para Formar Supercâmara Setorial," *Folha de São Paulo*, October 4, 1994.

98. This legislator, Maurílio Ferreira Lima, has tried since February 1992 to gain approval for a constitutional amendment extinguishing the armed forces and creating a *força de auto defesa*. He has joined with legislators from other South American countries to turn the whole region into a "non-belligerent" zone. The constitutional amendment he has tried to push through since then is published in *Diário do Congressional Nacional*, February 21, 1992, p. 1988.

99. Informative articles on the military lobby and the constitutional revision include "General Avalia Revisão da Constituição," *Correio Braziliense*, November 7, 1993; "Militares Exigem 'Tratamento Peculiar' na Revisão," *Jornal de Brasília*, December 25, 1993; "Militares Fazem o 'Lobby' Mais Ativo da Revisão," *Jornal do Brasil*, February 6, 1994; and "Lobby Militar Ganha Força no Congresso," *Estado de São Paulo*, February 8, 1994.

100. An informative article that lays out the objectives and obstacles of the unsuccessful constitutional revision is Peixoto and Rego, "A Revisão Constitutional."

CHAPTER 4

1. For an analysis of the labor legislation that Vargas introduced to co-opt a potentially independent and militant working-class movement, see Erickson, *The Brazilian Corporative State*, pt. 1; and Schmitter, *Interest Conflict*, 188–94. For a description of how the military regime sought to control the labor movement, see Mericle, "Corporatist Control of the Working Class."

2. This description of the CLT owes much to Erickson, *The Brazilian Corporative State*, pt. 1; French, *The Brazilian Workers' ABC*, chap. 5; and Collier and Collier, *Shaping the Political Arena*, 185–89.

3. The term literally refers to a hide blanket that absorbs shocks between the horse and the saddle. Schmitter, *Interest Conflict and Political Change*, 129, explains the origin of the term.

4. Analyses of how this developed include Erickson, *The Brazilian Corporative State*, chaps. 4–7; and Collier, "Popular Sector Incorporation."

5. Stepan, "Political Leadership."

6. See Anderson, "The Latin American Political System."

7. See Brasil, Lei 4.330 de 1 de junho de 1964.

8. Alves, *State and Opposition*, 51.

9. Most strikes declared legal by the labor courts after 1964 involved cases in which employers were over three months behind in paying their workers. See ibid., 52.

10. This is even admitted by one of the architects of the wage policy, Mário Henrique Simonsen. See Brasil, Ministério da Fazenda, "A Política Salarial dos Governos da Revolução," especially 80. In the period of the "miracle," the minimum wage lost 23 percent of its purchasing power. In 1979, after two years of strikes forced the government to concede wage adjustments, the minimum wage had only 61 percent of the purchasing power it had in 1960. See *Boletim DIEESE*, 14–15.

11. Alves, *State and Opposition*, 52.

12. The metallurgical workers emerged victorious insofar as they bargained directly with their employers and received an extra pay increase to compensate for the past under-estimation of inflation and the assurance that future calculations would start with this base.

13. This was by no means a unanimous view. Some leaders of the new unionism felt strongly that their energies should be focused on strengthening the organizational base of independent unions. Almeida, "*Novo Sindicalismo* and Politics," traces the evolution of the *novo sindicalismo* from a union movement to involvement in partisan politics. See also Keck, *The Workers' Party*.

14. See Brasil, Decreto Lei 1.632 de 4 de agosto de 1978, 12343–44. See also "Estudos Foram de Velloso, Prieto, Falção e Golbery," *O Globo*, August 5, 1978; and "EMFA Estuda Nova Lista dos que Não Podem Fazer Greve," *Jornal do Brasil*, August 8, 1978.

15. "Tratamento Rigoroso a Greve em Estatal," *Estado de São Paulo*, August 4, 1978.

16. The government could readily defend petroleum as essential to the country's operation, but it faced resistance in specifying banking as an essential activity. Government spokespersons maintained that functioning banking systems were fundamental to the viability of large industrial economies, with everything from workers' salaries to foreign exchange being linked to banks. Apart from this justification, the inclusion of banking was undoubtedly related to the militancy of this sector and the predominant role it played in the new labor movement. See "Atividade Bancária Não é Essencial," *Estado de São Paulo*, August 5, 1978; and "Apoio de Prieto Não Reduz Críticas à Lei de Greve," *Jornal do Brasil*, August 6, 1978.

17. See "Geisel Define Onde Greve é Intolerável," *Jornal de Brasília*, August 5, 1978.

18. The first National Security Law was issued (as Decree Law 314) on March 13, 1967, and was modified thereafter to conform to the changing tenor of the regime. See Alves, *State and Opposition*, 319.

19. Ronning and Keith discuss this in "Shrinking the Political Arena," 231.

20. See "Apoio de Prieto Não Reduz Críticas à Lei de Greve," *Jornal do Brasil*, August 6, 1978.

21. See "FIESP Quer Mudar Lei de Greve," *Jornal do Brasil*, August 5, 1978.

22. For a discussion of ARENA's strategy, see "Arena Manobra e Não Vota Lei de Greve," *Jornal de Brasília*, September 14, 1978; and "Lula Critica Atitude dos Arenistas no Congresso," *Folha de São Paulo*, September 15, 1978.

23. "Lei de Greve Tem Aprovação," *O Globo*, September 15, 1978; "Proibição de Greve Vai ao Plenário," *Jornal de Brasília*, September 15, 1978; "ARENA Mantêm o Boicote," *Folha de São Paulo*, September 28, 1978.

24. Articles that discuss the regime's selective application of existing laws include "Gov-

erno Envia Projeto," *Folha de São Paulo*, June 4, 1983; and "A CUT è Ilegal, mas . . . ,"
Gazeta Mercantil, August 19, 1983.

25. See Partido do Movimento Democrático Brasileiro, "Esperança e Mudança," 21–22, 27–30. This manifesto was passed in August 1982, before the elections of that year.

26. Skidmore, *The Politics of Military Rule*, 289.

27. It was mainly generals in the army ministry, the SNI, and SADEN (and not the navy or air force leadership) who mobilized over this question. This division among the service branches would undoubtedly strengthen the capacity of civilians to advance labor reforms.

28. Roughly 15 percent of Brazilian workers are unionized. See Schneider, "Brazil under Collor," 332.

29. For an overview of the new unionism, see Keck, "The New Unionism."

30. This and other findings from the same survey are reported in Muszynski and Mendes, "Democratização e Opinião Pública," 63.

31. Sandoval, "Labor Unrest in the 1980s," 14.

32. See "O Dedo do SNI," *Senhor* (May 29, 1985): 65.

33. For an expression of the army's viewpoint, see "Ainda Há Velhos Fantasmas em Brasília," *Senhor* (May 8, 1985): 31–34.

34. This is discussed in "SNI Faz Relatório sobre Greves," *Estado de São Paulo*, September 10, 1986.

35. As this author noticed, the ESG library contained several unpublished papers on labor issues in the New Republic written by students who had attended the ESG course "Curso de Altos Estudos de Política e Estratégia." See, for example, Arruda, "Direito de Greve," and Irene Heller Lopes da Silva, "Direito de Greve."

36. Initially, Labor Minister Pazzianotto also enjoyed support among widespread sectors. See "Pazzianotto: Prestígio em Alta," *Relatório Reservado* (October 14–20, 1985): 2.

37. Cruz, "Empresários, Economistas e Perspectivas." Military leaders were not as concerned about the organizational framework of the labor movement as they were about strikes. For example, they voiced little objection over proposals to eliminate the obligatory union tax and requirement that only one union represent workers in a single trade per territorial jurisdiction.

38. See "Pazzianotto Quer Reduzir Setores Onde Greve é Ilegal," *Folha de São Paulo*, August 1, 1985.

39. For a description of the proposal, see "O Que Muda com o Projeto de Lei do Governo," *Veja*, July 30, 1986.

40. Military personnel remained an exception.

41. Payne, "Working Class Strategies," 223–24.

42. See "Dura Negociação Nos Temas Trabalhistas," *Gazeta Mercantil*, June 8, 1987.

43. DIAP was formed in 1978, a decade before the constitution of the New Republic was signed. One of its first demands involved expanding the right of workers to strike.

44. Payne, *Brazilian Industrialists and Democratic Change*, 99–101, reports that 91 percent of the industrialists she surveyed regarded labor in this light.

45. See "Empresários Vão aos Militares," *Correio Brasiliense*, July 8, 1988.

46. See Brasil, Assembléia Nacional Constituinte, Comissão da Ordem Social, and Subcomissão dos Direitos dos Trabalhadores e Servidores Públicos, *Anteprojeto*.

47. See "Dura Negociação Nos Temas Trabalhistas," *Gazeta Mercantil*, June 8, 1987.

48. See "Comissão Vota por Unanimidade Artigo Mantendo Direito de Greve," *Folha de São Paulo*, October 17, 1987.

49. This point emerged clearly in an August 11, 1989, interview I conducted with two army lobbyists, Luis Reis de Mello and Gilberto Serra.

50. For a report of the army minister's remarks, see "Os Militares e a Constituinte," *Jornal de Brasília*, June 26, 1987. See also "Empresário Apóia os Militares," *Estado de São Paulo*, June 27, 1987.

51. In *Brazilian Industrialists and Democratic Change*, 106, Payne notes that business groups contributed to a fund totaling $35 million to defeat the job security measure.

52. See Articles 6–11 of the *Constitution of the Federative Republic of Brazil 1988*.

53. For a breakdown of how constitutional delegates voted, see Brasil, Assembléia Nacional Constituinte, *Diário da Assembléia Nacional Constituinte*, 7874–76. Among the "não" votes were many of Brazil's archconservatives. An article that discusses this vote is "Garantido o Direito de Greve e Vetada a Pluralidade Sindical," *Gazeta Mercantil*, March 2, 1988.

54. See "Garantido o Direito de Greve," *Gazeta Mercantil*, August 17, 1988. An incident that occurred during the presidential campaign of 1989 underscores the fact that it was reasonable for politicians to consider the electoral impact of how one voted on labor issues. DIAP had documented and published the voting records of all presidential candidates who had been Constituent Assembly members. It assigned an "F" or *nota zero* to Guilherme Afif Domingo from the Liberal Party (PL) based on his voting record on labor-related issues. Afif's competitors seized the opportunity to denounce him on this count. The most vociferous of them was Fernando Collor. With the DIAP document in hand, Collor blasted Afif on national television as an enemy of Brazil's long-suffering working class. Afif ended up with only 4.8 percent of all valid votes. This incident is analyzed in Gurgel and Fleischer, *O Brasil Vai às Urnas*, 83–86.

55. After sensing the mood in the Constituent Assembly with respect to this issue, the army lobby informed the army leadership that its only hope was to maneuver a strategy to postpone the vote, but that this would only delay the inevitable.

56. See "Militares Temem Aumento de Greves com Direitos da Nova Constituição," August 18, 1988, *Folha de São Paulo*.

57. See "Generalização de Greve Inquieta Militares," *Relatório Reservado* (August 22–28, 1988): 2.

58. As early as November 1988 the high command had prodded Sarney to issue an emergency measure to discourage strikes. Two factors prevented him from doing so. First, leaders of the new unionism threatened not to participate in the economic pact with the government and business under consideration at the time should the government put forth such a measure. Second, Sarney and his advisors expected that Congress would be more likely to endorse an ordinary bill (*projeto de lei*) proposing moderate restrictions on strikes rather than a presidential decree, which carried connotations of heavy-handedness on the part of the executive.

59. This *medida provisória* (MP 50) was published in its entirety in the *Jornal do Brasil*, April 28, 1989.

60. João Silveira, aide to Senator Ronan Tito, clarified their dilemma for me.

61. It should also be mentioned that the newly appointed minister of labor, Dorothea Werneck, also objected to MP 50. Part of her objection stemmed from the fact that President Sarney, under prodding from other cabinet ministers, had circumvented her authority as labor minister in formulating the *medida provisória*.

62. The new *medida provisória* had the number 59.

63. In this connection, Guimarães had already taken Tito to task for his support of another unpopular measure: to de-link social security benefits from the minimum wage. This incident is discussed in "De Novo, um Ataque ao Bolso," *Veja* (May 31, 1989).

64. The new law was published in Brasil, *Diário do Congresso Nacional*, 2188–89. For a point-by-point comparison of the new strike law to the government's proposal, see "Veja o Que Muda com a Nova Lei," *Jornal de Brasília*, June 23, 1989.

65. For a list of deputies and how they voted, see Brasil, *Diário do Congresso Nacional*, 2181–82.

66. The left's reservations are discussed in "Congresso Aprova Lei de Greve Mais Branda," *Correio Braziliense*, June 23, 1989.

67. "Ocupação Visa Mostrar Que Greves Não Serão Admitidas," *Folha de São Paulo*, March 12, 1987.

68. For a report of the military's protest, see "Nova Onda de Greves Preocupa o SNI," *Estado de São Paulo*, March 7, 1987; and "Ocupação Visa Mostrar Que Greves Não Serão Admitidas," *Folha de São Paulo*, March 12, 1987.

69. See "Sarney Chama o Urutu," *Veja* (March 18, 1987): 20.

70. See "Políticos Debatem Ação Militar," *Gazeta Mercantil*, March 12, 1987.

71. See "A Ordem Militar Não Altera o Produto," *Jornal do Brasil*, November 24, 1988; and "Eleições Mantêm o Grupo de Lula como Tendência Majoritária do PT," *Folha de São Paulo*, November 28, 1988.

72. A good description of the army's involvement at Volta Redonda is contained in Zaverucha, "The 1988 Brazilian Constitution."

73. "Generais Divergem de Ação de Exército," *Jornal do Brasil*, November 23, 1988.

74. See "Collor Anuncia os Três Futuros Ministros Militares," *Folha de São Paulo*, January 18, 1990; and "A Chegada dos Outros Inquilinos No Poder," *Jornal do Brasil*, March 16, 1990.

75. See "Greve em Setor Essencial Terá Resposta Dura," *Relatório Reservado* (September 10–16, 1990); "Collor Ouve Medeiros e Não Muda Lei de Greve," *Jornal do Brasil*, May 8, 1991.

76. See Collor, *Brasil: Um Projeto de Reconstrução Nacional*, 71.

77. See "Operação Bananeira," *Veja* (May 18, 1994): 18–21; and "Radicais Livres," *IstoÉ* (May 18, 1994): 18–22.

78. The results of this survey are given detailed coverage in "Direitos Trabalhistas Devem Mudar Pouco," *Folha de São Paulo*, October 17, 1993; and "Congresso Está Dividido sobre Aposentadoria," *Folha de São Paulo*, October 17, 1993.

CHAPTER 5

1. For example, Stepan, *Rethinking Military Politics*, 72; and Eliézer Rizzo de Oliveira, "Constituinte, Forças Armadas e Autonomia Militar," 159.

2. For an informative discussion on the relationship between modernization and professionalism, see Pion-Berlin and López, "A House Divided," 67.

3. See Norden, "Democratic Consolidation and Military Professionalism"; and Pion-Berlin, "Between Confrontation and Accommodation."

4. This is a central theme of Ames, *Political Survival*. Downs, *An Economic Theory of Democracy*, also views budgetary politics in these terms. The analysis presented here follows Downs's conception of budgetary decision making under the majority principle, 69–70.

5. Mainwaring, "Clientelism, Patrimonialism, and Economic Crisis," 12.

6. Despite the impressive level of sophistication it has attained for a developing country, the Brazilian defense sector employs only about fifty thousand workers. See Conca, "Third World Military Industrialization," 148. In this same study, Conca notes that many previous studies overstated considerably the size and financial importance of Brazil's arms industry. Similarly, in "The Politics of Arms Production," 220, Acuña and Smith underscore the enclave nature of Brazil's arms industry, namely, its failure to generate greater employment and spillover effects on civilian technology.

7. Conca, "Third World Military Industrialization," 158–59.

8. This rule is embodied in Article 166, paragraph 3 (I and II), of the constitution of 1988.

9. The framework for this analysis comes from Olson, *The Logic of Collective Action*.

10. Variations on this general logic exist. Legislators with presidential aspirations, and those from districts with a high concentration of constituents associated with the military, are more likely than other legislators to support defense spending. And there may be some legislators who are willing to risk electoral loss to support systemic needs. It should also be noted that my approach to understanding the decline of military budgets applies less in contexts where Congress by and large rubber-stamps budgets designed by executives, a common practice in many South American countries.

11. As noted previously, although the constitution bans immediate reelection to the presidency, ex-presidents in Brazil often continue to run for political office. For example, former president Sarney ran successfully for federal senator in 1990 and was a precandidate in the presidential race of 1994. The large-scale patronage he distributed as president helped lay the groundwork for these candidacies. It has also helped support the political fortunes of many of his family members.

12. The work of Ames, *Political Survival*, chap. 4, sheds light on this previous period of Brazilian democracy.

13. Ames points out that while all elected governments try to influence elections through public spending, Latin American governments tend to concentrate their efforts on doling out political patronage rather than enhancing overall macroeconomic results, as in advanced industrial democracies. See *Political Survival*, 9–33.

14. For a description of congressional budgetary powers in this period, see Baaklini, *The Brazilian Legislature*, 140–42.

15. Ames, *Political Survival*, 110. The armed forces' share in this figure is defined as the

total of all the military ministries and other military programs divided by the sum of all central government expenditures.

16. The military budget also tended to rise slightly in the first year of most governments.

17. Ames, *Political Survival*, 46.

18. Ibid., 65.

19. Stepan, *Rethinking Military Politics*, 57.

20. For a description of the limits the military regime imposed on congressional budgetary powers, see Baaklini, *The Brazilian Legislature*, 142–44; and Ronning and Keith, "Shrinking the Political Arena," 291.

21. When computing the military's budget share it is necessary to make some corrections to keep a constant baseline over time. Above all, spending not attributed to any public agency (*encargos financeiros da União, transferencias a estados, districto federal e municípios, reserva de contingencia*, etc.) needs to be excluded from the budget total because it incorporates the internal and external debt service, which increased greatly in the 1980s. I also exclude spending by the Ministry of Labor and Social Security because the constitution of 1988 incorporated in this ministry's expenditures the huge social security budget that had before been independent. After these corrections are made, defense expenditures stipulated in the federal budget law (*despesa fixada*) constituted an average of 29.88 percent of the federal budget from 1965 to 1975, and 18.76 percent from 1976 to 1985 (or 18.3 percent and 8.1 percent of the total, uncorrected budget, respectively). These data were compiled from Brasil, Secretaria de Planejamento e Coordenação da Presidência da República, *Anuário Estatístico do Brasil*, 1964–85. For figures (based on other sources) that depict the decline in military expenditures as a percentage of GNP during the latter period of authoritarian rule, see Stepan, *Rethinking Military Politics*, 73.

22. See Brasil, Instituto de Planejamento Econômico e Social, Directoria de Programação, *Retrospecto das Finanças da União, Tesouro Brasil 1970–1985*, 1987, p. 29.

23. In this connection, Grindle notes that all of the "bureaucratic-authoritarian" regimes showed some degree of restraint vis-à-vis military spending. She attributes this to the broader economic goals of the military officers that led these regimes and to the fact that they were well positioned to impose restrictions on the armed forces. See Grindle, "Civil-Military Relations," 269–70.

24. Cammack, "The 'Brazilianization' of Mexico?," 306. See Cammack, "Clientelism and Military Government in Brazil," for a discussion of how the military regime revived patronage politics to bolster its own standing.

25. Skidmore, *The Politics of Military Rule in Brazil*, 273.

26. Doubtless an additional, albeit difficult to measure, way democracy has reduced funds for the military is through increased corruption. Facing uncertain prospects of reelection, politicians have systematically used their posts for personal benefit.

27. The World Bank and IMF are discouraging countries in the region from investing heavily in the armed forces. In a similar vein, Robert McNamara proposed eliminating Latin America's armed forces and replacing them with United Nations troops in order to divert billions of dollars into economic development. The resentment of the Brazilian armed forces toward external pressure of this kind is discussed in "Flores Denuncia Pressões do Bird," *Jornal do Brasil*, May 22, 1992.

28. These data were compiled from Brasil, Secretaria de Planejamento e Coordenação da Presidência da República, *Anuário Estatístico do Brasil*, 1982–93. The same corrections made for earlier years, described in note 21, apply to this time period. Without these corrections (that is, by including social security spending and the government's internal and foreign debt service, which greatly increased during the 1980s, in the budget total), the budget share of all other types of expenditures is artificially compressed and the decline of military spending is vastly overstated. This is actually something the military do in order to strengthen their case. For example, if left uncorrected, the military's budget share in 1993 falls to 2.5 percent (instead of 14.27 percent).

29. It should also be noted that since such a large percentage of the military budget is spent on personnel and basic operating costs, small variations can have an appreciable impact on re-equipment and modernization programs.

30. The International Institute for Strategic Studies, *The Military Balance 1993–1994*, 227.

31. U.S. Arms Control and Disarmament Agency, *World Military Expenditures 1993–1994*, 55.

32. Two army lobbyists I interviewed in August 1989, Gilberto Serra and Luis Reis de Mello, admitted to being somewhat surprised by which legislators showed a greater inclination to back defense spending. For example, they pointed to PT deputy José Genoino, a consistent critic of the military's political prerogatives, as a solid supporter of funding for "professional" military pursuits.

33. See the following transcripts of these hearings: Brasil, Câmara dos Deputados, *O "AMX": Desenvolvimento e Construção de Aeronave de Ataque*; Brasil, Câmara dos Deputados, *A Marinha e a Defesa Nacional*; and Brasil, Câmara dos Deputados, *O Programa "VLS"-Veículo Lançador de Satélites*.

34. For this purpose, the navy prepared a document that compares defense expenditures across time and across countries. See Brasil, Ministerio da Marinha, "Orçamento das Forças Armadas: Quadros Comparativos." Brazilian military expenditures appear especially modest when expressed as a percentage of GDP.

35. Navy Minister Mário César Flores stated in a July 1992 interview with the author that lack of legislative interest led the committee twice to cancel a scheduled presentation in which he was to appear. Discouraged and somewhat insulted by this treatment, he threatened to call off the session entirely in the event of a third cancellation.

36. For a discussion of the role of the private arms lobby, see "Deputado Quer Formar Lobby para Aumentar Verbas das Forças Armadas," *Folha de São Paulo*, November 1, 1989.

37. For a discussion of these conflicts, see Conca, *Global Markets, Local Politics, and Military Industrialization*, chap. 7; and Franko-Jones, *The Brazilian Defense Industry*, chap. 8. See also Acuña and Smith, "The Politics of 'Military Economics,'" 13–17; Conca, "Technology, the Military, and Democracy," 167; Mauricio Broinizi Pereira, "Tiro Pela Culatra," 6–9; and "Urutus e Urubus," *IstoÉ* (October 27, 1993): 71.

38. The budgetary powers of Congress are covered in Articles 165 and 166 of the constitution of 1988. Figueiredo and Limongi, "O Processo Legislativo"; Longo, "O Processo Orçamentário"; and Serra, "A Crise Fiscal," provide useful explanations of the new bud-

getary procedures. For a discussion of the veto process, see "Veto Parcial de Sarney Poderá ser Derrubado," *Gazeta Mercantil*, January 3, 1989.

39. An exception to Congress's right to shift shares of the budget concerns the (considerable) portion of the budget devoted to the payment of the internal and external debt.

40. See Ames, "Wheeling, Dealing, Stealing, and Appealing," 3.

41. Figueiredo and Limongi, "O Processo Legislativo," 33.

42. Interviews with three individuals in particular helped me understand legislative and executive strategies toward defense spending under the Sarney government. The first of these interviews was conducted in Brasília in June 1989 with Deputy César Maia, vice president of the congressional budget committee. The latter two were done in July 1992 with Dalton Castello Branco, a *técnico* of SOF (Secretaria de Orçamento e Finanças or the Budget and Finance Secretariat) and João Ricardo C. de Souza, a legislative aide who specializes in military affairs.

43. See "Ameaça de Cortes," *Relatório Reservado* (October 17–23, 1988): 8; and "Orçamento: Leônidas Ataca," *Relatório Reservado* (December 5–11, 1988).

44. See "Orçamento de 90 Privilegia Militares," *Jornal do Brasil*, October 3, 1989, p. 1. This executive budget proposal assigned the military ministries (collectively) more money than any other single ministry.

45. "Comissão Vota Hoje Corte Nos Gastos dos Ministerios Militares," *Folha de São Paulo*, November 7, 1989. See also "Soldier Lobbyists Fight for Funds," *Latin American Weekly Report* (November 30, 1989): 5.

46. In particular, they proposed shifting shares away from the air force's subsonic fighter and the navy's nuclear submarine program. "Caça às Verbas: Deputados Fazem Emendas para Garantir Seus Votos," *IstoÉ Senhor* (November 15, 1989): 50.

47. See "Tinoco Justifica Corte em Gastos Militares," *Estado de São Paulo*, November 2, 1989.

48. See Weyland, "Democracy and Equity."

49. Although Sarney's action pushed legal boundaries and violated the widely recognized need for serious fiscal austerity, few legislators contested it because many of them also benefited from the funds he released. See "Sarney Muda Orçamento de 88 e Agrava Crise," *Relatório Reservado* (October 17–23, 1988): 8.

50. See "Verbas Militares: Sarney Cede a Pressão," *Relatório Reservado* (October 30–November 5, 1989): 8.

51. See "Pressões por Gastos Levam o Governo a Se Dividir," *Jornal do Brasil*, October 22, 1989; and "Congresso Em Fim de Festa Aprova Gastos," *Jornal do Brasil*, December 11, 1989. Such conduct brought Sarney criticism in the press, but may have furthered his own narrow political goals. Even after Sarney's appallingly poor presidential performance, he managed to win a Senate seat for himself, help two of his children be elected as congressional deputies in the Sarney family's home state of Maranhão, and make a fair showing as a precandidate in the 1994 presidential race.

52. "Forças Armadas Querem Reativar o Calha Norte," *Correio Braziliense*, October 26, 1992.

53. For a general description of how budget cuts under the Collor government affected the armed forces, see "A Caserna no Sufoco," *IstoÉ* (July 21, 1993): 34–41. For information

on an army survey conducted in 1992, which revealed 38 percent of all army servicemen to be engaged in second jobs, see "Moonlighting to Survive," *Latin American Regional Report–Brazil Report*, June 4, 1992, p. 3.

54. In 1991, the amendments presented involved a total of some U.S.$6.7 billion. Notably, the head of the budget committee, João Alves, authored an inordinate number of amendments proposing projects in his own electoral base. He was later subject to charges of corruption. See "A Máfia Dos Anões," *Veja* (October 23, 1991): 36–39.

55. See "Para Uso Ornamental," *Folha de São Paulo*, July 6, 1992. The leader of this effort, Deputy Israel Pinheiro, sought to divert some of these newly available funds to works in his electoral district.

56. See "Orçamento de 93 Não Inclui Verbas Secretas," *Jornal do Brasil*, December 8, 1992.

57. On congressional efforts to monitor this money, see "PT and PDT Querem Fiscalizar Verbas Nucleares Secretas," *Folha de São Paulo*, August 6, 1991; and "Deputado Quer Comissão para Fiscalizar Verba Secreta," *Jornal do Brasil*, August 8, 1991.

58. Salary parity among the branches (*isonomia*) would provide generals, legislators, and judges with roughly equal pay. Without *isonomia*, low-skilled employees of the Congress and judiciary earn far more than many military officers. The options for resolving this problematic situation are limited. A drastic upward increase of military pay is untenable given Brazil's financial situation, especially since fairness would mandate granting higher wages to all employees in the executive branch, not just the military. At the same time, the constitution prohibits the alternate option: a reduction of wages in the other two branches. For a discussion of this thorny issue, see Franko, "De Facto Demilitarization," 53.

59. Collor decreased the expected increase of 95.7 percent to 81 percent, the amount awarded to civilians. Given the tremendous inflation Brazil has experienced in recent years, these amounts are not as high as they may initially appear. See "Sem Privilégio," *IstoÉ Senhor* (December 26, 1990): 23.

60. The previous accord was signed in 1952 and endured until 1977, when the Geisel government abrogated it in reaction to U.S. pressure over human rights abuses. The military vehemently opposed a renewal of the accord for fear that it would shut down Brazil's already ailing domestic arms industry, whose development was spurred when the former accord was severed. This point was raised by many officers I interviewed in June and July of 1992. See also "Panelaço Em Marcha," *IstoÉ Senhor* (May 1, 1991): 20.

61. "Marcílio Promete Mais Verbas para o Exército," *Folha de São Paulo*, May 29, 1992.

62. "Governo Quer Recompor Plano Plurianual," *Correio Braziliense*, June 20, 1992.

63. Budget data in this series for 1994 are not yet available.

64. I present this figure to underscore the greater priority given to pork barrel spending over military spending. It would be incorrect to see this figure in terms of the budget series presented earlier, which is calculated from a different base. The continuation of patronage politics under the Franco presidency is discussed in "Um Atraso Federal," *Veja* (February 24, 1993): 18; and "Buraco no Caminho," *IstoÉ* (April 7, 1993): 24–25.

65. See "O Estado Empreitado," *Veja* (November 3, 1993): 36–40.

66. See "A Festa Continua," *IstoÉ* (July 13, 1994): 24–25.

67. On this incident, see "O Cumplô Mundial contra os Soldos," *Veja* (May 19, 1993): 22–23; and "Batalha Pelos Soldos," *IstoÉ* (May 19, 1993): 33.

68. See "Acordo com a Caserna," *IstoÉ* (May 26, 1993): 33. Several months later, Franco managed to extract a guarantee that sizable concessions be distributed over the course of 1994–98 to help all three service branches maintain their central strategic projects and purchase new arms and equipment. For details, see "Fim do Regime," *IstoÉ* (March 2, 1994): 67.

69. "Arrumem um General," *Veja* (May 26, 1993): 30–31.

70. "Congresso Recebe Orçamento Dia 2," *Jornal do Brasil*, April 22, 1994.

71. See Hunter, "Contradictions of Civilian Control," for a discussion of this problem.

72. The problem in this regard is not simply the amount spent on the military but its unpredictability. Projects begun under the expectation of future funding have been intermittently interrupted and resumed according to immediate political criteria rather than long-term planning and reasoned judgment. The officer corps as well as government technocrats in SOF have called attention to the senselessness of interrupting expensive projects in midcourse by denying them funds for political reasons. See "Orçamento de 90 Está Vulnerável, Diz Parente," *Folha de São Paulo*, November 26, 1989.

CHAPTER 6

1. For a quintessential geopolitical perspective of the region, see Golbery do Couto e Silva, *Geopolítica do Brasil*.

2. Fifty-nine percent of all of Brazil's territory lies within Amazônia. The border of the Amazon extends for nine thousand kilometers. For these and other dimensions, see Pompermayer, "The State and the Frontier," 89.

3. This principle was established with the Treaty of Madrid, which supplanted the Treaty of Tordesillas. See Tambs, "Geopolitics of the Amazon," 61.

4. See Therezinha de Castro, "Amazônia," 25; and Burns, *A History of Brazil*, 232–33.

5. See Bahiana, *As Forças Armadas*, 45; and Tambs, "Geopolitics of the Amazon," 77.

6. Hecht, "Cattle Ranching in Amazônia," 370–71.

7. By 1988, cattle ranches established under SUDAM's auspices covered a total of 8.4 million hectares. The average ranch equaled 24,000 hectares. See Mahar, "Government Policies and Deforestation," 12–15.

8. See Davis, *Victims of the Miracle*, 36, 90, 91.

9. The colonization project was largely unsuccessful. While the government succeeded in attracting large numbers of settlers to the region, the level of financial and technical assistance it provided the settlers was insufficient to compensate for problems like poor soils, difficult access to markets, and lack of storage.

10. Under the PIN, the one hundred kilometers of land along the federal highways (on each side) and along Brazil's borders became subject to federal control. Similarly, unclaimed lands previously under the control of individual states became the jurisdiction of the federal government. The administration and occupation of federal lands in the Ama-

zon rested with the National Security Council. Under Decree Law 1.164, the National Institute for Colonization and Agrarian Reform (INCRA), the agency assigned to mediate land disputes and to award titles, became subordinated to the National Security Council. See Bunker, *Underdeveloping the Amazon*, 109.

11. A particularly effective tactic to mobilize attention was to bring forest dwellers to international forums, where they related the hardships they had been forced to endure. The case of Chico Mendes is illustrative. Chico Mendes was a rubber tapper who had become head of the rubber tappers union in the state of Acre. North American groups, such as the Environmental Defense Fund, the World Wildlife Fund, and the Wildlife Federation, arranged for Mendes to testify at various international conferences. In 1987, Mendes was awarded a United Nations prize for promoting extractive reserves as a way to conserve the forest. When ranchers murdered Chico Mendes in December 1988, his death provoked an international outcry.

12. One of the first cases of this type involved the Northwest Brazil Integrated Development Pole. In March 1985, the World Bank suspended funds for the project. Heated controversy also surrounded the IDB and the paving of the BR-364 highway into the state of Acre. When the Brazilian government failed to comply with the environmental conditions it demanded, the IDB withdrew the loan in 1987.

13. The accusation of advanced countries trying to "freeze" the current structure of power is not unprecedented or limited to Amazon issues. It also finds expression in arguments defending Brazil's opposition to signing the Treaty for the Nonproliferation of Nuclear Weapons. See João Augusto de Araujo Castro, "The United Nations."

14. This coalition had also been instrumental in impeding agrarian reform in the Sarney government. It is important to note, however, that not the military but Brazil's agrarian elites and their formidable political and economic resources played the leading role in blocking the passage of proposals for land reform in the Sarney administration.

15. See Brasil, Ministério do Interior, *Projeto Calha Norte: Desenvolvimento e Segurança na Região ao Norte das Calhas Dos Rios Solimões e Amazonas*. See also Allen, "Calha Norte: Military Development"; and the volume edited by João Pacheco de Oliveira, *Projeto Calha Norte*.

16. Wood and Schmink, "The Military and the Environment," 99. See also "Sarney Destina a Mesma Terra a Exército e Índios," *Folha de São Paulo*, September 27, 1989.

17. See Albert, "Indian Lands." It is estimated that more than half of the nine thousand surviving members of the Yanomami have contracted diseases from contact with miners from 1987 to 1990.

18. See Articles 231 and 232 of the *Constitution of the Federative Republic of Brazil 1988*. See also Allen, "Brazil: Indians and the New Constitution."

19. See "Para Leônidas, Cultura Indígena é Baixíssima e Não é Respeitável," *Folha de São Paulo*, April 20, 1989.

20. The issue of demarcation has a long and complex history. The central criterion for demarcation has to do with usage patterns. Demarcation has been employed as a means to protect Indians as well as control them. Nevertheless, indigenous rights activists feel strongly that demarcation is essential for the cultural survival of indigenous groups. In re-

gions where land rights have not been secured, Indians have been subject to devastating diseases and violent encounters with intruders.

21. "Justiça Preserva a Reserva Original," *Folha de São Paulo*, February 17, 1990; and "Igreja e Políticos Saem em Defesa dos Índios Yanomami," *Gazeta Mercantil*, January 12, 1990.

22. See "Sarney Libera NCr$15 Mi para Funai Atender aos Ianomami," *Folha de São Paulo*, December 7, 1989.

23. See "Sarney Atende a Militares e Cancela a Viagem a Holanda," *Jornal do Brasil*, March 3, 1989.

24. See "Governo Brasileiro Desautoriza o Anuncio da Declaração de Haia," *Folha de São Paulo*, April 5, 1989.

25. Nine other countries, including Bolivia, Chile, and Costa Rica, had entered into such arrangements when they were proposed to Brazil during the Sarney government. "Troca da Dívida por Proteção à Natureza é Opção para o Brasil," *Jornal do Brasil*, November 6, 1989.

26. "Militares Recusam Fundação," *Jornal do Brasil*, March 9, 1989; "Denys: Ajuda Externa So Através de Doação," *Correio Braziliense*, April 7, 1989.

27. See "Relacões Brasil-EUA na Era Bush," *Folha de São Paulo*, January 8, 1989; and "Divida Externa: As Malvinas de Sarney," *IstoÉ Senhor* (June 14, 1989): 40–44.

28. For a discussion of the pressures exerted by NGOs on the lending decisions of the development banks, see "Brazil's Thriving Environmental Movement," *Technology Review* (October 1990): 45; and Rich, *Mortgaging the Earth*, 289.

29. Hecht and Cockburn, *The Fate of the Forest*, 120.

30. See Arnt and Schwartzman, *Um Artifício Orgânico*, 283–90, for a brief description and assessment of IBAMA.

31. Hurrell, "The Politics of Amazonian Deforestation," 209, briefly summarizes its limitations.

32. See Arnt and Schwartzman, *Um Artifício Orgânico*, 288.

33. See, for example, "Calha Norte é Condenado em Relatório à ECO-92," *Jornal de Brasília*, June 21, 1991.

34. "Ecologia de Resultados," *IstoÉ Senhor* (June 5, 1991): 22–26; and "Guerra dos Babacas," *Veja* (September 11, 1991): 76–77.

35. See "Governo Prioriza o Meio Ambiente," *Jornal do Brasil*, March 22, 1990.

36. Barbosa, "The 'Greening' of the Ecopolitics," 125.

37. Before Collor assumed the presidency in March 1990, he traveled to Europe and to the United States. During his visit to the United States, Collor and his aides were surprised to discover that the preoccupation of U.S. officials about the Amazon rain forest nearly equaled their concern over the external debt.

38. Hurrell, "The Politics of Amazonian Deforestation," 213.

39. See Goldemberg and Feiveson, "Denuclearization"; Krasno, "Brazil's Secret Nuclear Program"; and Redick, "Latin America's Emerging Non-Proliferation Consensus."

40. For articles about Lutzenberger, see "Ambientalistas Decidem dar Apoio à Gestão de José Lutzenberger," *Folha de São Paulo*, March 13, 1990; and "José Lutzenberger Aceita Secretariado e Propõe Diálogo entre Países," *Gazeta Mercantil*, March 5, 1990.

41. "Forças Armadas Serão Convocadas para Impedir Queimadas e Garimpos," *Gazeta Mercantil*, March 23, 1990.

42. From March 1990 to March 1991 (the first year of the Collor government), the rate of burning fell significantly. In relation to the year before, deforestation in the central Amazon region was reduced by approximately 50 percent and in other regions of the Amazon was reduced by 70 percent. In 1990, IBAMA collected the equivalent of U.S.$9 million in fines, 60 percent more than collected in the previous year under the Sarney administration. See "Measures to Stem Amazon Deforestation Assessed," Foreign Broadcast Information Service-LAT-91-026, February 7, 1991, pp. 33–34; "Pace of Amazon Region Deforestation Declining," FBIS-LAT-91-071, April 12, 1991, p. 28; and "Tensão Marca Relação entre Collor e Militares," *Folha de São Paulo*, May 11, 1990.

43. Albert, "Indian Lands," 61.

44. This won him great applause in the international press. See, for example, "Brazil Ends Orders That Cut Amazon Tribes's Land," *New York Times*, April 21, 1991.

45. Two weeks before, Collor approved seventy-one other Indian reserves, covering a total of 42,471 square miles.

46. Rabben, "Demarcation—and Then What?," 12.

47. In a June 1992 interview with the author, Jarbas Passarinho (then a senator) noted the difficulty of gaining congressional as well as military support for the measure. Deputies and senators from Amazonian states were its main congressional opponents. They had economic aspirations for the region and resented federal government interference in their states. Congressional concern about the Amazon is reflected in a parliamentary investigation (CPI) on the "Internationalization of the Amazon." See Brasil, Câmara dos Deputados, Comissão Parlamentar de Inquérito, *Relatório Final*.

48. In the same June 1992 interview with the author, Jarbas Passarinho emphasized that the 1988 constitution, which stipulates that Indians be returned to areas from which they are removed for emergency purposes, restricted what he could do legally to meet the army's demand of keeping the Yanomami out of the twenty kilometers of land on the border. This restriction is stated in Article 231, paragraph 5, of the *Constitution of the Federative Republic of Brazil 1988*.

49. "General Não Ve Risco Externo sobre Amazônia," *Folha de São Paulo*, January 12, 1992.

50. "Plano Ecológico de Collor Prevé Recrutamento Civil," *Jornal do Brasil*, September 21, 1990.

51. See "Collor Viaja para Ver Calha Norte," *Estado de São Paulo*, March 22, 1990.

52. The omission of civilian entities led to charges that the military had come to exercise complete domination over Calha Norte. Minister of the Navy Mário César Flores stated this in a July 1992 interview with the author.

53. See "Flores Diz Que Calha Norte Acabou," *Jornal do Brasil*, August 13, 1993. In a June 1992 interview with the author, FUNAI director Sydney Possuelo claimed that the military's de facto ability to control the northern border region was reduced appreciably by the budgetary squeeze on Calha Norte.

54. Sydney Possuelo, interview by author, June 1992.

55. A Yanomami rights group, the Comissão pela Criação do Parque Yanomami (Committee for the Creation of the Yanomami Park or CCPY), puts out a regular newsletter that frequently features stories of the health problems of the Indians. See Comissão pela Criação do Parque Yanomami-CCPY. Newsletter.

56. Albert, "Indian Lands," 60–61. In a July 1992 interview with the author, anthropologist João Pacheco de Oliveira attested to the disproportionate care given to the Yanomami. He attributed this partly to the media hype surrounding their plight.

57. On the movement of troops to the Amazon, see "A Floresta Verde-Oliva," *IstoÉ* (April 13, 1994): 40–42.

58. These incidents include a series of skirmishes between Brazilian soldiers and Colombian gold miners and guerrillas in 1991, a massacre of Yanomami Indians by gold miners in 1993, and, in the same year, jungle training exercises conducted by the U.S. Army in neighboring Guyana, which led to rumors that the United States was constructing military facilities bordering on the Brazilian Amazon.

59. See "PCB Tem Tarefa para Militar," *Jornal do Brasil*, April 22, 1989.

60. See "Forças Armadas Querem Reativar o Calha Norte," *Correio Braziliense*, October 26, 1992; and "Calha Norte Ganha Força No Governo Itamar," *Jornal do Brasil*, November 2, 1992.

61. See Brasil, Secretaria de Assuntos Estratégicos, *Sistema de Proteção de Amazônia*.

62. See Oswald, "Brazil's Amazon Protection System."

63. In fact, controversy and accusations of wrongdoing surrounding SIVAM led to the resignation of the air force minister and a senior presidential advisor in the first year of the Cardoso government.

64. "A Ocupação Tecnológica," *IstoÉ* (March 2, 1994): 62–66.

65. On this incident, see "Selvageria de Brancos," *IstoÉ* (August 25, 1993): 70–79; "Pouca Luz na Selva," *Veja* (September 1, 1993): 28–29; and "Massacre Exagerado," *IstoÉ* (September 9, 1993): 30. The killings attested to the fact that even on a reserve of 9.4 million hectares, the Indians remain vulnerable without the enforcement of judicial decisions. Two major operations to remove *garimpeiros* (gold miners) took place under the Franco government. These operations involved FUNAI, federal police, and the armed forces. See "A Resistencia na Selva," *Veja* (June 2, 1993): 61.

66. "Direitos dos Índios Na Mira da Revisão," *Jornal do Brasil*, February 12, 1994.

67. "Emenda Quer Resguardar a Amazônia," *Jornal de Brasília*, December 25, 1993.

68. Personal communication with Ana Valéria Nascimento Araújo Leitão, *assessora jurídica* (legal aide) for the Núcleo de Direitos Indígenas, September 19, 1994.

69. "O Abacaxi Amazônia," *IstoÉ* (September 29, 1993): 5–7.

CONCLUSION

1. For a clear explanation and rationale of this strategy, see Huntington, *The Soldier and the State*, 83–85.

2. The phenomenon of the "new professionalism," whereby the most technologically

advanced militaries of Latin America assumed power amid the social upheavals of the 1960s and 1970s, suggests that professionalism alone will not prevent the military from engaging in politics. See Stepan, "The New Professionalism."

3. See, for example, "As Fardas Falantes," *Veja* (December 15, 1993): 38.

4. See "Um Eterno Retorno," *IstoÉ* (July 29, 1992): 28–30.

5. See "Caso Lilian Desencadeia Pressão dos Militares," *Jornal do Brasil*, February 22, 1994; and "Ressaca Sem Fim," *IstoÉ* (March 2, 1994).

6. Fitch notes the existence of this phenomenon in Ecuador and Argentina as well. See "Military Role Beliefs in Latin American Democracies: Context, Ideology, and Doctrine in Argentina and Ecuador," 67–68.

7. Brasil, Ministério do Exército, *ECEME: Curso de Comando e Estado-Maior: Currículo* (1994), 10 and 12.

8. For a full list of these appointments, see "Tucano e Quepes: Reforma Ministerial Fortalece FHC e Militares," *IstoÉ* (March 9, 1994): 26. See also "Itamar Chama a Guarda," *IstoÉ* (March 30, 1994): 34–39. For a discussion of material concessions that Franco made to the armed forces, see "Acordo com a Caserna," *IstoÉ* (May 26, 1993): 33.

9. See "Aos Milicos, com Carinho," *IstoÉ* (January 5, 1994): 23. Notably, perhaps more than these appointments and other minor concessions, the saber rattling witnessed from roughly mid-1993 until mid-1994 subsided markedly as the economy improved and the military supported the presidential candidacy of Fernando Henrique Cardoso, who as former finance minister "represented" the government against the candidacy of socialist Luis Inácio (Lula) da Silva.

10. This compares, for example, with 6.5 percent of Argentine respondents and 19 percent of Chilean respondents who listed "combating crime" as their first choice. See *Latinobarómetro 1995*, questions P68 and P69.

11. See Chile, *Ley Orgánica Constitucional de las Fuerzas Armadas*.

12. The present discussion of the constitution and attempts to reform it draws heavily on the following sources: Constable and Valenzuela, "Chile's Return to Democracy"; Ensalaco, "In with the New, Out with the Old?"; Loveman, "¿Misión Cumplida?"; and Geisse and Ramírez Arrayas, *La Reforma Constitutional*. The book by Geisse and Ramírez systematically presents specific provisions of the 1980 charter and proposals of the democratic opposition to reform them.

13. For an excellent overview of the National Security Council see Atria, "El Consejo de Seguridad Nacional." For a succinct discussion of the authority the 1980 constitution granted the council, see Ensalaco, "In with the New, Out with the Old?," 423.

14. Loveman, "¿Misión Cumplida?" 42, describes the context in which Pinochet made this statement.

15. The final vote was 54.7 percent to 43 percent. Reforming rather than dismantling the 1980 constitution was the best that the democratic opposition could do since the maintenance of the charter was a central condition Pinochet extracted before agreeing to hold the 1988 plebiscite.

16. Aylwin earned 55.2 percent of the vote. Büchi came in second with 29.4 percent. The third candidate, Francisco Javier Errázuriz, who ran on a populist platform, came in last with 15.5 percent.

17. Had the Senate consisted of only elected officials, the Concertación would have enjoyed a 22 to 16 majority. But the presence of the designated senators (eight, following the death of one) gave the right-wing opposition a two-seat edge.

18. See "Consejo de RN Criticó a Los Senadores Disidentes," *El Mercurio*, January 23, 1993.

19. Articles that discuss this incident include "'Terremoto Grado Diez," *Hoy* (November 16–22, 1992): 10–13; "PS Propone Sancionar Relaciones de Espionaje entre Políticos y Militares," *Las Ultimas Noticias*, November 16, 1992; and "RN a la Justicia Militar," *Hoy* (November 30–December 6, 1992): 10–13.

20. See "Piñera Respalda a Allamand en Ley de FF.AA.," *La Época*, December 3, 1992.

21. Most political actors make calculations vis-à-vis more than one arena. For example, politicians participate in both the parliamentary and electoral arenas. The notion of nested games, or a network of games, is described in Tsebelis, *Nested Games*, 7–9, 160.

22. See "Juegos de Guerra," *El Mercurio*, November 4, 1990; "Aylwin Impone Su Autoridad," *Que Pasa* (November 5, 1990): 12–16; and "La Tensa Noche del Miércoles 31," *Hoy* (November 5–11, 1990).

23. See "Carabineros Lose Military Status," *Latin American Weekly Report* (November 15, 1990): 11.

24. See "No Part for Army in Anti-Terrorist Unit," *Latin American Regional Reports–Southern Cone*, May 30, 1991, p. 6.

25. Chile's second postauthoritarian president discovered firsthand that a government that cannot cashier a top military commander lacks control over one of the basic instruments of state power. This occurred over a crisis about the permanence of Chile's chief of police, General Rodolfo Stange, after new information implicated him in covering up the murder of three communist activists in 1985. For a discussion of the Stange case, see "¿Quién Manda a Quién?," *Hoy* (April 25–May 1, 1994): 16–18; and "Caso Stange: Locademia de Policía," *Hoy* (May 16–22, 1994): 8–11.

26. There is ample sentiment among center-left politicians to reform these provisions. See PAL (Programa de Asesoria Legislativa), "Proyecto de Ley que Modifica las Leyes Orgánicas Constitucionales."

27. In an interview with the author on February 9, 1995, in Santiago, Marco A. Riveros Keller, advisor to the RN party leadership, noted this.

28. *Estudios Públicos* published a reprint of the Rettig report and the armed forces' official response to it. See Comisión Nacional de Verdad y Reconciliación, *Informe de la Comisión Nacional de Verdad y Reconciliación*; and Las Fuerzas Armadas Chilenas *Respuestas de las Fuerzas Armadas y de Orden al Informe de la Comisión Nacional de Verdad y Reconciliación*.

29. On their objections, see "Viera-Gallo Pide al Gobierno que Considere la Posición del PS-PPD," *Las Ultimas Noticias*, August 23, 1993; "Manifesto La Senadora Laura Soto: La Ley Aylwin Está Totalmente Erosionada," *El Mercurio*, August 26, 1993.

30. See "Advierten Senadores de RN: La Ley Aylwin sin la Norma Del Secreto en un Absurdo," *El Mercurio*, August 21, 1993.

31. Pion-Berlin and Arceneaux, "Tipping the Civil-Military Balance."

32. Reported in "Army Rallies around Espinoza While Government Counts on Pinochet," *Latin American Regional Reports–Southern Cone*, August 10, 1995, p. 1.

33. "No Se Ha Logrado Plena Reconciliación Nacional," *El Mercurio Edición Internacional*, July 20–26, 1995.

34. See "Caso Contreras: Dos Estrategias para la Moneda," *Hoy* (June 19–25, 1995): 8–11.

35. For a description of the evolution of the arrangement between the military and CODELCO, see Rojas, "Chile y el Gasto Militar"; and Patillo, "Evolución y Estructura de Gasto."

36. Chile, Ministerio de Hacienda, Dirección de Presupuestos, *Estadísticas de las Finanzas Públicas, 1989–1993*, 59.

37. Ibid.

38. Felipe Agüero, personal communication, March 2, 1994. In light of declining budget shares, the military jealously guard the 10 percent cut they receive from copper sales. Top commanders frequently assert that their modernization programs would be arrested if the armed forces were to lose access to these funds. See "'No Hacemos Propuestas, sino Sugerencias," *Hoy* (May 30–June 5, 1994): 29.

39. See "CUT Pide Bajar Gasto Militar," *La Nación*, May 2, 1992; and "Ley Reservada del Cobre Debe Ser Eliminada, Afirmó Ministro Hales," *La Época*, December 20, 1992.

40. For an overview of government programs to increase equity among the population, see Chile, Ministerio de Planificación y Cooperación, *Avanzando en Equidad*. See also Ritter, "Development Strategy," especially chap. 5.

41. Alejandro Foxley, academic economist and minister of finance under the Aylwin government, articulates this concern in *La Economía Política de la Transición*, 7, 17.

42. Ffrench-Davis, "Desarrollo Económico y Equidad," 41.

43. CEPAL, "Una Estimación de la Magnitud de la Pobreza en Chile, 1987," especially 110.

44. The following government document outlines the Concertación's plan to reconcile considerations of economic growth with social welfare. See Chile, Ministério de Hacienda, Ministerio Secretaría General de Gobierno, *Crecimiento con Equidad*.

45. See Weyland, "'Growth with Equity.'"

46. Munck, "Democratic Stability," 7.

47. Wide-ranging social groups, including business and labor, came to oppose the military. At the outset of the civilian regime, 85 percent of the urban population had a negative image of military leaders, compared with 84 percent that had a positive image of political parties. See Catterberg, *Argentina Confronts Politics*, 56 and 93. For additional survey data on citizens' attitudes toward the military, see Fontana and Llenderrozas, "Resumen Encuesta"; Fraga, *La Cuestión Militar*, 239–59; and Murillo, "Argentina: Breaking the Praetorian Cycle," 9. For a direct comparison of public opinion in Chile and Argentina toward the military, see "Chilenos y Argentinos Opinan de Sus FF.AA," *La Nación*, October 18, 1992.

48. See Smith, *Authoritarianism and the Crisis of the Argentine Political Economy*, 224–66.

49. Cavarozzi, "Political Cycles in Argentina since 1955," 47.

50. For a more in-depth description of the alleged military-union pact and a discussion of its electoral effect on the Peronists, see López, *Ni la Ceniza Ni la Gloria*, 43–49; and McGuire, "Interim Government and Democratic Consolidation," 189–92. Adding to reservations about Luder's candidacy was the association of his party with the decision made by the Peronist government of Isabel Perón to sign decrees authorizing the military to annihilate leftist guerrillas and opposition forces.

51. Alfonsín won 52 percent of the vote, whereas the Peronists obtained only 40 percent.

52. This section draws on Huser, "Reforma Militar y Revisión del Pasado"; López, *Ni la Ceniza Ni la Gloria*; Norden, "Between Coups and Consolidation," chap. 4; and Pion-Berlin, "Between Confrontation and Accommodation."

53. President Alfonsín later put forth a decree opening the way for greater military participation in putting down internal disturbances, provided that the security problem exceed the capacity of the police and other civilian security forces. This decree came in the wake of the incident at La Tablada, in which a radical leftist group, the Movimiento Todos por la Patria, attacked an infantry regiment on January 23, 1989.

54. Much attention has been paid to the creation by Menem of a security agency (Secretaría de Seguridad y Protección a la Comunidad) to oversee the federal police, the maritime and river police, and the border police in emergency situations, thus removing the former from the Interior Ministry and the latter two from the Defense Ministry and placing them directly under the president. The rationale for the "super-secretariat" was that the government needed a central authority to respond quickly to regional uprisings and terrorist attacks. While the concentration of authority in a single agency is understandably disconcerting to many Argentines, the super-secretariat is squarely under the president's personal control and is directly answerable to him. It is not an example of creeping military autonomy.

55. Public opinion surveys suggested that by 1994, only 25 percent of all Argentine citizens favored the continuation of compulsory military service. For a breakdown of public opinion on this issue, see "Sondeo Favorable a la Eliminación del Servicio Militar Obligatorio," *La Nueva Provincia*, October 2, 1994. See also "Rebeldes con Causas," *Página 12*, May 28, 1994; "FF.AA. Acatan Fin de Servicio Militar Anunciado por Menem," *La Época*, June 12, 1994; and "Abolirán el Servicio Militar en Argentina," *El Mercurio*, June 11, 1994.

56. See Republica Argentina, "Mensaje Presidencial," 20.

57. Pion-Berlin, "Between Confrontation and Accommodation," 560.

58. Norden, "Between Coups and Consolidation," 211, reports that approximately four hundred new names were added to the list of those to be tried.

59. These rebellions are discussed and analyzed in Norden, "Between Coups and Consolidation," chaps. 5 and 6; Pion-Berlin and López, "A House Divided"; and Sain, *Los Levantamientos Carapintada*.

60. These figures on military expenditures are presented in Scheetz, "Military Expenditures in South America," table 4.

61. Ibid., table 5.

62. For a discussion of how budgetary restrictions affected the Argentine armed forces, see Fitch, "Military Role Beliefs in Latin American Democracies"; and Norden, "Democratic Consolidation and Military Professionalism."

63. U.S. Arms Control and Disarmament Agency, *World Military Expenditures and Arms Transfers*, 52.

64. Ibid.

65. See Franko, "De Facto Demilitarization," 44–50.

66. For these and other figures on the Argentine economy, see *Indicadores de Coyuntura* 329: 4; and Powers, "The Politics of Poverty in Argentina," 3.

67. See "Argentine Senate Backs Menem on a Second Term for President," *New York Times*, December 30, 1993; and "Menem Gains in Bid for New Term in Argentina," *New York Times*, April 14, 1994. See also Jones, "Argentine Public Opinion and Constitutional Reform."

68. For an interesting assessment of changing attitudes within the military, see Fitch, "Military Role Beliefs in Latin American Democracies." See also Fontana, "Argentine Security Interests and Perspectives," and "Percepciones Militares Acerca del Rol de las Fuerzas Armadas."

69. For such a view, see Fontana, "Argentine Security Interests and Perspectives," and "Percepciones Militares acerca del Rol de las Fuerzas Armadas."

70. Agüero, "The Military and Limits to Democratization," 158–59.

71. For an analysis of the transfer of power to civilians in Peru, see Cotler, "Military Interventions."

72. See Obando, "El Poder de los Militares," 79–80. Obando adds that had Sendero Luminoso not advanced so rapidly in the early 1980s, leading the Belaúnde government to cede increasing responsibility to counterinsurgency forces, the army may well have found its role restricted even further.

73. Scheetz, "Military Expenditures in South America," table 4.

74. Ibid., table 5.

75. The percentage of the *valid* vote (not counting null and void ballots) that García obtained was 53.1 percent. But since García failed to receive "50-percent-plus-one" of the *total* vote, the threshold defined for victory in Peru, a second round of voting would have been necessary had the main opposition candidate (Alfonso Barrantes from the Izquierda Unida) not conceded the election to García. For an informative discussion of the rise of Alan García and the election of 1985, see Crabtree, *Peru under García*, chap. 3.

76. On the creation of the Defense Ministry, see Agüero, "The Military and the Limits to Democratization," 158–59; and Crabtree, *Peru under García*, 111.

77. A strong expression of this perspective is Obando, "El Poder de los Militares."

78. See Mauceri, "Military Politics and Counter-Insurgency."

79. See McClintock, "The Prospects for Democratic Consolidation," 134.

80. Scheetz, "Military Expenditures in South America," table 5.

81. Ibid., table 4.

82. See McClintock, "The Prospects for Democratic Consolidation," 134.

83. For a graph that depicts García's changing popularity over time, see Crabtree, *Peru under García*, 159.

84. For a discussion of this incident, see ibid., 204.

85. McClintock, "The Prospects for Democratic Consolidation," 144.

86. Throughout 1992, Fujimori could claim an approval rating of 60 percent or higher. See McClintock, "The Breakdown of Constitutional Democracy," 1.

87. Ibid. In this regard, it should be noted that a large number of institutionalist officers—those seeking to keep the military out of conflictual domestic situations for the sake of protecting corporate integrity—object to the politicization of the military that has resulted from the Fujimori coup. Fujimori's use of the military as a power base has politicized promotions and purges. It has also fragmented authority within the institution. For example, since December 1990, the *jefe político-militar* (civil-military chief) of each region reports directly to military zone commanders, responsible for operational decisions, rather than to the joint command in Lima. An article that expresses the disquiet of professionally minded officers toward such developments is "Las Heridas del Ejército Peruano," *Que Hacer* 81 (January–February 1993): 8–15.

88. Obando makes this argument in "El Poder de los Militares," 82.

89. Mauceri describes the expansion of the military's counterinsurgency role in "Military Politics and Counter-Insurgency," 99–102. The same author notes, however, that even in this sphere, where officers and soldiers enjoy an inordinate level of privilege, the Peruvian legislature overturned a presidential decree that would have restricted the judgment of all military personnel in the country's many emergency zones to military courts, and it is likely to rescind other decrees of this kind.

90. Quoted in "Pérez de Cuéllar Joins the Race," *Latin American Regional Reports–Andean Group*, October 13, 1994, pp. 6–7.

91. See "Amnesty Law Causes Uproar," *Latin American Weekly Report* (June 29, 1995): 287; "Protests Grow against Amnesty," *Latin American Weekly Report* (July 6, 1995).

92. Tocqueville, *Democracy in America*. See especially vol. 1: chaps. 4 and 15; vol. 2: bk. 2, chap. 1, and bk. 4, chap. 1.

BIBLIOGRAPHY

Abreu, Hugo. *O Outro Lado do Poder*. Rio de Janeiro: Editora Nova Fronteira, 1979.

Abugattas, Luis A. "Populism and After: The Peruvian Experience." In *Authoritarians and Democrats: Regime Transition in Latin America*, edited by James M. Malloy and Mitchell A. Seligson, 121–43. Pittsburgh: University of Pittsburgh Press, 1987.

Acuña, Carlos, and Catalina Smulovitz. "¿Ni Olvido ni Perdón? Derechos Humanos y Tensiones Cívico-Militares en la Transición Argentina." Paper prepared for presentation at the 16th International Congress of the Latin American Studies Association, Buenos Aires, February 1991.

Acuña, Carlos H., and William C. Smith "The Politics of Arms Production and the Arms Race among the New Democracies of Argentina, Brazil, and Chile." In *Security, Democracy, and Development in U.S.-Latin American Relations*, edited by Lars Schoultz, William C. Smith, and Augusto Varas, 199–240. Miami: University of Miami, North-South Center, 1994.

———. "The Politics of 'Military Economics' in the Southern Cone: Comparative Perspectives on Democracy and Arms Production in Argentina, Brazil, and Chile." Paper prepared for presentation at the 18th International Congress of the Latin American Studies Association, Atlanta, Georgia, March 10–12, 1994.

Agüero, Felipe. "La Autonomía de las Fuerzas Armadas." In *Chile en El Umbral de los Noventa: Quince Años que Condicionan el Futuro*, edited by Jaime Gazmuri, 163–88. Santiago: Planeta Espejo de Chile, 1988.

———. "Democracia en España y Supremacía Civil." *Revista Española de Investigaciones Sociológicas* 44 (October–December 1988): 23–49.

———. "The Assertion of Civilian Supremacy in Post-Authoritarian Contexts: Spain in Comparative Perspective." Ph.D. diss., Duke University, 1991.

———. "The Transition to Democracy and the Military: Chile since the Plebiscite of 1988." Paper prepared for presentation at the 16th International Congress of the Latin American Studies Association, Washington, D.C., April 4–6, 1991.

———. "The Military and the Limits to Democratization in Latin America." In *Issues in Democratic Consolidation: The New South American Democracies in Comparative Perspective*, edited by Scott Mainwaring, Guillermo O'Donnell, and J. Samuel Valenzuela, 153–98. Notre Dame: University of Notre Dame Press, 1992.

———. "Debilitating Democracy: Political Elites and Military Rebels in Venezuela." In *Lessons from Venezuela*, edited by Louis W. Goodman, Johanna Mendelson, Moisés Naim, and Joseph Tulchin, 136–62. Baltimore: Johns Hopkins University Press, 1995.

———. "Chile: South America's Success Story?" *Current History* (March 1993): 130–35.

———. *Soldiers, Civilians and Democracy: Post-Franco Spain in Comparative Perspective*. Baltimore: Johns Hopkins University Press, 1995.

Alario, Margarita. "Environmental Policy Enactment under the Military: Some Generaliza-

icies: Global and Regional Dimensions, edited by Elizabeth G. Ferris and Jennie K. Lincoln, 153–64. Boulder: Westview Press, 1981.

Brasil. Decreto Lei 1.632 de 4 de agosto de 1978. *Diário Oficial* (August 4, 1978): 12343–44.

Brasil. Decreto Lei 2.010 de 12 de janeiro de 1983. *Diário Oficial* (January 13, 1983): 761–63.

Brasil. *Diário do Congresso Nacional* (June 23, 1989).

Brasil. Lei 4.330 de 1 de junho de 1964. *Diário Oficial* (June 3, 1964).

Brasil. Assembléia Nacional Constituinte. *Diário da Assembléia Nacional Constituinte*. March 2, 1988.

———. *Quadro Comparativo*. Brasília: Centro Gráfico do Senado Federal, July 1988.

Brasil. Assembléia Nacional Constituinte. Comissão da Ordem Social, and Subcomissão dos Direitos dos Trabalhadores e Servidores Públicos. *Anteprojeto*. Brasília: Centro Gráfico do Senado Federal, June 1987.

———. *Relatório*. Brasília: Centro Gráfico do Senado Federal, June 1987.

———. *Substitutivo*. Brasília: Centro Gráfico do Senado Federal, June 1987.

Brasil. Assembléia Nacional Constituinte. Comissão da Organização Eleitoral, Partidária e Garantias das Instituições. *Emendas Oferecidas ao Substitutivo*. Brasília: Centro Gráfico do Senado Federal, June 1987.

———. *Relatório Preliminar e Substitutivo*. Brasília: Centro Gráfico do Senado Federal, June 1987.

———. *Substitutivo*. Brasília: Centro Gráfico do Senado Federal, June 1987.

Brasil. Assembléia Nacional Constituinte. Comissão da Organização Eleitoral, Partidária e Garantias das Instituições and Subcomissão da Defesa do Estado, da Sociedade e de Sua Segurança. *Anteprojeto*. Brasília: Centro Gráfico do Senado Federal, June 1987.

Brasil. Câmara dos Deputados. *Projeto de Lei no. 2.146 de 1989 (do Poder Executivo)*. Mensagem no. 177/89.

———. *A Marinha e a Defesa Nacional. Palestra para as Comissões de Defesa Nacional da Câmara dos Deputados e do Senado Federal*. [Testimony before the Committee of National Defense of the Chamber of Deputies and the Federal Senate.] Brasília, May 11, 1989.

———. *O "AMX": Desenvolvimento e Construção de Aeronave de Ataque. Palestra para as Comissões de Defesa Nacional da Câmara dos Deputados e do Senado Federal*. [Testimony before the Committee of National Defense of the Chamber of Deputies and the Federal Senate.] Brasília, May 31, 1989.

———. *O Conselho de Defesa Nacional e a SADEN/PR. Palestra para as Comissões de Defesa Nacional da Câmara dos Deputados e do Senado Federal*. [Testimony before the Committee of National Defense of the Chamber of Deputies and the Federal Senate.] Brasília, June 8, 1989.

———. *O Programa "VLS"—Veículo Lançador de Satélites. Palestra para as Comissões de Defesa Nacional da Câmara dos Deputados e do Senado Federal*. [Testimony before the Committee of National Defense of the Chamber of Deputies and the Federal Senate.] Brasília, June 14, 1989.

———. *Projeto de Lei no. 1.862 de 1991 (do Poder Executivo)*. Mensagem no. 504/91.

———. *Análise do Projeto de Lei no. 1862 de 1991 (do Poder Executivo)*. Analysis of proposed law no. 1862/1991.

———. *Projeto de Lei no. 1.887 de 1991*. Brasília: Centro Gráfico do Senado Federal, September 9, 1991.

———. *Projeto de Lei no. 4349 de 1993*. Brasília: Centro Gráfico do Senado Federal, December 6, 1993.

Brasil. Câmara dos Deputados. Comissão da Defesa Nacional. *Audiência Pública*. [Testimony of the minister of aeronautics, Sócrates da Costa Monteiro, before the Comissão da Defesa Nacional, on the need for air defense in the Brazilian Amazon.] June 5, 1991.

———. *Audiência Pública*. [Testimony of the minister of justice, Jarbas Passarinho, and the secretary of the federal police, Romeu Tuma, before the Comissão da Defesa Nacional, on

the demarcation of the Yanomami reserve and the issue of national sovereignty.] December 12, 1991.
———. *Sinopse de Palestra Proferida pelo Exmo. Sr. Ministro das Relações Exteriores.* [Testimony of the foreign minister, Francisco Rezek, before the Comissão da Defesa Nacional, on the Earth Summit held in Rio de Janeiro in 1992.] 1992.
———. *O Público e o Privado: As Razões e os Segredos de Estado e as Liberdades Individuais.* [Seminar: Intelligence Activities in a Democratic State—The Case of Brazil.] May 18, 1994.
———. *Serviço de Inteligência em Outros Países.* May 18, 1994.
———. *O Papel do Legislativo Brasileiro nas Questões de Inteligência.* May 19, 1994.
———. *Serviços de Inteligência no Brasil.* May 19, 1994.
———. *As Atividades de Inteligência Civil para o Brasil: A Perspectiva do Ministério das da Justiça.* May 25, 1994.
———. *As Atividades de Inteligência Civil para o Brasil: A Perspectiva do Ministério das Relações Exteriores.* May 25, 1994.
———. *As Atividades de Inteligência no Brasil: Um Breve Retrospecto Histórico.* May 26, 1994.
Brasil. Câmara dos Deputados. Comissão Parlamentar de Inquérito. *Relatório Final.* [Transcripts of hearings on the existence of clandestine airports and religious missions in the Amazon.] June 1991.
Brasil. Congreso Nacional. Revisão da Constituição Federal. *Apresentacão de Proposta Revisional.* 1993.
———. *Parecer no. 66, de 1994—RCF.* Brasília: Centro Gráfico do Senado Federal, 1994.
Brasil. Instituto de Planejamento Econômico e Social. Directoria de Programação. *Retrospecto das Finanças da União, Tesouro Brasil 1970–1985.* Brasília: Instituto de Planejamento Econômico e Social, 1987.
Brasil. Ministério do Exército. AMAN *[Academia Militar das Agulhas Negras]: Plano do Ensino.* Brasília: Ministério do Exército, 1989.
———. *ECEME [Escola de Comando e Estado Maior do Exército]: Curso de Comando e Estado-Maior: Currículo.* Brasília: Ministério do Exército, 1985, 1989, 1994.
Brasil. Ministério do Exército. Centro de Comunicação Social do Exército. *Temas Constitucionais: Subsídios.* Brasília: Ministério do Exército, 1987.
Brasil. Ministério da Fazenda. "A Política Salarial dos Governos da Revolução." In *Palestras e Conferências do Ministro Mário Henrique Simonsen,* 77–93. Rio de Janeiro: Ministério da Fazenda, 1977.
Brasil. Ministério do Interior. *Projeto Calha Norte: Desenvolvimento e Segurança na Região ao Norte das Calhas dos Rios Solimões e Amazonas.* Brasília: Ministério do Interior, 1985.
Brasil. Ministério da Marinha Brasileira. "Orçamento das Forças Armadas: Quadros Comparativos." N.d. Photocopy.
Brasil. Secretaria de Assuntos Estratégicos. *Coletânea de Assuntos de Especial Interesse da SAE.* Brasília: Secretaria de Assuntos Estratégicos, 1993.
———. *Sistema de Proteção de Amazônia.* N.d. Photocopy.
Brasil. Secretaria de Planejamento e Coordenação da Presidência da República. *Anuário Estatístico do Brasil.* Rio de Janeiro: Fundação Instituto Brasileiro de Geografia e Estatística-IBGE, 1982–93.
Brito, Alexandra Barahona de. "Truth and Justice in the Consolidation of Democracy in Chile and Uruguay." *Parliamentary Affairs* 46.4 (October 1993): 579–93.
Bruneau, Thomas C. "Consolidating Civilian Brazil." *Third World Quarterly* 7.4 (October 1985): 973–87.
———. "Brazil's Political Transition." In *Elites and Democratic Consolidation in Latin America and Southern Europe,* edited by John Higley and Richard Gunther, 257–81. Cambridge: Cambridge University Press, 1992.
Bruszt, Laszló, and David Stark. "Paths of Extrication and Possibilities of Transformation." Working papers, Transitions from State Socialism, Cornell University, 1991.

Bunker, Stephen. *Underdeveloping the Amazon: Extraction, Unequal Exchange, and the Failure of the Modern State.* Chicago: University of Chicago Press, 1985.
———. "Policy Implementation in an Authoritarian State: A Case from Brazil." *Latin American Research Review* 8.1 (1988): 33–58.
Burns, E. Bradford. *A History of Brazil.* New York: Columbia University Press, 1970.
Camargo, Aspásia, and Walter de Goés. *Meio Século de Combate: Diálogo com Cordeiro de Farias.* Rio de Janeiro: Editora Nova Fronteira, 1981.
Cammack, Paul. "Clientelism and Military Government in Brazil." In *Private Patronage and Public Power: Political Clientelism and the Modern State,* edited by Christopher Clapham, 53–75. New York: St. Martin's, 1982.
———. "The 'Brazilianization' of Mexico?" *Government and Opposition* 23.3 (Summer 1988): 305–20.
Cardoso, Fernando Henrique. "Entrepreneurs and the Transition Process: The Brazilian Case." In *Transitions from Authoritarian Rule: Comparative Perspectives,* edited by Guillermo O'Donnell, Philippe C. Schmitter, and Laurence Whitehead, 137–53. Baltimore: Johns Hopkins University Press, 1986.
Carvalho, José Murilo de. "As Forças Armadas na Primeira República: O Poder Desestabilizador." Cadernos do Departamento de Ciência Política, Universidade Federal do Minas Gerais 1 (March 1974): 113–88.
———. "Forças Armadas e Política, 1930–1945." Paper prepared for presentation at the seminar "A Revolução de 1930," Rio de Janeiro, September 22–25, 1980.
———. "Os Militares, a Constituinte e a Democracia." *Presença* 8 (August 1986): 38–44.
———. "Militares e Civis: Um Debate além da Constituinte." Cadernos de Conjuntura 10. Rio de Janeiro: Instituto Universitário de Pesquisas do Rio de Janeiro, 1987.
Castro, Celso Corrêa Pinto de. *O Espírito Militar: Um Estudo de Antropologia Social na Academia Militar das Agulhas Negras.* Rio de Janeiro: Zahar, 1990.
———. "A Origem Social Dos Militares: Novos Dados para uma Antiga Discussão." *Novos Estudos* 37 (November 1993): 225–31.
Castro, João Augusto de Araujo. "The United Nations and the Freezing of the International Power Structure." *International Organization* 26.1 (Winter 1972): 159–66.
Castro, Therezinha de. "Amazônia: O Grande Desafio Geopolítico." *A Defesa Nacional: Revista de Assuntos Militares e Estudo de Problemas Brasileiros* 697 (September–October 1981): 23–37.
Catterberg, Edgardo. *Argentina Confronts Politics: Political Culture and Public Opinion in the Argentine Transition to Democracy.* Boulder: Lynne Rienner Publishers, 1991.
Cavarozzi, Marcelo. "Political Cycles in Argentina since 1955." In *Transitions from Authoritarian Rule: Latin America,* edited by Guillermo O'Donnell, Philippe C. Schmitter, and Laurence Whitehead, 19–48. Baltimore: Johns Hopkins University Press, 1986.
Centro Ecumênico de Documentação e Informação. *De Angra a Aramar: Os Militares a Caminho da Bomba.* Rio de Janeiro: CEDI, 1988.
CEPAL [Economic Commission for Latin America and the Caribbean]. "Uma Estimación de la Magnitud de la Pobreza en Chile, 1987." *Colección Estudios CIEPLAN (Corporación de Investigaciones Económicas para Latinoamerica]* 31 (March 1990): 107–29.
Chagas, Carlos. 113 *Dias de Angústia: Impedimento e Morte de um Presidente.* Pôrto Alegre: L & PM Editores, 1979.
———. *A Guerra das Estrelas, 1964–1985: Os Bastidores das Sucessões Presidenciais.* Pôrto Alegre: L & PM Editores, 1985.
Chalmers, Douglas A. "Parties and Society in Latin America." In *Friends, Followers, and Factions,* edited by Steffen W. Schmidt et al., 401–21. Berkeley: University of California Press, 1977.
———. "The Politicized State in Latin America." In *Authoritarianism and Corporatism in Latin America,* edited by James M. Malloy, 23–45. Pittsburgh: University of Pittsburgh Press, 1977.

Child, Jack. "Geopolitical Thinking." In *The Military and Democracy: The Future of Civil-Military Relations in Latin America*, edited by Louis W. Goodman, Johanna S. R. Mendelson, and Juan Rial, 143–63. Lexington: Lexington Books, 1990.

Chile. *Ley Orgánica Constitucional de las Fuerzas Armadas*. Ley no. 18.948. Santiago: Diário Oficial, February 27, 1990.

Chile. Ministerio de Hacienda. Dirección de Presupuestos. *Estadísticas de las Finanzas Públicas, 1989–1992*. Santiago: Ministerio de Hacienda, 1993.

Chile. Ministerio de Hacienda. Ministerio Secretaria General de Gobierno. *Crecimiento con Equidad: Balance y Proyección Econômico-Social del Gobierno del Presidente Aylwin, 1990–1992*. Santiago: Ministerio de Hacienda, 1993.

Chile. Ministerio de Planificación y Cooperación. *Avanzando en Equidad: Un Proceso de Integración al Desarrollo: 1990–1992*. Santiago: Ministerio de Planificación y Cooperación, 1992.

Coelho, Edmundo Campos. *Em Busca da Identidade: O Exército e a Política na Sociedade Brasileira*. Rio de Janeiro: Editora Forense-Universitária, 1976.

———. "A Instituição Militar no Brasil: Um Ensaio Bibliográfico." *Boletim Informativo e Bibliográfico de Ciências Sociais* 19 (1985): 5–20.

Cohen, Youssef. "Democracy from Above: The Political Origins of Military Dictatorship in Brazil." *World Politics* 40.1 (October 1987): 30–54.

———. *The Manipulation of Consent: The State and Working-Class Consciousness in Brazil*. Pittsburgh: University of Pittsburgh Press, 1989.

Collier, Ruth Berins. "Popular Sector Incorporation and Political Supremacy: Regime Evolution in Brazil and Mexico." In *Brazil and Mexico: Patterns in Latin Development*, edited by Sylvia Ann Hewlett and Richard S. Weinert, 57–109. Philadelphia: Institute for the Study of Human Issues, 1982.

Collier, Ruth Berins, and David Collier. *Shaping the Political Arena: Critical Junctures, the Labor Movement, and Regime Dynamics in Latin America*. Princeton: Princeton University Press, 1991.

Collor, Fernando. *Brasil: Um Projeto de Reconstrução Nacional*. Brasília: Secretaria de Imprensa da Presidência da República, 1991.

Comisión Nacional de Verdad y Reconciliacíon. *Informe de la Comisión Nacional de Verdad y Reconciliacíon*. Reprinted in *Estudios Públicos* 41 (Summer 1991).

Comissão pela Criação do Parque Yanomami-CCPY (Brasília). Newsletter. Various issues January 1992–August 1994.

Comissão Pró-Índio de São Paulo. Departamento Jurídico. "Emendas Colocam em Risco Direitos e Interesses dos Povos Indígenas." *Informe Jurídico* 29–30 (February 1994): 1–2.

———. "Os Direitos Indígenas e a Revisão Constitucional: Quadro Geral das Propostas Revisionais Afetas aos Direitos dos Índios." *Informe Jurídico* 29–30 (February 1994): 3–10.

Comitê PMDB: Candidatura pró Ulysses e Waldir. "Segurança: Uma Nova Polícia Militar." Informativo especial. July 1989.

Conca, Ken. "Global Markets, Local Politics, and Military Industrialization in Brazil." Ph.D. diss., University of California, Berkeley, 1992.

———. "Technology, the Military, and Democracy in Brazil." *Journal of Interamerican Studies and World Affairs* 34.1 (Spring 1992): 141–77.

———. "Third World Military Industrialization and the Evolving Security System." In *The Highest Stakes: The Economic Foundations of the Next Security System*, edited by Wayne Sandholtz, Michael Borrus, John Zysman, Ken Conca, Jay Stowsky, Steven Vogel, and Steve Weber, 141–64. New York: Oxford University Press, 1992.

Conniff, Michael. "The Tenentes in Power: A New Perspective on the Brazilian Revolution of 1930." *Journal of Latin American Studies* 10.1 (May 1978): 61–82.

Constable, Pamela, and Arturo Valenzuela. "Chile's Return to Democracy." *Foreign Affairs* 68.5 (Winter 1989–90): 169–86.

Constituição da República Federativa do Brasil 1988. Rio de Janeiro: Bloch Editores, 1988.

Constitution of Brazil 1967 (as amended by Constitutional Amendment No. 1 of October 17,
    1969). Washington, D.C.: General Secretariat, Organization of American States, De-
    partment of Legal Affairs.
Constitution of the Federative Republic of Brazil 1988. Brasília: Senado Federal, n.d.
Cook, Karen Schweers, and Margaret Levi, eds. *The Limits of Rationality.* Chicago: University
    of Chicago Press, 1990.
Cotler, Julio. "Military Interventions and 'Transfer of Power to Civilians' in Peru." In *Transi-
    tions from Authoritarian Rule: Latin America,* edited by Guillermo O'Donnell, Philippe
    C. Schmitter, and Laurence Whitehead, 148–72. Baltimore: Johns Hopkins University
    Press, 1986.
Crabtree, John. *Peru under García: An Opportunity Lost.* Pittsburgh: University of Pittsburgh
    Press, 1992.
Cruz, Sebastião C. Velasco e. "Empresários, Economistas e Perspectivas da Democratização
    no Brasil." In *A Democracia no Brasil: Dilemas e Perspectivas,* edited by Fábio Wan-
    derley Reis and Guillermo O'Donnell, 256–81. São Paulo: Vértice, 1988.
Dahl, Robert A. *A Preface to Democratic Theory.* Chicago: University of Chicago Press, 1956.
———. *Who Governs: Democracy and Power in an American City.* New Haven: Yale University
    Press, 1961.
———. *Polyarchy: Participation and Opposition.* New Haven: Yale University Press, 1971.
———. *Dilemmas of Pluralist Democracy.* New Haven: Yale University Press, 1982.
D'Araujo, Maria Celina, Gláucio Ary Dillon Soares, and Celso Castro, eds. *Visões do Golpe: A
    Memória Militar sobre 1964.* Rio de Janeiro: Relume Dumara, 1994.
Davis, Shelton H. *Victims of the Miracle: Development and the Indians of Brazil.* Cambridge:
    Cambridge University Press, 1977.
Degregori, Iván Carlos, and Carlos Rivera. "Perú 1980–1993: Fuerzas Armadas, Subversión y
    Democracia." Lima: Instituto de Estudios Peruanos, documento de trabajo 53, July 1994.
Downs, Anthony. *An Economic Theory of Democracy.* New York: Harper & Row, 1957.
Dreifuss, René. *A Conquista do Estado: Acão Politica e Golpe de Classe.* Petrópolis: Editora
    Vozes, 1981.
———. "Nova República. Novo Exército?" In *Nova República: Um Balanço,* edited by Flavio
    Koutzii, 168–93. Pôrto Alegre: L & PM Editores, 1986.
———. "Um Governo Renovador e as Forças Militares." In *PT: Um Projeto Para o Brasil,* edited
    by Francisco Weffort, 123–79. São Paulo: Editora Brasiliense, 1989.
———. *O Jogo da Direita.* Petrópolis: Editora Vozes, 1989.
Eckstein, Harry. "Case Study and Theory in Political Science." In *Handbook of Political Sci-
    ence.* Vol. 7, *Strategies of Inquiry,* edited by Fred I. Greenstein and Nelson Polsby, 79–
    137. Reading: Addison-Wesley, 1975.
Ensalaco, Mark. "In with the New, Out with the Old? The Democratising Impact of Constitu-
    tional Reform in Chile." *Journal of Latin American Studies* 26.2 (May 1994): 409–29.
Erickson, Kenneth Paul. *The Brazilian Corporative State and Working Class Politics.* Berkeley:
    University of California Press, 1977.
Ferguson, Yale. "Cooperation in the Amazon: The Politics of Regional Integration." In *The Dy-
    namics of Latin American Foreign Policies: Challenges for the 1980s,* edited by Jennie K.
    Lincoln and Elizabeth G. Ferris, 37–55. Boulder: Westview Press, 1984.
Fernandes, Heloisa Rodrigues. *Política e Segurança.* São Paulo: Editora Alfa-Omega, 1974.
———. "O Militar Como Categoria Social." Ph.D. diss., Universidade de São Paulo, 1977.
Ferreira, Oliveiros. "As Forças Armadas na Constituição." *Política e Estratégia* 3.3 (July–
    September 1985): 391–436.
———. "Forças Armadas, Para Quê? Uma Apreciação Histórica." *Política e Estratégia* 4.3 (July–
    September 1986): 318–41.
———. *Forças Armadas, para quê?* São Paulo: Editora GRD, 1988.
Ffrench-Davis, Ricardo. "Desarrollo Econômico y Equidad en Chile." *Colección Estudios*

CIEPLAN (Corporación de Investigaciones Económicas para Latinoamerica] 31 (March 1991): 31–51.

Figueiredo, Argelina Cheibub, and Fernando Limongi. "O Processo Legislativo e a Produção Legal No Congresso Pós-Constituinte." *Novos Estudos* 38 (March 1994): 24–37.

Finer, Samuel. *The Man on Horseback: The Role of the Military in Politics.* New York: Praeger, 1962.

Fishman, Robert. "Rethinking State and Regime: Southern Europe's Transition to Democracy." *World Politics* 42.3 (April 1990): 422–40.

Fitch, J. Samuel. "Military Professionalism, National Security, and Democracy: Lessons from the Latin American Experience." Paper prepared for presentation at the 15th International Congress of the Latin American Studies Association, San Juan, Puerto Rico, September 21–23, 1989.

———. "Democracy, Human Rights, and the Armed Forces in Latin America." In *United States–Latin American Relations in the 1990s: Beyond the Cold War*, edited by Jonathan Hartlyn, Carlos Portales, Lars Schoultz, and Augusto Varas, 181–213. Chapel Hill: University of North Carolina Press, 1992.

———. "Military Role Beliefs in Latin American Democracies: Military Doctrine, Ideology, and Context in Argentina and Ecuador." Interim performance report 3, United States Institute of Peace, 1993.

———. "Military Role Beliefs in Latin American Democracies: Context, Ideology, and Doctrine in Argentina and Ecuador." Paper prepared for presentation at the 19th International Congress of the Latin American Studies Association, Washington, D.C., September 28–30, 1995.

Fitch, J. Samuel, and Andrés Fontana. "Military Policy and Democratic Consolidation in Latin America." Paper prepared for presentation at the 16th International Congress of the Latin American Studies Association, Washington, D.C., April 4–6, 1991.

Fleischer, David. "From Non-competitive to Competitive Elections to the 1987–88 Constituent Assembly." Paper prepared for presentation at the Academia de Humanismo Christiano, Santiago, March 23, 1988.

Flores, Mário César. "Maritimidade: Causa de Progresso ou de Risco?" *Revista Marítima Brasileira* 101.7–9 (July–September 1981): 41–64.

———. "A Estrutura Básica do Ministério da Marinha—Uma Revisão Conveniente." *Revista Marítima Brasileira* 104 (April–June 1984): 11–34.

———. "O Preparo da Marinha dos Próximos 10 a 30 Anos." *Revista Marítima Brasileira* 108 (January–March 1988): 13–21.

———. "A Sociedade e as Forças Armadas." Photocopy, adopted from public address at the Brazilian Navy Academy, September 6, 1988.

———. *Bases para uma Política Militar.* Campinas: Editora de Unicamp, 1992.

Flynn, Peter. *Brazil: A Political Analysis.* Boulder: Westview Press, 1978.

Fontana, Andrés. "Argentine Security Interests and Perspectives." Fundación Simón Rodriguez, May 20, 1993. Photocopy.

———. Percepciones Militares Acerca del Rol de las Fuerzas Armadas en Argentina." Fundación Simón Rodriguez, May 1993. Photocopy.

Fontana, Andrés, and Elsa Llenderrozas. "Resumen Encuesta: Actitudes y Opiniones de la Población en Relación a la Profesión Militar, las Fuerzas Armadas, y Temas de Seguridad." Buenos Aires: Fundación Simón Rodriguez, 1992. Photocopy.

Fortes, Luiz Roberto Salinas, and Milton Meira Do Nascimento, eds. *A Constituinte em Debate.* São Paulo: Sofia Editora, 1986.

Fox, M. Louise. *Poverty Alleviation in Brazil, 1970–87.* Internal discussion paper: Latin America and the Caribbean Region, report IDP-072. Washington, D.C.: World Bank, 1990.

Foxley, Alejandro. *La Economia Política de la Transición: El Camino de Diálogo.* Santiago: Ediciones Dolmen, 1993.

Fraga, Rosendo, with the collaboration of Raúl Alberto Gaticia. *La Cuestión Militar en los Noventa*. Buenos Aires: Centro de Estudios Unión para la Nueva Mayoria, 1991.

Franko, Patrice. "De Facto Demilitarization: Budget-Driven Downsizing in Latin America." *Journal of Interamerican Studies and World Affairs* 36.1 (Spring 1994): 37–74.

Franko-Jones, Patrice. *The Brazilian Defense Industry*. Boulder: Westview Press, 1992.

French, John D. *The Brazilian Workers' ABC: Class Conflict and Alliances in Modern São Paulo*. Chapel Hill: University of North Carolina Press, 1992.

Fuentes, Claudio S. "Los Efectos de una Nueva Realidad Internacional en las Fuerzas Armadas de América Latina: El Caso Chileno." Paper prepared for presentation at the 18th International Congress of the Latin American Studies Association, Atlanta, Georgia, March 10–12, 1994.

Fundação Getúlio Vargas. Centro de Pesquisa e Documentação. *Dicionário-Histórico Biográfico Brasileiro, 1930–1983*. Rio de Janeiro: Editora Forense-Universitária, 1984.

Geddes, Barbara. "Democratic Institutions as a Bargain among Self-Interested Politicians." Paper prepared for presentation at the 86th Annual Meeting of the American Political Science Association, San Francisco, August 30–September 2, 1990.

———. *Politician's Dilemma: Building State Capacity in Latin America*. Berkeley: University of California Press, 1994.

Geddes, Barbara, and John Zaller. "Sources of Popular Support for Authoritarian Regimes." *American Journal of Political Science* 33.2 (May 1989): 319–47.

Geisse, Francisco, and José Antonio Ramírez Arrayas. *La Reforma Constitutional*. Santiago: CESOC [Centro de Estudios Sociales], 1989.

Goés, Walder de. *O Brasil do General Geisel: Estudo do Processo de Tomada de Decisão no Regime Militar-Burocrático*. Rio de Janeiro: Editora Nova Fronteira, 1978.

———. "O Novo Regime Militar no Brasil." *Dados* 27.3 (1984): 361–75.

———. "Os Militares e a Transição Política." Paper prepared for presentation at the 9th Annual Meeting of ANPOCS [Associação Nacional de Pós-Graduação e Pesquisas em Ciências Sociais], Aguas de São Pedro, São Paulo, October 1985.

———. "Militares e Política: Uma Estratégia para a Democracia." In *A Democracia no Brasil: Dilemas e Perspectivas*, edited by Fábio Wanderley Reis and Guillermo O'Donnell, 229–55. São Paulo: Vértice, 1988.

Goldemberg, Jose, and Harold A. Feiveson. "Denuclearization in Argentina and Brazil." *Arms Control Today* 24.2 (March 1994): 10–14.

Goldman-Solingen, Etel. "A Study in the Political Economy of Technological Development: Brazil's Nuclear Program." Ph.D. diss., University of California, Los Angeles, 1987.

Gomes, Mercio Pereira. *Os Índios e o Brasil*. Petrópolis: Editora Vozes, 1988.

Grindle, Merilee S. "Civil-Military Relations and Budgetary Politics in Latin America." *Armed Forces and Society* 13.2 (Winter 1987): 255–75.

Gurgel, Antônio de Padua, and David Fleischer. *O Brasil Vai às Urnas: Retrato da Campanha Presidencial*. Brasília: Thesaurus Editora, 1990.

Hagopian, Frances. "The Politics of Oligarchy: The Persistence of Traditional Elites in Contemporary Brazil." Ph.D diss., Massachusetts Institute of Technology, 1986.

———. "'Democracy by Undemocratic Means'? Elites, Political Pacts, and Regime Transition in Brazil." *Comparative Political Studies* 23.2 (July 1990): 147–70.

Hayes, Robert A. *The Armed Nation: The Brazilian Corporate Mystique*. Tempe: Arizona State University, Center for Latin American Studies, 1989.

Hecht, Susanna B. "Cattle Ranching in Amazônia: Political and Ecological Considerations." In *Frontier Expansion in Amazônia*, edited by Marianne Schmink and Charles H. Wood, 366–98. Gainesville: University of Florida Press, 1984.

Hecht, Susanna, and Alexander Cockburn. *The Fate of the Forest: Developers, Destroyers and Defenders of the Amazon*. London: Verso, 1989.

Hilton, Stanley E. "The Armed Forces and Industrialists in Modern Brazil: The Drive for Military Autonomy (1889–1954)." *Hispanic American Historical Review* 62.4 (1982): 629–73.

———. "The Brazilian Military: Changing Strategic Perceptions and the Question of Mission." *Armed Forces and Society* 13.3 (Spring 1987): 329–51.

Hunter, Wendy. "Back to the Barracks? The Military in Post-Authoritarian Brazil." Ph.D. diss., University of California, Berkeley, 1992.

———. "The Brazilian Military after the Cold War: In Search of a Mission." *Studies in Comparative International Development* 28.4 (Winter 1994): 31–49.

———. "Contradictions of Civilian Control: Argentina, Brazil and Chile in the 1990s." *Third World Quarterly* 15.4 (December 1994): 635–55.

———. "Politicians against Soldiers: Contesting the Military in Post-Authoritarian Brazil." In *Comparative Politics* 27.4 (July 1995): 425–43.

Huntington, Samuel P. *The Soldier and the State.* Cambridge, Mass.: Harvard University Press, 1957.

———. *Political Order in Changing Societies.* New Haven: Yale University Press, 1968.

———. *The Third Wave: Democratization in the Late Twentieth Century.* Norman: University of Oklahoma Press, 1991.

Hurrell, Andrew. "The Politics of Amazonian Deforestation." *Journal of Latin American Studies* 23.1 (February 1991): 197–215.

Huser, Herbert C. "Reforma Militar y Revisión del Pasado: The Civil-Military Relationship in Democratic Argentina." Paper prepared for presentation at the 18th International Congress of the Latin American Studies Association, Atlanta, Georgia, March 10–12, 1994.

Ianni, Octávio. *Colonização e Contra-Reforma Agrária na Amazônia.* Petrópolis: Editora Vozes, 1979.

Indicadores de Coyuntura 329. Fundación de Investigaciones Económicas Latinoamericanas, November 1993.

International Institute for Strategic Studies. *The Military Balance 1993–1994.* London: Brassey's, 1993.

Janowitz, Morris. *The Military in the Political Development of New Nations.* Chicago: University of Chicago Press, 1964.

Johnson, John J. *Political Change in Latin America: The Emergence of the Middle Sectors.* Stanford: Stanford University Press, 1958.

Jones. Mark P. "Argentine Public Opinion and Constitutional Reform." Paper prepared for presentation at the 89th Annual Meeting of the American Political Science Association, New York City, September 1–4, 1994.

Karl, Terry Lynn. "Dilemmas of Democratization in Latin America." *Comparative Politics* 23.1 (October 1990): 1–21.

Karl, Terry Lynn, and Philippe C. Schmitter. "Modes of Transition in Latin America, Southern and Eastern Europe." *International Social Science Journal* 128 (May 1991): 269–84.

Keck, Margaret E. "Update on the Brazilian Labor Movement." *Latin American Perspectives* 11.1 (Winter 1984): 27–34.

———. "The New Unionism in the Brazilian Transition." In *Democratizing Brazil: Problems of Transition and Consolidation,* edited by Alfred Stepan, 252–98. New York: Oxford University Press, 1989.

———. "Brazil." In *Prospects for Democracy in Latin America,* edited by Forrest D. Colburn, 252–96. Center of International Studies Monograph Series 1. Princeton: Princeton University Press, 1990.

———. *The Workers' Party and Democratization in Brazil.* New Haven: Yale University Press, 1992.

Kenworthy, Eldon. "Coalitions in the Political Development of Latin America." In *The Study of Coalition Behavior: Theoretical Perspectives from Four Continents,* edited by Sven Groennings, E. W. Kelley, and Michael Leiserson, 103–40. New York: Holt, Rinehart and Winston, 1970.

Keohane, Robert, and Joseph Nye. *Power and Interdependence: World Politics in Transition.* Boston: Little, Brown, 1977.

Knight, Jack. *Institutions and Social Conflict*. Cambridge: Cambridge University Press, 1992.

Krasner, Stephen. "Punctuated Equilibrium: An Approach to the Evolution of State-Society Relations." Department of Political Science, Stanford University, 1982. Photocopy.

———. "Sovereignty: An Institutional Perspective." *Comparative Political Studies* 21.1 (April 1987): 66–94.

Krasno, Jean. "Brazil's Secret Nuclear Program." *Orbis* 38.3 (Summer 1994): 425–37.

Kucinski, Bernardo. *Abertura, a História de uma Crise*. São Paulo: Editora Brasil Debates, 1982.

Lagoa, Ana. *O SNI: Como Nasceu, Como Funciona*. São Paulo: Editora Brasiliense, 1983.

Lamounier, Bolívar. "Ideology and Authoritarian Regimes: Theoretical Perspectives and a Study of the Brazilian Case." Ph.D. diss., University of California, Los Angeles, 1974.

Latinobarómetro 1995: Datos Preliminares. Ann Arbor: University of Michigan, Institute for Social Research, Survey Research Center, 1995.

Levi, Margaret. *Of Rule and Revenue*. Berkeley: University of California Press, 1988.

Levine, Robert. *The Vargas Regime: The Critical Years, 1934–38*. New York: Columbia University Press, 1970.

Lima, Antonio Carlos de Souza. "Militares, Indios e Fronteiras Politicas." Paper prepared for presentation at the 13th annual meeting of ANPOCS [Associação Nacional de Pós-Graduação e Pesquisas em Ciências Sociais], Caxambu, Minas Gerais, October 23–27, 1989.

Lima, Olavo Brasil de, Jr. "Mudança Política e Processo Decisório: Análise da Política Orçamentária Brasileira." *Dados* 14 (1977): 141–63.

Linz, Juan J. "The Future of an Authoritarian Situation or the Institutionalization of an Authoritarian Regime: The Case of Brazil." In *Authoritarian Brazil: Origins, Policies, and Future*, edited by Alfred Stepan, 233–54. New Haven: Yale University Press, 1973.

Lipset, Seymour Martin, and Stein Rokkan. "Cleavage Structures, Party Systems, and Voter Alignments: An Introduction." In *Party Systems and Voter Alignments: Cross National Perspectives*, edited by Seymour Martin Lipset and Stein Rokkan, 1–64. New York: Free Press, 1967.

Longo, Carlos Alberto. "O Processo Orçamentário: Tendências e Perspectivas." *Revista de Economia Política* 14.2 (April–June 1994): 40–52.

López, Ernesto. *Ni la Ceniza Ni la Gloria: Actores, Sistema Político y Cuestión Militar en los Años de Alfonsín*. Buenos Aires: Universidade Nacional de Quilmes, 1994.

Loveman, Brian. "¿Misión Cumplida? Civil Military Relations and the Chilean Political Transition." *Journal of Interamerican Studies and World Affairs* 33.3 (Fall 1991): 35–74.

———. *The Constitution of Tyranny: Regimes of Exception in Spanish America*. Pittsburgh: University of Pittsburgh Press, 1993.

———. "'Protected Democracies' and Military Guardianship: Political Transitions in Latin America, 1978–1993." *Journal of Interamerican Studies and World Affairs* 36.2 (Summer 1994): 105–89.

Lowenthal, Abraham F., and J. Samuel Fitch, ed. *Armies and Politics in Latin America*. New York: Holmes & Meier, 1976.

Lowi, Theodore. "American Business, Public Policy, Case Studies and Political Theory." *World Politics* 16.4 (July 1964): 677–715.

Lukes, Steven. *Power: A Radical View*. London: Macmillan, 1974.

Macedo, Ubiratan Borges de. "Forças Armadas—Segurança Interna ou Externa." *Política e Estratégia* 4.3 (July/September 1985): 455–60.

Mahar, Dennis. "Government Policies and Deforestation in Brazil's Amazon Region." Environment Department working paper 7. Washington, D.C.: World Bank, 1988.

Mainwaring, Scott. "Political Parties and Democratization in Brazil and the Southern Cone." *Comparative Politics* 21.1 (1988): 91–120.

———. "Clientelism, Patrimonialism, and Economic Crisis: Brazil since 1979." Paper prepared for presentation at the 16th International Congress of the Latin American Studies Association, Washington, D.C., April 4–6, 1991.

——. "Brazilian Party Underdevelopment." *Political Science Quarterly* 107 (Winter 1992–93): 677–707.

Mainwaring, Scott, and Timothy R. Scully. "Parties and Democracy in Latin America: Different Patterns, Common Challenges." In *Building Democratic Institutions: Parties and Party Systems in Latin America*, edited by Scott Mainwaring and Timothy R. Scully, 459–74. Stanford: Stanford University Press, 1995.

Malheiros, Tania. *Brasil: A Bomba Oculta*. Rio de Janeiro: Gryphus, 1993.

Malloy, James M. "The Politics of Transition in Latin America." In *Authoritarians and Democrats: Regime Transition in Latin America*, edited by James M. Malloy and Mitchell A. Seligson, 235–58. Pittsburgh: University of Pittsburgh Press, 1987.

March, James G. "The Power of Power." In *Varieties of Political Theory*, edited by David Easton, 39–70. Englewood Cliffs: Prentice-Hall, 1966.

March, James G., and Johan P. Olsen. "The New Institutionalism: Organizational Factors in Political Life." *American Political Science Review* 78.3 (September 1984): 734–49.

——. *Rediscovering Institutions: The Organizational Basis of Politics*. New York: Free Press, 1989.

Martine, George. "Internal Migration in Brazil." *Texto para Discussão* 12. Brasília: IPEA/IPLAN [Instituto de Planejamento Econômico e Social, Instituto de Planejamento], 1989.

Martins, José de Souza. "The State and the Militarization of the Agrarian Question in Brazil." In *Frontier Expansion in Amazonia*, edited by Marianne Schmink and Charles H. Wood, 463–90. Gainesville: University of Florida Press, 1984.

——. *A Militarização da Questão Agrária no Brasil*. Petrópolis: Editora Vozes, 1985.

——. "Impasses Políticos dos Movimentos Sociais na Amazônia." *Tempo Social. Revista de Sociologia da USP [Universidade de São Paulo]* 1.1 (First semester 1989): 131–48.

Martins, Luciano. "The 'Liberalization' of Authoritarian Rule in Brazil." In *Transitions from Authoritarian Rule: Latin America*, edited by Guillermo O'Donnell, Philippe C. Schmitter, and Laurence Whitehead, 72–94. Baltimore: Johns Hopkins University Press, 1986.

Mauceri, Philip. "The Military, Insurgency and Democratic Power: Peru, 1980–1988." Papers on Latin America 11, Institute of Latin American and Iberian Studies, Columbia University, 1989.

——. "Military Politics and Counter-Insurgency in Peru." *Journal of Interamerican Studies and World Affairs* 33.4 (Winter 1991): 83–109.

McCann, Frank D. "The Formative Period of Twentieth-Century Brazilian Army Thought, 1900–1922." *Hispanic American Historical Review* 64.4 (November 1984): 737–65.

——. "The Military." In *Modern Brazil: Elites and Masses in Historical Perspective*, edited by Michael L. Conniff and Frank D. McCann, 47–80. Lincoln: University of Nebraska Press, 1989.

——. "The Brazilian Army 1889–1985: Conservative or Revolutionary?" Paper prepared for presentation at the 17th International Congress of the Latin American Studies Association, Los Angeles, California, September 24–27, 1992.

McCleary, Rachel M. "The International Community's Claim to Rights in Brazilian Amazonia." *Political Studies* 39 (1991): 691–707.

McClintock, Cynthia. "The Prospects for Democratic Consolidation in a 'Least Likely' Case: Peru." *Comparative Politics* 21.2 (January 1989): 127–48.

——. "Peru." In *Prospects for Democracy in Latin America*, edited by Forrest D. Colburn, 17–21. Monograph series 1, Center of International Studies, Princeton University, 1990.

——. "The Breakdown of Constitutional Democracy in Peru." Paper prepared for presentation at the 18th International Congress of the Latin American Studies Association, Atlanta, Georgia, March 10–12, 1994.

McDonough, Peter. *Power and Ideology in Brazil*. Princeton: Princeton University Press, 1981.

McGuire, James W. "Interim Government and Democratic Consolidation: Argentina in Comparative Perspective." In *Between States: Interim Governments and Democratic Transitions*, edited by Juan Linz and Yossi Shain, 179–210. Cambridge: Cambridge University Press, 1995.

Mericle, Kenneth S. "Corporatist Control of the Working Class: Authoritarian Brazil since 1964." In *Authoritarianism and Corporatism in Latin America*, edited by James M. Malloy, 303–38. Pittsburgh: University of Pittsburgh Press, 1977.

Mettenheim, Kurt von. "The Brazilian Voter in Democratic Transition, 1974–1982." *Comparative Politics* 23.1 (October 1990): 23–44.

The Military Balance 1992–1993. London: The International Institute for Strategic Studies, 1992.

Miyamoto, Shiguenoli. "Do Discurso Triunfalista ao Pragmatismo Ecumênico. Geopolítica e Política Externa no Brasil Pós-64." Ph.D. diss., Departamento de Ciência Política, Universidade de São Paulo, 1985.

———. "Conselho de Segurança Nacional e Política Brasileira." *Tempo e Presença* (September 1987): 11–12.

———. "Diplomacia e Militarismo: O Projeto Calha Norte e a Ocupação do Espaço Amazônico." *Revista Brasileira de Ciência Política* 1.1 (March 1989): 145–63.

Morris, Michael. *International Politics and the Sea: The Case of Brazil*. Boulder: Westview Press, 1981.

Moura, Maria da Glória Veiga. "Considerações Sobre os Direitos dos Trabalhadores." In *Constituinte: Temas em Análise* 1, edited by Vânia Lomônaco Bastos and Tânia Moreira da Costa. Caderno do Centro de Estudos e Acompanhamento da Constituinte/UnB, (1988): 87–93.

Munck, Gerardo L. "Democratic Stability and Its Limits: An Analysis of Chile's 1993 Elections." *Journal of Interamerican Studies and World Affairs* 36.2 (Summer 1994): 1–38.

Murillo, Maria Victoria. "Argentina: Breaking the Praetorian Circle (or the Hope of Democracy)." Paper prepared for presentation at the 17th Congress of the Latin American Studies Association, Los Angeles, California, September 24–27, 1992.

Muszynski, Judith, and Antonio Manuel Teixeira Mendes. "Democratização e Opinião Pública no Brasil." In *De Geisel a Collor: O Balanço da Transição*, edited by Bolívar Lamounier, 61–80. São Paulo: IDESP [Instituto de Estudos Sociais e Políticos] Editora Sumaré, 1990.

Needler, Martin C. "Military Motivations in the Seizure of Power." *Latin American Research Review* 10.3 (Fall 1975): 63–79.

Norden, Deborah L. "Democratic Consolidation and Military Professionalism: Argentina in the 1980s." *Journal of Interamerican Studies and World Affairs* 32.3 (Fall 1990): 151–76.

———. "Between Coups and Consolidation: Military Rebellion in Post-Authoritarian Argentina." Ph.D. diss., University of California, Berkeley, 1992.

———. "Keeping the Peace: Outside and In: Argentina's UN Missions." *International Peacekeeping* 2.3 (Autumn 1995): 330–49.

———. *Military Rebellion in Argentina: Between Coups and Consolidation*. Lincoln: University of Nebraska Press, 1996.

Nordlinger, Eric A. *Soldiers in Politics: Military Coups and Governments*. Englewood Cliffs, N.J.: Prentice-Hall, 1977.

North, Douglass C. *Institutions, Institutional Change, and Economic Performance*. Cambridge: Cambridge University Press, 1990.

Nosso Século: Memória Fotográfica do Brasil no Século 20. São Paulo: Abril Cultura, 1980.

Nunn, Frederick M. *Latin American Militarism in World Perspective*. Lincoln: University of Nebraska Press, 1992.

Obando, Enrique. "El Poder de los Militares." In *El Poder en el Peru*, edited by Augusto Alvarez Rodrich, 75–85. Lima: Editorial Apoyo, 1993.

O'Donnell, Guillermo A. *Modernization and Bureaucratic-Authoritarianism: Studies in South American Politics*. Berkeley: Institute of International Studies, University of California, Berkeley, 1973.

———. "Introduction to the Latin American Cases." In *Transitions from Authoritarian Rule: Latin America*, edited by Guillermo A. O'Donnell, Philippe C. Schmitter, and Laurence Whitehead, 3–18. Baltimore: Johns Hopkins University Press, 1986.

———. "Challenges to Democratization in Brazil." *World Policy Journal* 5 (Spring 1988): 281–300.

———. "Delegative Democracy." *Journal of Democracy* 5.1 (January 1994): 55–69.

———. "On the State, Democratization and Some Conceptual Problems (A Latin American View with Glances at Some Post-Communist Countries)." Kellogg Institute, South Bend, Indiana, Working paper 192, April 1993.

———. "Transições, Continuidades e Alguns Paradoxos." In *A Democracia no Brasil: Dilemas e Perspectivas*, edited by Fábio Wanderley Reis and Guillermo O'Donnell, 41–71. São Paulo: Vértice, 1988.

O'Donnell, Guillermo A., and Philippe C. Schmitter. *Transitions from Authoritarian Rule: Tentative Conclusions about Uncertain Democracies*. Baltimore: Johns Hopkins University Press, 1986.

Oliveira, Ariovaldo Umbelino de. *Integrar Para Não Entregar: Políticas Públicas e Amazônia*. Campinas: Papirus, 1988.

Oliveira, Eliézer Rizzo de. "Constituinte, Forças Armadas e Autonomia Militar." In *As Forças Armadas no Brasil*, edited by Eliézer Rizzo de Oliveira et al. Rio de Janeiro: Espaço e Tempo, 1987.

———. "Transição Política e Aparelho Militar." Paper prepared for presentation at the Conference on Civil-Military Relations and Democracy in Latin America, American University, Washington, D.C., 1987.

———. *De Geisel a Collor: Forças Armadas, Transição e Democracia*. São Paulo: Papirus, 1994.

Oliveira, João Pacheco de. "Segurança das Fronteiras e o Novo Indigenismo: Formas e Linhagem do Projeto Calha Norte." Paper prepared for the 13th Annual Meeting of ANPOCS [Associação Nacional de Pós-Graduação e Pesquisas em Ciências Sociais], Caxambu, Minas Gerais, October 23–27, 1989.

———, ed. *Projeto Calha Norte: Militares, Índios, e Fronteiras*. Rio de Janeiro: Editora UFRJ [Universidade Federal de Rio de Janeiro], November 1990.

Olson, Mancur. *The Logic of Collective Action: Public Goods and the Theory of Groups*. Cambridge, Mass.: Harvard University Press, 1965.

———. "A Theory of the Incentives Facing Political Organizations: Neo-Corporatism and the Hegemonic State." *International Political Science Review* 7.2 (April 1986): 165–89.

Oswald, Michael S. "Brazil's Amazon Protection System: Security and 'Sustainable' Development for the 1990s?" April 21, 1994. Photocopy.

PAL (Programa de Asesoria Legislativa). "Proyecto de Ley que Modifica las Leyes Orgánicas Constitutionales de las Fuerzas Armadas y de Carabineros de Chile." Bitacora Legislativa 81. Santiago: PAL, 1993.

Parker, Phyllis. *Brazil and the Quiet Intervention: 1964*. Austin: University of Texas Press, 1979.

Partido do Movimento Democrático Brasileiro. "Esperança e Mudança: Uma Proposta de Governo Para o Brasil." *Revista do PMDB* 2.4 (October–November 1982).

Partido dos Trabalhadores. *Lula Presidente: Uma Revolução Democrática no Brasil. Bases do Programa de Governo*. São Paulo: Partido dos Trabalhadores, 1994.

Pattillo, Guillermo. "Al Gasto Militar en Chile en la Década de los Ochenta." Working paper 229, Centro de Estudios de Desarrollo, Santiago, 1991.

———. "Evolución y Estructura de Gasto de las Fuerzas Armadas de Chile, 1970–1990." *Fuerzas Armadas y Sociedad* 7.2 (April–June 1992): 1–13.

Payne, Leigh A. "Working Class Strategies in the Transition to Democracy in Brazil." *Comparative Politics* 23.2 (January 1991): 221–38.

———. *Brazilian Industrialists and Democratic Change*. Baltimore: Johns Hopkins University Press, 1994.

Pedreira, Fernando. *Brasil Política 1964–1975*. São Paulo: DIFEL, 1975.

Peixoto, Antonio Carlos. "O Clube Militar e os Confrontos no Seio das Forças Armadas (1945–1964)." In *Os Partidos Militares No Brasil*, edited by Alain Rouquié, 71–113. Rio de Janeiro: Editora Record, 1980.

Peixoto, João Paulo M., and Antonio Carlos Pojo do Rego. "A Revisão Constitucional e a Reforma do Estado Brasileiro." *Revista de Administracão Pública* 28.3 (July/September 1994): 132–54.

Pereira, Luiz Carlos Bresser. "Experiências de um Governo." Cadernos de Conjuntura 16, Instituto Universitário de Pesquisas do Rio de Janeiro, 1988.

Pereira, Mauricio Broinizi. "Tiro Pela Culatra." *Teoria & Debate* 14 (May 1991): 6–9.

Perruci, Gamaliel, Jr. "Environment and the 'National Interest': The National Security State in the Brazilian Amazon." Paper prepared for presentation at the 18th International Congress of the Latin American Studies Association, Atlanta, Georgia, March 10–12, 1994.

Pion-Berlin, David. "The National Security Doctrine, Military Threat Perception and the 'Dirty War' in Argentina." *Comparative Political Studies* 21 (1988): 382–407.

——. "A House Divided: Segmented Professionalism and Security Ideology in the Argentine Army, 1984–1989." Paper prepared for presentation at the 15th International Congress of the Latin American Studies Association, San Juan, Puerto Rico, September 21–23, 1989.

——. "Between Confrontation and Accommodation: Military and Government Policy in Democratic Argentina." *Journal of Latin American Studies* 23.3 (October 1991): 543–71.

——. "Military Autonomy and Emerging Democracies in South America." *Comparative Politics* 25.1 (October 1992): 83–102.

——. "To Prosecute or to Pardon? Human Rights Decisions in the Latin American Southern Cone." *Human Rights Quarterly* 16.1 (February 1994): 105–30.

Pion-Berlin, David, and Craig Arceneaux. "Tipping the Civil-Military Balance: Human Rights Policy and Institutions in Democratic Argentina and Chile." Paper prepared for presentation at the 19th International Congress of the Latin American Studies Association, Washington, D.C., September 28–30, 1995.

Pion-Berlin, David, and Ernesto López. "A House Divided: Crisis, Cleavage, and Conflict in the Argentine Army." In *The New Argentine Democracy: The Search for a Successful Formula*, edited by Edward C. Epstein, 63–96. Westport: Praeger, 1992.

Pittmann, Howard T. "Geopolitics and Foreign Policy in Argentina, Brazil and Chile." In *Latin American Foreign Policies: Global and Regional Dimensions*, edited by Elizabeth G. Ferris and Jennie K. Lincoln, 165–78. Boulder: Westview Press, 1981.

Pompermayer, Malori José. "The State and the Frontier in Brazil: A Case Study of the Amazon." Ph.D. diss., Stanford University, 1979.

Potash, Robert A. "The Alfonsin Administration in Argentina: A Retrospective." Paper prepared for presentation at the 15th International Congress of the Latin American Studies Association, Miami, December 1989.

Power, Timothy. "Perfil Dos Ex-Arenistas No Congresso Nacional: Quadros Estatísticos." Department of Government and International Studies, University of Notre Dame, 1990. Photocopy.

——. "Politicized Democracy: Competition, Institutions, and 'Civic Fatigue' in Brazil." *Journal of Interamerican Studies and World Affairs* 33.3 (Fall 1991): 75–112.

——. "The Political Right and Democratization in Brazil." Ph.D. diss., University of Notre Dame, 1993.

Powers, Nancy. "The Politics of Poverty in Argentina in the 1990s." 1994. Photocopy.

Price, David. *Before the Bulldozer: The Nambiquara Indians and the World Bank*. Washington, D.C.: Seven Locks Press, 1989.

Proença, Domício, Jr. "Tecnologia Militar e Os Militares na Tecnologia: O Caso da Politica Nacional de Informática." M.A. thesis, COPPE (Coordenação de Programas de Pós-Graduação de Engenharia], Universidade Federal do Rio de Janeiro, November 1987.

Przeworski, Adam. "Some Problems in the Study of the Transition to Democracy." In *Transitions from Authoritarian Rule: Comparative Perspectives*, edited by Guillermo O'Donnell, Philippe C. Schmitter, and Laurence Whitehead, 47–63. Baltimore: Johns Hopkins University Press, 1986.

Pye, Lucian. *Aspects of Political Development*. Boston: Little, Brown, 1966.

Rabben, Linda. "Demarcation—and Then What?" *Cultural Survival Quarterly* 17.2 (Summer 1993): 12–14.

Rabkin, Rhoda. "The Aylwin Government and 'Tutelary' Democracy: A Concept in Search of a Case?" *Journal of Interamerican Studies and World Affairs* 34.4 (Winter 1992–93): 119–95.

Ramos, Alcida. "Report on the Inspection Trip to the Yanomami and Makushi Area in Roraima by the Citizens' Action Committee." June 9–12, 1989. Photocopy.

——. "An Economy of Waste: Amazonian Frontier Development and the Livelihood of Brazilian Indians." Paper prepared for presentation at the 39th Annual Conference of the Center for Latin American Studies, "Economic Catalysts to Ecological Change," University of Florida, Gainesville, February 9–10, 1990.

Redick, John R. "Latin America's Emerging Non-Proliferation Consensus." *Arms Control Today* 24.2 (March 1994): 3–9.

"Região Amazônica: Um Outro Brasil, Quase Sem Brasileiros." *A Defesa Nacional* 634 (November–December 1970): 157–60.

Reis, Elisa P., and Zairo B. Cheibub. "Political Values of Elites and Democratic Consolidation." Paper prepared for presentation at the 16th World Congress of the International Political Science Association, Berlin, August 21–25, 1994.

Reis, Fábio Wanderley. "Consolidação Democrática e Construção do Estado." In *A Democracia no Brasil. Dilemas e Perspectivas*, edited by Fábio Wanderley Reis and Guillermo O'Donnell, 13–40. São Paulo: Vértice, 1988.

Remmer, Karen L. "Neopatrimonialism: The Politics of Military Rule in Chile, 1973–1987." *Comparative Politics* 21.2 (January 1989): 149–70.

Republica Argentina. "Mensaje Presidencial del Dr. Carlos Saúl Menem a la Honorable Asamblea Legislativa en la apertura del 113er Período de Sesiones Ordinarias." Buenos Aires: Presidencia de la Nación and H. Senado de la Nación, Dirección Publicaciones, March 1, 1995.

Respuestas de las Fuerzas Armadas y de Orden al Informe de la Comisión Nacional de Verdad y Reconciliación. Reprinted in *Estudios Públicos* 41 (Summer 1991).

Rich, Bruce. *Mortgaging the Earth: The World Bank, Environmental Impoverishment, and the Crisis of Development*. Boston: Beacon Press, 1994.

Ritter, Archibald R. M. *Development Strategy and Structural Adjustment in Chile: From the Unidad Popular to the Concertación, 1970–92*. Ottawa: The North-South Institute, 1992.

Riz, Liliana de. "Argentina: El Enigma Democrático." *Nueva Sociedad* 129 (January–February 1994): 6–12.

Roberts, J. Timmons. "Crisis and Environment." *Hemisphere* 6.1 (Winter/Spring 1994): 26–30.

Rodrigues, Leôncio Martins. *Quem é Quem na Constituinte: Uma Análise Sócio-Política dos Partidos e Deputados*. São Paulo: Oesp-Maltese, 1987.

Rojas, Francisco. "Chile y el Gasto Militar: Un Criterio Histórico y Jurídico de Asignación." In *Gasto Militar en América Latina: Procesos de Decisiones y Actores Claves*, edited by Francisco Rojas, 239–77. Santiago: Centro Internacional para el Desarrollo Económico (CINDE) and Facultad Latinoamericano de Ciencias Sociales (FLACSO), 1994.

Ronning, Neale C., and Henry H. Keith. "Shrinking the Political Arena: Military Government in Brazil since 1964." In *Perspectives on Armed Politics in Brazil*, edited by Henry H. Keith and Robert A. Hayes, 225–51. Tempe: Center for Latin American Studies, Arizona State University, 1976.

Rouquié, Alain. "Demilitarization and the Institutionalization of Military-Dominated Polities in Latin America." In *Transitions from Authoritarian Rule: Comparative Perspectives*, edited by Guillermo O'Donnell, Philippe C. Schmitter, and Laurence Whitehead, 108–36. Baltimore: Johns Hopkins University Press, 1986.

———. *The Military and the State in Latin America*. Berkeley: University of California Press, 1989.

Sain, Marcelo Fabián. *Los Levantamientos Carapintada, 1987–1991*. Vols. 1 and 2. Buenos Aires: Centro Editor de América Latina, 1994.

Sandoval, Salvador Antonio Mireles. "Labor Unrest in the 1980s: A Quantitative Analysis of Strike Waves in Brazil." Paper prepared for presentation at the 16th International Congress of the Latin American Studies Association, Washington, D.C., April 4–6, 1991.

———. *Social Change and Labor Unrest in Brazil since 1945*. Boulder: Westview Press, 1993.

Sandroni, Paulo, ed. *Constituinte, Economia e Política da Nova República*. São Paulo: Cortez, 1986.

Santilli, Paulo. "Terra Indígena: Princípios Constitucionais e Arranjos Institucionais." In *Aconteceu* special edition 17: *Povos Indígenas no Brasil*. São Paulo: Centro Ecumênico de Documentação e Informação-CEDI, 1985–86.

———. "Tratado de Cooperação Amazônica: Um Instrumento Diplomático a Serviço da Retórica Nacionalista." *Tempo e Presença* 244–45 (August–September 1989): 40–45.

Santos, Wanderley Guilherme dos. "The Calculus of Conflict: Impasse in Brazilian Politics and the Crisis of 1964." Ph.D. diss., Stanford University, 1979.

———. "Fronteiras do Estado Mínimo: Indicações Sobre o Híbrido Institucional Brasileíra." In *O Brasil e as Reformas Políticas*, edited by João Paulo dos Reis Velloso, 49–94. Rio de Janeiro: José Olympio, 1992.

Schattschneider, E. E. *The Semi-Sovereign People: A Realist's View of Democracy in America*. Hinsdale: Dryden Press, 1969.

Scheetz, Thomas. "Military Expenditures in South America." Paper prepared for presentation at the United Nations Disarmament Conference, Asunción, Paraguay, January 1993.

Schmink, Marianne. "Land Conflicts in Amazônia." *American Ethnologist* 9.2 (1982): 341–57.

———. "Contesting the Amazon, 1979–1989." Paper prepared for presentation at the workshop on Amazonian Ecological Disorder: A 1989 Assessment, Rio de Janeiro, August 27–September 1, 1989.

Schmitter, Philippe C. *Interest Conflict and Political Change in Brazil*. Stanford: Stanford University Press, 1971.

———. "The 'Portugalization' of Brazil?" In *Authoritarian Brazil: Origins, Policies, Future*, edited by Alfred Stepan. New Haven: Yale University Press, 1973.

———. "Democratic Theory and Neo-Corporatist Practice." *Social Research* 50.4 (Winter 1983): 885–928.

———. "The Consolidation of Political Democracy in Southern Europe." Department of Political Science, Stanford University, 1988. Photocopy.

———. "Democracy, Democratization and Military Power." European University Institute and University of Chicago, n.d. Photocopy.

Schmitter, Philippe C., and Terry Lynn Karl. "What Democracy Is and Is Not." *Journal of Democracy* 2.3 (Summer 1991): 75–88.

Schneider, Ben Ross. *Politics within the State: Elite Bureaucrats and Industrial Policy in Authoritarian Brazil*. Pittsburgh: University of Pittsburgh Press, 1991.

———. "Brazil under Collor: Anatomy of a Crisis." *World Policy Journal* 8.2 (Spring 1991): 321–50.

Schneider, Ronald M. *The Political System of Brazil: Emergence of a "Modernizing" Authoritarian Regime, 1964–1970*. New York: Columbia University Press, 1971.

Selcher, Wayne A. "Brazil in the World: Multipolarity as Seen by a Peripheral ADC Middle Power." In *Latin American Foreign Policies: Global and Regional Dimensions*, edited by Elizabeth G. Ferris and Jennie K. Lincoln, 81–101. Boulder: Westview Press, 1981.

———. "Brazil's Foreign Policy: More Actors and Expanding Agendas." In *The Dynamics of Latin American Foreign Policies: Challenges for the 1980s*, edited by Jennie K. Lincoln and Elizabeth G. Ferris, 101–23. Boulder: Westview Press, 1984.

———. "Contradictions, Dilemmas, and Actors in Brazil's Abertura, 1979–1985." In *Political*

Liberalization in Brazil: Dynamics, Dilemmas, and Future Prospects, edited by Wayne A. Selcher, 55–95. Boulder: Westview Press, 1986.

Serra, José. "A Crise Fiscal e as Diretrizes Orçamentárias." *Revista de Economia Política* 9.4 (October–December 1989): 137–55.

Shepsle, Kenneth A. "Studying Institutions: Some Lessons from the Rational Choice Approach." *Journal of Theoretical Politics* 1.2 (1989): 131–47.

Shugart, Matthew Soberg, and John M. Carey. *Presidents and Assemblies: Constitutional Design and Electoral Dynamics.* Cambridge: Cambridge University Press, 1992.

Sigmund, Paul E. "Chile." In *Prospects for Democracy in Latin America*, edited by Forrest D. Colburn, 13–16. Monograph series 1, Center of International Studies, Princeton University, 1990.

Silva, Golbery do Couto e. *Geopolítica do Brasil.* Rio de Janeiro: José Olympio Editora, 1967.

Silva, Irene Heller Lopes da. "Direito de Greve e Lei de Negociações Coletivas." Paper written for course of the Escola Superior de Guerra, Curso de Altos Estudos de Política e Estratégia, Trabalho Especial, 1987. Photocopy.

Silva, José Gomes da. *A Reforma Agrária no Brasil: Frustração Camponesa ou Instrumento de Desenvolvimento?* Rio de Janeiro: Zahar Editores, 1971.

———. *Caindo por Terra: Crises da Reforma Agrária na Nova República.* São Paulo: Busca Vida, 1987.

Skidmore, Thomas E. *Politics in Brazil, 1930–1964: An Experiment in Democracy.* New York: Oxford University Press, 1967.

———. "Workers and Soldiers: Urban Labor Movements and Elite Responses in Twentieth-Century Latin America." In *Elites, Masses, and Modernization in Latin America, 1850–1930*, edited by Virginia Bernhard, 79–126. Austin: University of Texas Press, 1979.

———. *The Politics of Military Rule in Brazil: 1964–1985.* Oxford: Oxford University Press, 1988.

Smith, William C. *Authoritarianism and the Crisis of the Argentine Political Economy.* Stanford: Stanford University Press, 1989.

Sódre, Nelson Werneck. *A História Militar do Brasil.* 3d ed. Rio de Janeiro: Civilização Brasileira, 1979.

———. *Do Tenentismo ao Estado Novo: Memórias de um Soldado.* Petrópolis: Editora Vozes, 1986.

———. *Do Estado Novo à Ditadura Militar: Memórias de um Soldado.* 2d ed. Petrópolis: Editora Vozes, 1988.

Souza, Maria do Carmo Campello. "The Contemporary Faces of the Brazilian Right: An Interpretation of Style and Substance." In *The Right and Democracy in Latin America*, edited by Douglas A. Chalmers, Maria do Carmo Campello de Souza, and Atilio A. Boron, 99–127. New York: Praeger, 1992.

Stepan, Alfred. *The Military in Politics: Changing Patterns in Brazil.* Princeton: Princeton University Press, 1971.

———. "The New Professionalism of Internal Warfare and Military Role Expansion." In *Authoritarian Brazil: Origins, Policies, Future*, edited by Alfred Stepan, 47–65. New Haven: Yale University Press, 1973.

———. *The State and Society in Peru: Peru in Comparative Perspective.* Princeton: Princeton University Press, 1978.

———. "Political Leadership and Regime Breakdown: Brazil." In *The Breakdown of Democratic Regimes: Latin America*, edited by Juan J. Linz and Alfred Stepan, 110–37. Baltimore: Johns Hopkins University Press, 1978.

———. "Paths toward Redemocratization: Theoretical and Comparative Considerations." In *Transitions from Authoritarian Rule: Comparative Perspectives*, edited by Guillermo O'Donnell, Philippe C. Schmitter, and Laurence Whitehead, 64–84. Baltimore: Johns Hopkins University Press, 1986.

———. *Rethinking Military Politics: Brazil and the Southern Cone.* Princeton: Princeton University Press, 1988.

———, ed. *Democratizing Brazil: Problems of Transition and Consolidation*. New York: Oxford University Press, 1989.

Stockholm International Peace Research Institute. *SIPRI Yearbook 1992: World Armaments and Disarmament*. New York: Oxford University Press, 1992.

Stumpf, André Gustavo, and Merval Pereira Filho. *A Segunda Guerra: Sucessão de Geisel*. São Paulo: Editora Brasiliense, 1979.

Tambs, Lewis A. "Geopolitics of the Amazon." In *Man in the Amazon*, edited by Charles Wagley, 45–87. Gainesville: University of Florida Press, 1974.

Teixeira, Maria Lúcia, and Werneck Vianna. *A Administração Do "Milagre": O Conselho Monetário Nacional 1964–1974*. Petrópolis: Editora Vozes, 1987.

Thelen, Kathleen, and Sven Steinmo. "Historical Institutionalism in Comparative Politics." In *Structuring Politics: Historical Institutionalism in Comparative Analysis*, edited by Sven Steinmo, Kathleen Thelen, and Frank Longstreth, 1–32. New York: Cambridge University Press, 1992.

Tocqueville, Alexis de. *Democracy in America*, edited by Francis Bowen and Phillips Bradley. 2 vols. New York: Vintage, 1945.

Tsebelis, George. *Nested Games: Rational Choice in Comparative Politics*. Berkeley: University of California Press, 1990.

U.S. Arms Control and Disarmament Agency. *World Military Expenditures and Arms Transfers 1993–1994*. Washington, D.C.: ACDA Publications, 1995.

Valenzuela, Arturo. "A Note on the Military and Social Science Theory." *Third World Quarterly* 7.1 (January 1985): 132–42.

Varas, Augusto, ed. *La Autonomía Militar en América Latina*. Caracas: Editorial Nueva Sociedad, 1988.

———. *Democracy Under Siege: New Military Power in Latin America*. New York: Greenwood Press, 1989.

Varas, Augusto, and Claudio Fuentes. *Defensa Nacional, Chile 1990–1994: Modernización y Desarrollo*. Santiago: FLACSO [Facultad Latinoamericano de Ciencias Sociales], 1994.

Venturini, Danilo. *A Questão Fundiária do Brasil: Exposição na Câmara dos Deputados*. Brasília: Câmara dos Deputados, 1984.

Viana Filho, Luís. *O Governo Castelo Branco*. Rio de Janeiro: José Olympio Editora, 1975.

Viola, Eduardo J. "O Movimento Ecológico no Brasil (1974–1986): Do Ambientalismo à Ecopolítica." Working paper 93, University of Notre Dame, Kellogg Institute, 1987.

Vita, Alvaro de. *Constituição, Constituinte*. São Paulo: Atica, 1987.

Wallerstein, Michael. "The Collapse of Democracy in Brazil: Its Economic Determinants." *Latin American Research Review* 15.3 (1980): 3–40.

Wesson, Robert, ed. *The Latin American Military Institution*. New York: Praeger, 1986.

Weyland, Kurt. *Democracy without Equity: Failures of Reform in Brazil*. Pittsburgh: University of Pittsburgh Press, 1996.

———. "The Rise and Fall of President Collor and Its Impact on Brazilian Democracy." *Journal of Interamerican Studies and World Affairs* 35.1 (1993): 1–38.

———. " 'Growth with Equity' in Chile's New Democracy?" *Latin American Research Review* 32.1 (Spring 1997), forthcoming.

Wirth, John. "Tenentismo in the Brazilian Revolution of 1930." *Hispanic American Historical Review* 44.2 (May 1964): 171–79.

Wood, Charles H., and Marianne Schmink. "The Military and the Environment in the Brazilian Amazon." *Journal of Political and Military Sociology* 21 (Summer 1993): 81–105.

World Bank. *Argentina: From Insolvency to Growth*. Washington, D.C.: World Bank, 1993.

Wright, Robin W. "The Politics of 'Divide and Conquer.' The Baniwa, Mining Development and the *Projeto Calha Norte*." Paper prepared for presentation at the 13th Annual Meeting of ANPOCS [Associação Nacional de Pós-Graduação e Pesquisas em Ciências Sociais], Caxambu, Minas Gerais, October 23–27, 1989.

Zagorski, Paul W. *Democracy vs. National Security: Civil-Military Relations in Latin America.* Boulder: Lynne Rienner Publishers, 1992.

——. "Civil-Military Relations and Argentine Democracy: The Armed Forces under the Menem Government." *Armed Forces and Society* 20.3 (Spring 1994): 423–37.

Zaverucha, Jorge. "Os Militares e a Conjuntura Nacional." In *Cadernos de Conjuntura* 44. Rio de Janeiro: Instituto Universitário de Pesquisas do Rio de Janeiro, September 1991.

——. "Civil-Military Relations during the Process of Transition: Spain, Argentina, and Brazil." Ph.D. diss., University of Chicago, 1991.

——. "The 1988 Brazilian Constitution or How to Harm the Civilian Control over the Military." Paper prepared for presentation at the 15th Annual Meeting of ANPOCS [Associação Nacional de Pós-Graduação e Pesquisas em Ciências Sociais], Caxambu, Minas Gerais, October 15–18, 1991.

——. "The Degree of Military Political Autonomy during the Spanish, Argentine and Brazilian Transitions." *Journal of Latin American Studies* 25.2 (May 1993): 283–99.

——. *Rumor de Sabres: Tutela Militar ou Controle Civil?* São Paulo: Editora Ática, 1994.

Zirker, Daniel. "Democracy and the Military in Brazil: Elite Accommodation in Cases of Torture." *Armed Forces and Society* 14.4 (1988): 587–605.

——. "The Civil-Military Mediators in Post-1985 Brazil." *Journal of Political and Military Sociology* 19 (Summer 1991): 47–73.

——. "The Military Ministers and Political Change in Post-Authoritarian Brazil." *Revue Canadienne des Études Latino-Américaines et Caraïbes* 18.35 (1993): 87–110.

Zirker, Daniel, and Marvin Henberg. "Amazônia: Democracy, Ecology, and Brazilian Military Prerogatives in the 1990s." *Armed Forces and Society* 20.2 (Winter 1994): 259–81.

INDEX

ABIMDE. *See* Brazilian Association of
   Defense Materiel Industries
Accomarca (Peru) massacre, 166
Acre (state), 118, 129
Advisory Secretariat of National Defense
   (SADEN), 55, 58, 61, 62, 69, 125
Afif Domingo, Guilherme, 194 (n. 54)
Air force, 19–20, 45, 48, 61, 104, 118
Air Force Intelligence Center (CISA), 34
Air Force Ministry, 32, 44, 45–47, 59, 61
Albuquerque Lima, Alfonso Augusto de, 29,
   180 (n. 15)
Alfonsín, Raúl: and human rights trials,
   22–23, 39, 159, 161; and military influence,
   158, 159, 162, 171, 209 (n. 53)
Allamand, Andrés, 152
Allende Gossens, Salvador, 152
Alves, João, 200 (n. 54)
Amazon Ministry, 133, 136
Amazon Protection System (SIPAM),
   134
Amazon region, 4, 141; military interest in,
   2, 22, 68, 116, 117, 118, 121–22, 138; Collor
   government and, 2, 117, 128–33, 138;
   indigenous reserve lands, 68, 124–25,
   129–31, 136–37; Sarney government and,
   117, 122–27; Franco government and, 117,
   133–38; military bases in, 118, 122, 123,
   131–32, 134; territorial disputes in, 118, 134;
   economic development in, 118–21; environmental destruction in, 119, 120, 126,
   129, 204 (n. 42); environmental protection
   efforts, 120–21, 123, 125, 126–29, 131, 132–33,
   134–35, 137, 138; Brazilian territory in, 201
   (n. 2)
Amazon River, 118
Amazon Surveillance System (SIVAM), 133,
   134–35, 137

American Revolutionary Popular Alliance
   (APRA), 165, 166
Ames, Barry, 8
Amnesty decree (1979), 23, 37, 39
"Amphibians," 28
ANC. *See* National Constituent Assembly
Annibal Pacheco, Carlos, 131
Anti-Militarist Movement (MAM), 63
APRA. *See* American Revolutionary Popular
   Alliance
"April package" (1977), 37
ARENA. *See* National Renovating Alliance
Argentina, 1; Brazilian nuclear agreement
   with, 2, 128; trials for human rights abuses,
   22–23, 39, 159, 161–62; defense spending,
   96, 103, 162–63; Brazilian rapprochement
   with, 121–22; military rule in, 158; military
   influence in, 159–61, 163, 169, 170, 171, 172;
   Congress of, 161
Arinos de Mello Franco, Afonso, 183 (n. 2)
Armed Forces General Staff (EMFA), 45–46,
   184 (n. 11); ministerial status, 32–33, 34, 63
Arms industry, 98, 107, 196 (n. 6)
Army: intervention in politics, 6–8, 19–20;
   and public approval, 21; military regime
   and, 27, 30–31, 32; promotion and retirement system, 28, 30; internal conflicts,
   28–29; education and training, 31–32, 144;
   control of military police, 35, 50, 51–53,
   59; presidents and, 43; and drafting of
   1988 constitution, 44; and proposed Ministry of Defense, 45, 61; and internal security responsibility, 48, 67, 144; and labor
   strikes, 81, 85, 87, 89, 90, 91; and Amazon
   region, 116, 118
Army academy (AMAN), 31
Army Intelligence Center (CIE), 34
Army Ministry, 32, 44, 45–47, 53, 59, 61